THE VITAL PARTS OF A MONEY-MAKING MACHINE

INSPIRATION (and how far to trust it)

CAPITAL (how much you really need and when you'll really need it)

PROTECTION (against rip-offs)

PARTNERS (and how to know if you really need them)

BIG CORPORATIONS (and how to make them work for you)

MERCHANTS (and the secrets of getting them to give you shelf space)

THE PUBLIC (and the fine art of THE BIG SELL)

... All in the book that puts you in the driver's seat on the road to your first million (for starters)—

HOW TO TURN YOUR IDEA INTO A MILLION DOLLARS

DON KRACKE had his first million-dollar idea in 1967. Since then he has formed a company called Group X which takes ideas—his own and others'—and develops them for market.

ROGER HONKANEN is an advertising executive with wide experience in marketing. A former newspaper reporter, magazine editor, and film producer, he is currently working on a textbook for operators of small businesses.

Ⓜ MENTOR (0451)

ALL ABOUT BUSINESS

☐ **GOING FOR IT: How to Succeed as an Entrepreneur by Victor Kiam.** The story of spectacular success, his full-speed-ahead guide is packed with winning business advice. Victor Kiam is the entrepreneurial wizard whose unorthodox advertising campaigns made the world his marketplace—and his name a household word. (148517—$4.95)

☐ **DOING BUSINESS WITH THE JAPANESE by Mitchell F. Deutsch.** There is a logic behind Japanese business practices—and this book will show you how to recognize and use it to your own advantage. Designed to help American executives bridge the East-West "knowledge gap," this step-by-step guide to negotiation offers a wealth of invaluable advice.
(623495—$4.50)

☐ **HOW TO START AND MANAGE YOUR OWN BUSINESS by Gardiner G. Greene. Revised and Updated.** Step-by-Step instructions for a successful small business operation: how to choose an ad agency, how to obtain government aid, how to incorporate and form partnerships, plus much more. (625846—$4.95)

☐ **HOW TO KEEP SCORE IN BUSINESS: Accounting and Financial Analysis for the Non-Accountant by Robert Follett.** A practical and realistic look at the financial workings of the business world designed to give nonfinancial managers the knowledge necessary to succeed on the job. Presents the primary financial reports and statements, main analysis tools, key vocabulary terms, significant trend indicators, useful ratios, and financial danger signals that all managers should be familiar with. Charts, glossary, and index included. (626338—$3.95)

☐ **HOW TO TURN YOUR IDEA INTO A MILLION DOLLARS by Don Kracke with Roger Honkanen.** A step-by-step guide to researching, patenting, financing, manufacturing, marketing and distributing new products. Appendices (Inventor's Checklist, Sources, Typical Marketing Plan) and Index included.
(626060—$4.95)

Prices slightly higher in Canada

Buy them at your local bookstore or use this convenient coupon for ordering.

NEW AMERICAN LIBRARY
P.O. Box 999, Bergenfield, New Jersey 07621

Please send me the books I have checked above. I am enclosing $_____
(please add $1.00 to this order to cover postage and handling). Send check or money order—no cash or C.O.D.'s. Prices and numbers are subject to change without notice.

Name_____

Address_____

City _____ State _____ Zip Code _____
Allow 4-6 weeks for delivery.
This offer is subject to withdrawal without notice.

HOW TO TURN YOUR IDEA INTO A MILLION DOLLARS

Don Kracke
with
Roger Honkanen

A MENTOR BOOK
NEW AMERICAN LIBRARY
NEW YORK AND SCARBOROUGH, ONTARIO

COPYRIGHT © 1977, 1979 BY DON KRACKE

All rights reserved. For information address Doubleday & Company, Inc., 245 Park Avenue, New York, New York 10167.

Library of Congress Catalog Card Number: 79-88469

This is an authorized reprint of a hardcover edition published by Doubleday & Company, Inc.

MENTOR TRADEMARK REG. U.S. PAT. OFF. AND FOREIGN COUNTRIES
REGISTERED TRADEMARK—MARCA REGISTRADA
HECHO EN WINNIPEG, CANADA

SIGNET, SIGNET CLASSIC, MENTOR, ONYX, PLUME, MERIDIAN AND NAL BOOKS are published *in the United States* by
NAL PENGUIN INC.,
1633 Broadway, New York, New York 10019,
in Canada by The New American Library of Canada Limited,
81 Mack Avenue, Scarborough, Ontario M1L 1M8

FIRST MENTOR PRINTING, NOVEMBER, 1979

7   8   9   10   11   12   13   14

PRINTED IN CANADA

Contents

INTRODUCTION 1
How the author and his wife got an idea and then did something about it.

I HOW TO HAVE AN IDEA 10
Ideas don't just happen. You have to work for them. And there are some tricks you should know.

II WHAT'S A GOOD IDEA? 19
Some great ideas are born losers. How do you tell if yours is one of them?

III PATENT IT, FAST! 32
Getting legal protection for your idea. What it costs, what it does, how to do it.

IV THE PLAINTIVE PLAINTIFF 48
Getting legal protection doesn't automatically mean you're protected.

V RESEARCH AND RIP-OFFS 58
Those "Inventors Wanted" ads may be selling real help or just a scam. Here's how to tell the difference.

VI DOING YOUR HOMEWORK 71
Calculating wholesale and retail price, including manufacturing, packaging, selling and shipping.

VII WHICH WAY TO GO 89
Many roads lead to the marketplace, but some are better than others.

VIII IMAGINE, IF YOU WILL ... 120

A professional presentation can help sell your idea. Here's how to make one.

IX A MIRACLE. JUST A LITTLE ONE 130

Turning a major marketer's interest into a lot of free help. It's called leverage.

X LET'S MAKE A DEAL 140

How much to ask for, how much to expect when you sell your idea.

XI THE WONDERFUL WORLD OF MERCHANDISING 154

Using advertising, packaging and publicity to sell your product.

XII WHO'S GOT THE MONEY? 174

Marketing your idea means spending money. Here's how to finance at least part of your venture.

XIII SERENDIPITY-DOO-DAH 184

After all the hard work is done, there's one more factor to consider: luck.

XIV YOU HAVE REACHED ROCK BOTTOM 190

How a hot rock turned into a cool million in one year. The story of the Pet Rock.

APPENDIX I THE INVENTOR'S CHECKLIST 201

The step-by-step outline and checklist to follow in taking your idea to market.

APPENDIX II SOURCES 207

APPENDIX III A TYPICAL MARKETING PLAN 220

INDEX 223

HOW TO TURN YOUR IDEA INTO A MILLION DOLLARS

INTRODUCTION

How the author and his wife got an idea and then did something about it.

Overnight success takes about a year. Or longer.

This book, for example. It had all the ingredients of a sure-fire overnight best seller when I got the idea for it in 1970. It's a how-to book that strikes a responsive chord with, as nearly as I can tell, one out of three people in the world at any given moment. It promises to give you all the real inside dope on turning your idea or invention into a lot of money. All secrets revealed, nothing held back. And it's illustrated by the real-life frustrations, adventures, incredible good luck and gawdawful disasters experienced by my wife, Margaret, and me on our way to doing just that: turning a simple little idea into an international success. How could the book miss?

So, how come it's 1977 before this overnight best seller finally makes its way into print? Aha! Already you've grasped a basic concept at the very core of what I have to tell you. Simply *having* an idea is a long, long way from doing something about it. And it's an even longer way from doing the *right* things about it.

What I'm going to try to do in this book is give you an idea of what all those right things are. Margaret and I learned by doing a lot of the wrong things first, making some expensive mistakes. You won't have to do that, I hope. You'll have the benefit of all our blunders when you decide to turn your bright idea into your personal ticket to freedom.

I might as well tell you right now that it's not going to be easy, though, no matter how well you learn the tricks of the

1

trade. Marketing an invention is no get-rich-quick scheme. It takes time. The learning process you'll have to go through is really tough. It's exhausting and frightening work much of the time, no matter how good your idea or how marketable your invention. There's incredible pressure to understand incomprehensible new things quickly and deal with totally mystifying problems at a dead run. Developing an idea is hard. It takes guts and a certain amount of knowledge.

But it *can* be done. *You* can do it.

Believe me, I know. Since that first success I've developed more than forty other inventions, and I'm still at it. Along the way I've found that there are some rules that apply every time out. There are things you have to do, things you'd better avoid if you want to give an idea—any idea—a good running shot at success.

For whatever comfort it might be worth, when we started we didn't know what we were getting into either. You couldn't possibly be more uninformed about the mysteries of this business than Margaret and I were. You could have inscribed our entire collected knowledge of the subject on the head of a pin with a shaving brush. That was the jumping off place for our crash course in business administration.

What we learned came from experience, some of it bitter, some of it exhilarating, most of it from our very first idea: Rickie Tickie Stickies. You've seen them. They're those ubiquitous little stick-on vinyl flowers that even now keep turning up on cars, trash cans, mailboxes and a lot of other places I'd really rather not think about. We took that idea and turned it into more than two and a half million dollars in retail sales in the first year.

People began to assume we were rich and smart. My mother-in-law, along with a few million other people, watched us babble for seven whole minutes one night on the Walter Cronkite network news—more time than Vietnam got that evening! We've been interviewed on radio and television, been in magazines and newspapers more times than I can count. That's exhilarating experience.

On the other hand, some of the experience has been less than exhilarating. A lot less. We had to hock just about everything to make our idea work. I've been told at least a hundred times, "You're really lucky to have come up with such a great overnight success." Lucky, hell. At one point, we had the house, two cars, a mountain lot *and* the kids' educa-

INTRODUCTION

tion fund all used as collateral to back our idea. Everything we had been able to save over fifteen years of working was on the line. And this was quite a while before we had any real indication of commercial success.

I suppose before we get down to the nitty gritty, we ought to take a moment for a little background on the whole Rickie Tickie Stickies thing, how it happened, what we did with it. A quick case history of what can happen to an idea.

It all started in 1967. Remember 1967? Kind of a down year. The Vietnam war had the whole country pretty well divided and unhappy. It wasn't an election year, so nobody was running around telling us how much better it was going to be in just a little while. There was restlessness. And, in the middle of all this, the hippies arrived and invaded San Francisco's Haight-Ashbury district with unheard-of-notions. Like "peace" and "love." Flower-power was where it was all *at*. And, just in time, too. The country was crying out for a little fun. Everybody, God knows, *wanted* to smile a little. But, there was just not a whole lot to smile about.

Then one day in March, we were driving down a Los Angeles freeway when we noticed that something new was going on. A movement, of sorts. Every once in a while, we'd see a car that had been decorated with wild, bright designs. Then we saw three in a row. They were mostly kind of scribbly and amateurish. But, they were somethnig to make you feel good for a moment, something to smile at. We did. Other drivers did, too.

As we talked about the motivation behind those kooky bits of color, the idea began to dawn: maybe the world was ready for some kind of bright, good looking, easy to use, fun bit of madness to stick on cars and things.

The result of that first freeway discussion was Rickie Tickie Stickies, the flowers that became part of the American scene from Maine to Texas to Washington and all points between in just a few months.

And that wasn't the end of it. Shortly, they found their way to such diverse places as Sweden, Argentina, Japan, Mexico, Germany and Canada. Our silly little flowers even turned up on taxicabs in Cairo and phone booths in Tel Aviv. For all we know, big rumbling tanks faced off on both sides of the Suez Canal with Rickie Tickie Stickies stuck on their sides. (I think there's a message in there somewhere, but I haven't been able to figure it out yet.) It became an international fad—longer lasting than hula hoops, lots more fun than bomb throwing.

In between that freeway discussion and the international fad, of course, there was plenty of feverish activity. One of our earliest decisions wasn't really a decision at all. It was more like an acceptance of the facts. We decided to market the idea ourselves. It wasn't so much that we were choosing the most effective way to retain control of this idea that might be the key to our fortune, it was mainly that there was no one standing around in the wings ready to do the job for us. Many inventors come to the same "decision" the same way.

It took us until July—four months—to have our first sample run made. Three thousand Stickies: a thousand flowers, a thousand paisleys, a thousand polka dots. There were some good reasons it took so long for such a relatively simple task. One was a full-time job. Another was a family of four children, at that time ages three through eight, who felt they ought to get a little attention once in a while.

By August we had covered our station wagon with flowers. And the garbage cans and the mailbox. The crazy Krackes were the laughingstock of the neighborhood. Our children were very apologetic about their strange parents, and prospects weren't all that bullish for our new idea. Pepsi Cola already had turned us down as a premium after keeping us dangling for more than three months. And every day brought new problems we couldn't understand. What we did then set a pattern that served us very well whenever we were stumped. *We would ask an expert.* Remember that.

If you get nothing else out of this book, remember that. It's probably the most valuable single tip you'll ever get about marketing an invention. No matter what kind of business problem you're puzzling over, there's somebody who will be happy to help you figure it out. Why? Because in the process of helping you solve your problem, he hopes to stir up some business for himself.

Pretty soon the word got around that we were in the stick-on flower business—whatever *that* was. Neighborhood kids started turning up at the door asking if they could buy one. So we negotiated.

"How much?" they asked.

"Fifty cents," I said.

INTRODUCTION

"Too much," they replied.

"What do you think they're worth," I countered. (This is called market research when the big companies do it.)

"A nickel," they said.

"How about a quarter?"

Pause.

"Okay," they replied.

"Go ask your parents," I advised, hoping to avoid being run out of the neighborhood.

Then parents started dropping by wondering if we had any "extras." Now, we had vaguely assumed all along that our natural market probably was teen-agers and the hippie fringe because, after all, who else would buy stick-on flowers? But these were PTA women, housewives, nice middle-class suburban mothers. Not a hippie in the bunch!

Under the pressure of our new business, Margaret reluctantly began to cut down her heavy schedule of community affairs. So, she resigned from the board of the League of Women Voters and got another little surprise. On their way out the door at the end of the meeting that day, one after another of the board members stopped and asked if Margaret would sell her a flower or two. Bemused, she found herself standing at the door of our house selling our product to the departing members. We began to sense we might have a little more on our hands than just a mini-fad.

By September we had named our product Rickie Tickie Stickies. I've often been asked why such a dumb name. Mainly, it was my little joke at the time. It seemed to me that when new products came out, they all had the same kind of name. Something short and meaningless, like Fab or Tab or Gag or something. Yechhhhh!

I was determined to look for an alternative to that kind of thinking. No security of mediocrity for me! Besides, I owned the company. I was the boss. I could, by gosh, pick any kind of dumb name I wanted. Six months from then, what difference would it make?

The name Rickie Tickie Stickies just popped up one day. It was a happy name. We had a happy product. Once stuck in your mind, it was hard to forget. And, then there was something a little poetic about being Kracke from Rickie Tickie Stickies. I always fondly hoped to make the cover of *Business Week* with that caption. Never did.

Another rule we broke right away was the one that says

your product's name has to be very, very legible and easily readable at a minimum of fifty paces. Since we were in complete control, we naturally decided to have a totally illegible type face designed for our packages. As it finally turned out, neither a ridiculous name, nor an illegible type face was any deterrent to our product's success.

Meanwhile, we had begun learning another in the endless succession of lessons: It costs real money to get an idea off the ground. Even a simple idea like ours.

I found it would cost $300 to have a special die made to cut out the shape of the Stickies after they had been printed. Okay. No big deal. Then the printer wanted $1,000 in advance for the first batch of prototypes. After all, he had a family to feed, too. So, we dipped into the savings and paid the man.

Then we started thinking about a display box for stores carrying our product. As a general rule, you'll sell a lot more of an item like ours if it's out on the counter in a display box, rather than just stocked on the store's shelves. But, the price was $1,800 for 500 of the display boxes we had in mind. That's $3.60 each, just to hold some packets of Stickies! This was getting to be a lot more expensive than we had anticipated.

At this point, I took advantage of a friend of mine. He was vice-president for merchandise at Buffums', a chain of high-quality department stores in Southern California. I had a product, a package, an idea for a display box that sounded too expensive, and not a clue as to what to do next. Not only did my friend, Bill Johns, give me a lot of valuable advice, he also gave me an order for $900 worth of Stickies. That was a great day.

However, we didn't have enough product to fill his order. To get the cost of the Stickies down to where we could break even, at least, we had to triple our second order from the printer. Another $2,500 in advance. Bill agreed that our proposed display box was a necessity. There goes that $1,800. Having an apparently successful new idea was no longer all that much fun. It had gone beyond the swagger stage and was starting to cut into hard-earned savings. And that was, we were to discover, only the beginning of that particular lesson.

Meanwhile, we were trying to expand. Reasoning, that if

the first store we approached was a department store, we figured the next one should also be a department store. Obviously, you don't have to be too clever right at the beginning. We checked our credit cards. We owed the most to the Broadway, another chain of department stores. They became our next target. With twenty-four stores in those days, they represented a real gold mine, if we could make a sale.

Margaret—the housewife who didn't like selling Girl Scout cookies—called the stores' corporate office to find out when the gift and stationery buyer had visiting hours. We had learned a little bit already: that buyers had regularly scheduled hours to look at new products and that gift and stationery was the best department for us since they tended to carry a lot of impulse-type items and were usually in the heaviest traffic area of any given store.

Twenty minutes after Margaret was admitted to the buyer's office, Rickie Tickie Stickies had an order for one box (cost: $48) for each of the twenty-four stores. We were in the big leagues! Or, at least, we thought we were at the time.

And we kept at the only other sales effort we knew at the time. It was pretty simple and straightforward stuff. Margaret loaded up the station wagon and drove around to retail stores. Overcoming a powerful urge not to stop at all, she would walk in, present the package and ask for an order. Strangely, nine out of ten people actually did buy a box to "give it a try." Better still, quite a few of them began calling back for reorders, which meant that customers were coming into the retail stores and buying the funny little flowers often enough to make it worth the shelf space.

So it went, inch by inch. As you already know, we survived somehow. The Stickies took off like a bat, and from the time they first appeared on our station wagon until the end of 1968, more than 180 million of these little flowers had been sold for more than $20 million at retail. Of course, we didn't sell all those flowers and they weren't all Rickie Tickie Stickies, since by then there were many competitive producers out there who hopped onto the bandwagon as soon as it started to roll. In the warm, soft light of retrospect, I guess our experience was a classic example of how "it can be done," as I told you earlier. But there were an awful lot of times when it didn't seem like such a good idea anymore. Which brings us to an important topic.

Most inventors are convinced that having the idea is all it

takes. They're willing to reap all the rewards and benefits, but they're usually unprepared to take their financial lumps. The fact is that you can lose money. Real money. *Your* money! It is quite possible to lose a bundle on an idea. I've done it. Other people have done it. I know a guy who developed a thundering success of an idea in the novelty field. He must have made a million dollars on it. That was six or seven years ago. The next time I heard about him, a mutual friend told me the guy was desperately trying to unload a hundred thousand four-color posters that had turned out to be a turkey after he'd invested in printing them. Any idea is a gamble, and any gambler can lose as well as win.

Even if your idea is a success, it takes a long, long time for the money to come in. You have to be patient. Even once you're in production and your invention is out there on the retail shelves of America, it takes months before you even get noticed. More than a year after we reached the market with Rickie Tickie Stickies, we were still being "discovered" here and there all over the country. Newspaper and magazine articles were being written about our "new" product months after we were sick and tired of it. It could very easily be a year or more after the launching of your product before you get a dime back for your efforts. It takes that long, sometimes, to take up the financial slack.

Please don't misunderstand me. I'm not trying to talk you out of developing your invention. For all the turmoil and tumult, running our company was fun, rewarding and unbelievably educational. Sure there were periods of flux and growth which were hard on all of us. We got over the rough spots and tried to set policies that would avoid insoluble problems.

And we worked hard to establish good relationships with our suppliers and our customers. We tried not to take ourselves too seriously. Our communications were on as informal a level as we could maintain and still function in a businesslike way. (I didn't realize how informal I had become with our sales representatives until one of them told me he was collecting our "memos" to publish someday as—what did he call it?—folk humor.)

There's one final lesson we learned in the process of marketing our "million-dollar idea." If you are going to take your idea to market, you're going to need the wholehearted co-operation of your family. If it's not a team effort, you're going to be facing a real uphill struggle.

After all, there are risks. At times you will have a lot of money on the line—maybe the entire family savings, as we did. Unless the whole family is completely behind your idea and involved as an integral part of your fight to make it a success, they're going to resent it. Rightfully so. It's *their* future you're mortgaging, too, you know. You're going to need their moral support. You're going to need their understanding. You're going to need their strong backs, unflagging strength and a whole lot of legwork. With the family on your side, working for the same goals, half the battle is already won.

That leads us to the case at hand—your idea. Your success. Your dream. Since our success with the flowers, people keep coming to me with ideas. The auto mechanic who works on our car, the wife of an associate, the waiter at a favorite restaurant. These inventors come from everywhere, all of them with what they consider a great idea. Almost none of them has a clue about what to do next.

This book, then, is directed to all of those creators—all of you—who have tucked away in the back of your minds, an idea. An idea that will free you from the dull routines of your job. An idea that you know will work if it just has a chance.

To you, I say, "Do it!"

Here's how.

I
HOW TO HAVE AN IDEA

Ideas don't just happen. You have to work for them. And there are some tricks you should know.

I'll make you a bet right here and now. I'll bet you that by the time you finish reading this book, you'll have an idea you won't be able to resist taking to market. I've seen it happen over and over again. I'll be babbling along to someone trying to explain to him how to have ideas and suddenly he'll get this funny look on his face. I'll become aware that he's no longer listening. He's just had an idea. So will you.

I'll give you an example, which may be telling tales out of school since it involves the editor at Doubleday who worked with us on this book. I was talking to Karen about how many people have ideas and how little most of them know about what to do next, what steps to take after that. She said she was fascinated by the whole process and wished she could come up with a great invention, make a million dollars and retire. She wondered how people go about having all those marvelous flashes of genius.

"Nothing to it," I said. "You want to have an idea right now? A good one?"

She smiled. "Sure, why not?"

"Okay, how many manuscripts do you get in here every week? Dozens? A hundred?"

"A lot," she said. "Doubleday probably looks at thousands of manuscripts a year."

"And how do they come to you?" I pressed. "I'll bet most

HOW TO HAVE AN IDEA

of them are all wrapped up in brown paper with string and tape. You can probably tell that somebody with about eleven thumbs wrapped it up on his kitchen table, right?" (Writers never seem to be very good at wrapping things. Or tidy, either. I understand that Thomas Wolfe delivered the manuscript of *Look Homeward, Angel* to his editor, Max Perkins, in a big corrugated cardboard grocery box. There were thousands of sheets of messy paper, words scribbled in the margins, blots and splotches all over everything.)

Karen allowed that it was true, that the manuscripts did seem to have that worried-over-and-bundled-up-carefully-in-too-much-of-everything look.

"Uh huh. And when you want to send the manuscript back to the writer, what do you do?" I asked. "You probably send it down to the mailroom where somebody else who has about eleven thumbs hauls out the brown paper and string and tape and wraps it up again."

"Something like that," Karen admitted.

"Okay, how about having some kind of foldable cardboard box, just the right size for a book manuscript. You buy it flat, pop it open, stick the manuscript in it, close it up with some locking tabs and mail it off. Push-pull, click-click. Just like that. The manuscript stays nice and neat, the package looks tidy and professional, and it only takes about thirty seconds for you to pack up the whole thing and be done with it."

Karen got that old familiar look on her face.

"Hey," she said, "that might work!"

Of course it would work. It would probably even sell. Maybe not a million dollars' worth, but enough to bring in a nice royalty. By the time you read this, somebody may already have the mailer on the market. Karen, for all I know.

Anyway, there are three lessons to be learned from the example to the manuscript mailer.

First, there's more to inventing something than meets the eye. If you think about it carefully—and Karen did—you'll realize that she didn't really invent anything at all in our conversation!

"Hey, wait a minute," she said. "I didn't invent that mailer. *You* did!"

"Nope," I said. "Neither of us did." You see, simply figuring out that something needs to be invented—a manuscript mailer, for instance—doesn't constitute inventing it. Just because you have a notion that a foldable mailer would be a good idea, don't think you've actually invented it. You're a long way from that, yet. You still have to work out all the details of how it would function, how it would be manufactured, how much it would cost, where it would be sold, how it would be distributed and how many you would expect to sell, to name just a few of the chores you still have to do before you have invented anything.

There are a lot of people wandering around this earth firmly convinced they've invented something, when all they've really done is figured out some new product that *needs* to be invented. That's daydreaming, not inventing.

The second lesson to be learned from our example of Karen's manuscript mailer is that you don't have to be a specialist to come up with a valid, marketable idea. All it takes is a little bit of creative thinking—the kind you use every day for other purposes. There's no mystery to it. You can do it. Your kids can do it. Your dimwitted neighbor can do it.

But probably the most important lesson to be learned from our example is the third one: You don't have ideas by sitting around and waiting for the muse of inventions to land on your shoulder. If you're going to wait around for a fit of inspiration to strike, you'd better bring your lunch. It's going to be a long, long wait. You've actually got to set out to invent something, lay out the ground rules and the information and then try to work out the invention. Getting started shouldn't be too hard. You can just look around you and you'll see a million things that need to be invented. Think about the problems you run into everyday, then solve them.

For instance, you probably have a paper towel dispenser in your kitchen. And you probably hate it as much as I do. When I try to tear off a paper towel, I generally wind up with a towel and a half. Or two towels. Or the whole roll falls off into the cat's water dish. And it looks tacky, a little piece of cheap plastic amid all the shiny chrome and enamel of the kitchen appliances. There has to be a better way.

Or how about your steam iron? Every time you try to fill it with water, you dribble it all over the counter and it spills down the side of the iron. Then little hidden droplets of water collect in the nooks and crannies and when you start to iron with it, the water droplets spill out and make a big, damp blot on the thing you're ironing. When it's time to empty the iron, you make more steam than the Orient

HOW TO HAVE AN IDEA

Express pulling out of Istanbul. And, of course, there's always a little water that won't come out. It stays inside the iron, rusting out the delicate little innards so that every now and then a belch of brown gunk comes out on your ironing along with the steam. There has to be a better way.

I could give you more examples, but I think you get the idea. There are millions of things standing around waiting to be invented. All you have to do is sit down, figure out what they are, then invent them.

There are people who make their entire living either coming up with ideas or developing the ideas of other people. They work for companies that live or die on the basis of their new products. Toy companies, for instance, are almost totally dependent on a new crop of great ideas every year. Buyers for major chain stores are constantly involved in the development of new items to add to their line of wares. A friend of mine, Bob Clower, is one of those latter people. You'll meet him from time to time in this book because of that fact and because he's articulate and intelligent about his work. As a housewares buyer for Sears, he's developed some tricks of the trade that could be valuable to you.

"I read every women's magazine and shelter magazine every month," Bob told me. "I'm interested in what new trends seem to be forming, for one thing. For another thing, I look at all the ads very carefully. Advertising creative directors and art directors who do those ads supply me with a lot of ideas for new directions to be thinking about. I don't look so much at the product these people are featuring, but rather I look at the props and decorative details they use in their layouts. These people are paid to be innovative, creative and appealing to the consumer. So I look for the little details they use to establish some interest with their consumer audience. More often than not, those details can translate into either new product directions or improvements. Because of my interest in housewares I read the food ads carefully. I also look at a lot of television for the same reason. For a long time I didn't even own a set until I realized that it was the best way to stay current with the new trends. Watching TV commercials is now a part of my job.

"I buy and read every new kind of cookbook that comes out," Bob continued. "That's how we got into the fondue pot business. We were the first mass merchant to offer a fondue pot in a catalogue. That was in January 1966. When I listed them in 1965 they were part of a Portuguese copper line, and I thought they were some kind of chafing dishes and said so to our customers. But by reading a cookbook, I learned what fondue was and that you needed a fondue pot for it. It was good business for us for years."

The same kind of thinking Bob uses to recognize new ideas can be used by you to come up with new ideas.

There's a human factor to ideas which even some of the big companies recognize. A vice-president of Mattel spent time explaining their 250-man development groups, but then he admitted, "The key to development of any one single product usually is one person. It's the one person who is really pushing for it. He may have a team of ten or so people working for him, but it's usually one person's drive that makes it happen." In other words, even at one of the gigantic companies that dominate an industry, it's one key individual who makes a new product happen. You, sitting in your kitchen, can do the same thing Mattel does. In fact, if there's a lesson to be learned at all from the big companies, it's this: You, working alone, with limited resources, can do very nearly anything they can do. You can do their kind of thinking. You can come up with the same product they can, and you can market it.

As long as we're on the subject of the human factor in the business of inventions, there's a fascinating story Bob Clower told me about some research that was done recently. Instead of researching products and public reaction to products, this time the mind probers were working on something more basic. One of the best, most innovative people at a major manufacturer was selected by his company to create a test that would isolate individuals with intuitive imagination. They wanted a test that would tell them whether someone was likely to be a good inventor or not.

After working intensively for three years with some of the finest psychiatrists, psychologists and behavioral scientists in the country, they concluded it was not possible to isolate such individuals. There was simply no neatly delineated, easily recognizable pattern to good inventors. Which is simply a very costly, highly sophisticated, carefully measured way of saying what I told you earlier: Anybody can be an inventor.

For his own part, Bob Clower has devised a simpler way of finding good inventors. He likes to find people who have had door-to-door selling success—people who have made their living that way for at least three years. He believes you'll find certain basic characteristics in those persons that also are found in most successful inventors. Not the least of those characteristics is perseverance. A super-successful door-to-door salesman knows that he can sell three out of every ten homes he calls on, if he's really cooking. More importantly, he knows he *will not* make a sale at seven out of the ten. He's aware that he'll fail fully 70 per cent of the time. He is therefore prepared to spend a lot of time being told "no" for the few times he hears the magical word "yes."

That kind of thinking reflects a high degree of intellectual fortitude. It takes a special kind of courage to be turned down time after time and keep going back for those three out of ten who won't turn you down.

Finally, a door-to-door salesman is an intruder. He knows it, he can deal with it. So is an inventor an intruder. The inventor constantly finds himself intruding on some manufacturer who's really too busy to be listening to yet another idea. (George Parker, vice-president of creative services at Hallmark, gave me a beautiful image of what happens to someone in his position when he's listening to somebody's great new idea. As George says, the inventor has to understand that the guy he's trying to sell his idea to is sitting there behind his desk with a great big thought balloon over his head like in the cartoons. In the balloon is one word: "Risk." The inventor is barging in on the man, trying to shake up the order of things, offering him a swell chance to take a Big Risk. No wonder it's hard to sell ideas.) The inventor also finds himself intruding on the marketplace, which is already glutted with products, new and old. And he's intruding on the consumer who is reasonably satisfied with things the way they are and really not that interested in having to change his world around to accommodate a new product, even a good one that will help him.

George pointed out another reason an inventor needs intellectual fortitude. The poor inventor may have a marvelous idea he's trying to sell and still may strike out time after time. The fact that the idea is rejected, George pointed out, doesn't necessarily mean it's a bad idea. It may just mean that the idea doesn't fit the company's particular needs. The inventor has to have enough courage and enough faith in his idea to keep trying until he finds a company that a) recognizes the worth of his invention, and b) needs that specific invention for its product line. A successful idea, George explained, really is one that meets two interlocking needs: a public need for that product and a company's need for that kind of product in the line.

Every once in a while, there will be a great idea that meets all the requirements, and it still flunks. George gave a classic example that happened at Hallmark a few years ago. A lady had made a hobby of hand painting incredibly intricate and lovely designs on eggs—sort of like the elaborate Russian Easter eggs of a century ago. One day she showed up at George's office with some of her hand-painted eggs and suggested that they might make beautiful illustrations for a line of Easter cards or, perhaps, a book on the art of egg designing. The eggs really were lovely. And he *could* use a nice new line of Easter cards. So George sent a professional photographer out to her home to take photos of the eggs.

The results were frustrating. Somehow photography was unable to capture the beauty of the eggs. It simply didn't translate from the three-dimensional work of art to the two-dimensional photograph. After a year of trying, Hallmark finally had to conclude there was simply no way to make it work. They had to turn down the Egg Lady despite the fact that the idea met a need both in the market and in the Hallmark line.

When you're thinking about ideas, by the way, don't succumb to the traditional inventor's syndrome of "Oh, well, somebody must have thought of that already." In the first place, you ought to make it your business to find out if it's been thought of already. (Part of what happens when you go to get a patent involves finding an answer to that question, by the way.)

Anyway, if it's not on the market, it probably never has been thought of. Even a bad idea, if it's backed by enough determination, will show up on the market at least briefly. As someone who's interested in new inventions and ideas, you'll probably notice it. Even ideas that have been thought of before may still be viable if you've got some new angle. A Mattel executive noted, "Mattel starts a lot of projects that are subsequently abandoned for one reason or another. However, someone still could come in with basically the same idea, but with some small differences, a fresh approach, and make the sale to us. It's worth it to Mattel to make a royalty agreement," he added, "rather than try to fight any legal battles with an inventor." Even though there is solid proof of having had basically the same idea much earlier, Mattel and most of the other big companies, would rather pay the inventor and get a clear title to the new or newly modified idea.

That also brings up another point. When you're having your idea, try to develop it horizontally as well as vertically. In other words, don't just work out all the details of the invention for a single application. Try to think of different directions to go with your basic idea, different modes, different styling and so forth. For example, if you're working on some new kind of design for a table lamp and you're using a floral motif, work out some other motifs too. Why? Because the guy you try to sell your idea to may be totally turned off by flowers but really hot for zodiac figures. That's kind of a dumb example, but something as dumb as that has been known to make the difference between an idea sold and an idea rejected. Honest.

Horizontal development means thinking of other applications for your idea, too. When you've got the basic idea in mind, spend some time thinking of *all* the different ways it could be used. Even silly ones. It could lead you into a whole new marketing direction in addition to the one you were already thinking about.

Whatever you do, don't stop trying to have ideas. Even if you've got a good one that you're working on, keep thinking of more and don't lose good ones that spring to mind at odd moments. I keep something I call (rather inelegantly) my "creative crap file." It's nothing more than a collection of odd bits of paper on which I've scribbled down ideas that have occurred to me and seem to have some promise. If I don't write them down or sketch them when they come to me, I'll lose them. At the moment I'd guess that there are more than two hundred reasonably viable ideas in the file, waiting to be developed when I can fit them into the schedule with the stuff that's already in the works.

With luck, you can start a good file of creative crap, too. I say "with luck" because I think anybody who is in the idea business is fortunate. Inventing and marketing new products is one of the most challenging, rewarding ways I can imagine to make a living. I enjoy it immensely and I'd like to see you share some of that enjoyment. There's really no way of knowing exactly how many of us inventors and potential inventors are out there. The nearest thing to a statistic is the fact that last year 75,000 new patents were granted to some 120,000 people who applied.

Next year, I hope you're one of them.

II
WHAT'S A GOOD IDEA?

Some great ideas are born losers. How do you tell if yours is one of them?

If you weren't already interested in inventions, you wouldn't be reading this book. After all, no matter how easy I try to make it, learning the ins and outs of becoming a successful inventor isn't exactly light entertainment. You could have more fun watching a grease job.

So, since you're here instead of watching TV or catching a good movie, I can only assume you're pretty serious about this whole business of making money with your idea. Good for you! That means you're ready to start thinking about the first hurdle on your way to success—figuring out just how good this idea of yours really is.

It doesn't count that your Uncle Ernie thinks it's the greatest thing since the invention of the inside straight. It's not enough that your neighbor says everybody would want one. Your uncle and your neighbor—wonderful persons though they may be—are a little less than totally objective about your invention. And marketing experts they're probably not. You need something a little more concrete to go on before you sink the family fortune, or at least a lot of the family's time and effort, into your invention.

The question at hand, then, is the one at the top of this chapter: "What's a good idea?" I'll give you a short answer.

I don't know.

Nobody does.

There simply is no surefire way of telling if you have a good idea on your hands. Believe me, if I knew a foolproof way of finding that out, I would have retired a long, long time ago. I also would have saved myself all kinds of trouble down through the years because I've spent plenty of time and money chasing what turned out to be bad ideas. Anybody in the idea business who says he hasn't done that at least once is probably lying at least a little.

All is not lost, however. You may not be able to tell a good idea when you've got it, but a *loser* you can tell. No guesswork and gambling about it. There are some reasonably concrete requirements for a good idea, and if your invention doesn't meet those requirements, it's a loser. I still can't guarantee that your idea will be a success if it meets all the requirements, of course. All I can do is give you a way to tell whether you've got a turkey on your hands.

No, there isn't any nice, simple rule that you can write down on a piece of paper and carry around in your wallet. The key is a little more complicated. It is an understanding of how business works.

It isn't enough that your product seems desirable to a lot of people. Nor is it enough that the price seems right. It has to be both of those things at the same time—and one thing more. It must be profitable to the seller, the manufacturer, and all the other various people along the line of distribution. Every successful product is a three-cushion shot that touches all of these points: desirability, value and profitability. If somebody offers you prunes at a good price, but what you really wanted was plums, there's no sale. On the other hand, if somebody offers you the plums you want, but at $100 a pound, there's no sale either. And unless everybody from the farmer to the grocer can make a fair profit of the transaction, nobody's going to offer you either one—plums or prunes.

Let's take a look at the first of the three points, desirability. It's the toughest, the most subjective of all the three points you have to meet. Not that the definition is difficult. If anything, it's simplistic: A product is desirable if a market exists for it. But simplistic or not, big companies spend millions of dollars every year trying to see if their products fit that magic definition. To give you a few examples of the kind of testing that goes on:

WHAT'S A GOOD IDEA?

Fisher-Price is one of the giant toy companies. Every year, it adds approximately twenty new items to its line. In other words, twenty times a year, Fisher-Price has to go through all the steps of developing and marketing a new product. Those twenty winners are selected from among some two thousand new ideas reviewed every year by Fisher-Price, so the early discards are pretty much on the basis of their own feelings about the market. (When I say "they," I'm referring to the triumvirate at the company in charge of selecting and developing new ideas: the president, the vice-president for new products and vice-president for marketing. They work with a twelve-person staff.) Previous experience with a similar product, feedback from their retailers or sales organization, analysis of market trends, sometimes just gut instinct honed by many years in the business tell them to drop this idea or that one. Eventually they narrow the field down to twenty ideas that they believe will be winners.

Do they just dive right into production and distribution and merchandising? Hardly. The next step is to mount a full-bore research project on each of the twenty ideas. No matter *how* sure they are of a product, nothing goes to market without some form of testing. There's just too much at stake. Basically, the research they do falls into one of three different levels of sophistication.

With ideas they're pretty sure of, they'll do a fairly unsophisticated kind of testing. They'll have artists make up some fairly well-finished drawings or "comps" (short for "comprehensive drawings") of the products. They'll show these artists' renderings to a few hundred people who seem to fit the profile of Fisher-Price's market—the right number of children, the right income, education and so forth. And they'll interview test subjects about the product. Would they buy it? How do they think their children would like it? What would they consider a fair price to pay? Things like that. Perhaps no more than a dozen or so questions, depending on the kind of information they're seeking.

The next level of sophistication is basically the same kind of testing, with one important difference. In this level of testing, Fisher-Price will actually make a model of the new toy. The model will be practically identical to the way the toy will look when it's manufactured. These models will be photographed—perhaps even with children. Now the interviews are conducted with these photographs of the product instead of the artists' renderings. The test subjects need to use less of their imagination to figure out what the toy will be like, so their reactions are likely to be more accurate reflections of how they'll feel about the real toy. Again, their answers to the test questions will be carefully analyzed to get an idea of how popular the toy will be, what the price level ought to be and to ferret out any unnoticed drawbacks about the toy. Naturally, it's more expensive to make a model and have it photographed than to just do a drawing, so this level of sophistication costs a bit more than the lower level.

The most sophisticated type of testing is reserved for toys about which Fisher-Price has some doubts. (Obviously, they couldn't have any really serious doubts or the toy wouldn't have made it this far.) For this type of research, the toys will actually be produced as prototypes, either handmade models or production items from a short test run in the factory. They'll be as much like the real thing as possible—so much so that you and I probably couldn't tell the difference. These samples will then be given out to groups of children who have been brought by their parents to the test labs. While the kids play with the toys, the researchers will watch their reactions through one-way mirrors, which is fun. Later they'll probe the parents' reactions, too.

In the process of finding out whether a market exists for any given toy, Fisher-Price regularly spends as much as $50,000 for research. Sometimes they can get by more cheaply, but if they think they need it, they'll spend the top dollar just to be sure. They could lose many times that much if they make a million of the toy and wind up selling only a hundred thousand.

At Mattel, another of the giants in the toy industry, they sort of back into the question of desirability. The first stage in development of a new idea at Mattel is to look at some segment of the toy business and select a price level for a new toy to be marketed by Mattel in that segment. A typical starting point, according to a Mattel vice-president, might be a suggestion from the marketing department saying, "We need for year after next a ten-dollar doll with lots of 'action' features." (Note that lead time. If you try to sell your idea to a giant company, you'll learn that "next Christmas" is at least two years off.)

In other words, Mattel looks for holes in the toy market and seeks to fill them with products. Work doesn't begin until

WHAT'S A GOOD IDEA?

the need for some specific type of toy is established. The idea people keep current on new materials and novel mechanisms, and at weekly conferences they attempt to fit these new things into ideas that fill the current product need. At these meetings, the marketing people play a very important part. Even before a new toy is beyond the hand-waving, sketch-making stage, the marketing experts are working out the TV promotion possibilities, the advertising and packaging ideas and other related possibilities of the toy.

Needless to say, some very heavy research is going on at all times. And, of course, they're constantly testing new ideas in very much the same way Fisher-Price does—with one significant difference. At Mattel, they may go so far as to make a quicky TV commercial on the new toy, then test *that* instead of testing the toy (or in addition to testing the toy).

As you can see, marketing is the name of the game at Mattel. And it seems to work. Along the way to becoming the biggest in the business, they developed two of the most famous (or infamous, depending on your viewpoint) toys in the industry: the Barbie Doll and Hot Wheels. In some ways, Mattel has revolutionized the whole business of selling toys.

It's worth pointing out at this stage that you can do some of the same sort of testing. Almost all market research is aimed at finding out to whom the product appeals, how appealing it is and whether or not the price is right. No matter how sophisticated the techniques used to find the answers, the questions are usually variations on those same themes. Those are all questions you can ask, too.

There are several ways you can ask the questions. For one, you might simply do a short questionnaire requiring only yes/no or one-word answers, then buttonhole people at a shopping center someplace and ask them your questions.

You might want to do an "in-depth interview" kind of study where you get a group of people together and steer the discussion into areas you're interested in. (This is more difficult, since you'll want to tape record and transcribe the whole discussion so you can analyze it all later.) Needless to say, you want your panel to be unbiased strangers, not friends who'll tell you what they think you want to hear. There are even a couple of variations on this "in-depth" research: (1) you might have a picture or a sample of the product for them to discuss, or (2) you might simply get the discussion rolling on the general market your product fits into, without showing or bringing up a specific product.

The advantage of the "in-depth" research over the questionnaire study is that you can turn up problems you didn't think of and learn product advantages you hadn't thought about. The disadvantage is that this is a highly subjective kind of study, and unless you're pretty well-grounded in market research, you could jump to some unjustified conclusions. If you use it, take the comments at face value and don't try to read more into them than that.

The questionnaire study is much simpler and less likely to mislead you. Here's an example of the kind of questionnaire you might use:

1. Do you like the product?
2. Do you think that the price is about correct?
3. What feature do you like most about it?
4. What feature do you like least about it?
5. Any comments?

You'll also need to know who it is you're talking to. You don't care about names and addresses, of course. And people are more likely to answer your questions if they feel they are anonymous. But you do need to know some basic information about them so you'll want to ask these questions:

1, Age.   (Check one)   18 to 24
                        25 to 39
                        40 to 65
                        Over 65

2. Income.   (Check one) $10,000 or under
                           $10,000 to $20,000
                           $20,000 to $30,000
                           Over $30,000

3. Education.   (Check one)   8 years or less
                              9 to 12 years
                              13 to 16 years
                              More than 16 years

4. Male or female
5. Other questions pertinent to your product, such as marital status, whether or not the respondent has children and so forth.

Keep the questionnaire short. The shorter it is, the more willing people are to answer your questions and the more interviews you can complete in a given time. Avoid quesitons that require long, narrative answers. Ideally, you'll have a sample of the product on hand. Otherwise, you'll have to make do with a picture of it. And if you have a sample, be prepared to replace it from time to time after it is dropped or broken by all the handling.

Get as many interivews as you can because that cuts down on the amount of error introduced by a couple of non-typical responses. And be sure you hit more than one location when you are doing your research. (If you do all of it at one shopping center, or even at a couple of places in the same general part of town, you could build in an unnecessary bias in your sample. You could wind up with a heavy sample of well-educated, wealthy respondents, for instance.)

Your specific product may indicate special variations on the questions, of course. But you'll have to work that out on your own. Just remember that the object of the research is to give you insights into how well received your product is likely to be. It may take some time and effort and involve a certain amount of expense, but it could pay handsome dividends if it uncovers some problems you didn't know about.

If you're systematic about your interviews and keep careful records of the answers, you could have a valuable sales tool to use later on when you try to sell your idea to some manufacturer or when you try to raise some financial backing. Careful research, properly handled, can be very, very impressive.

While we're on the subject of research, I have to point out that it is hardly infallible. "Market research is not a science, by any means," said Bob Hicks, vice-president for new products at Fisher-Price. "At best it can sort out the extremes. It can't tell you ahead of time whether to expect 200,000 sales or 800,000 sales. All it can do is tell you you'll probably do somewhere in that area."

There have also been some monumental flops in the research business. Seymour Popiel, the inventor of the Vegomatic and the Pocket Fisherman (a compact, collapsible fishing rod/reel combination) and a number of other hugely successful products is the last person in the world I'd expect to get stung by bad research results. Seymour is not only the master of his very specialized kind of marketing—TV promos with their high advertising budgets and heavy promotions—but he invented it. He carried the midway pitchman out of the carnival and put him on television, with fantastic success.

He has made research a cornerstone of that success, developing it to a very fine art in all his promotions.

Anyway, Seymour—like the rest of us—noticed the introduction of a new product called a trash compactor a few years ago. Brought out by Sears and Whirlpool, jointly, it was making heavy inroads in the kitchen-appliance market. So when an inventor called on him one day, Seymour was ready to listen to the man's description of a nonelectrical, low-priced trash compactor. It was a fascinating concept. The basis of the unit was a kitchen stool with a cylindrical base. You put the trash and garbage in the cylindrical part, then put the stool down on it and scrunch the garbage by sitting on it or standing on it.

It looked like a great idea to the idea expert. But part of Seymour's success is due to the fact that he never—but *never*—markets anything without doing a lot of research. He made samples and had them tested by experts. The garbage scruncher was probed by consumer panels, home economists, engineers and marketing experts. It was restyled three times before it passed muster, but finally all the tests were positive. It was going to be a winner for sure.

Seymour produced his usual batch of hard-selling television commercials, manufactured 50,000 of the new gadgets, put the commercials on the air and stood back to make room for the thundering herd of buyers.

There was a deafening silence. Nobody bought the things. To this day, no one really understands what went wrong except that somehow the research produced a clinker. Seymour, eternally the pragmatist, didn't bother to spend another fortune finding out how come he lost all that money. He closed out the remaining garbage stools at $12.99 each, washed his hands of the whole thing and moved on to bigger and better things.

Fisher-Price had a big research failure in reverse a while ago. They brought out a toy called the "Family Farm" —basically a hundred-year-old idea in modern dress. It was a toy farm, with buildings and equipment and livestock and people all done in plastic. The price was pegged at about $14 or $15 at retail and conventional wisdom said it wouldn't be much of a seller at that price. The rule of thumb in those days was that any toy with a price tag over $10 would probably be a slow mover. Research results confirmed it. The best

Fisher-Price figured on selling was maybe 150,000 units a year.

What the research didn't show—*couldn't* show—was that the year the toy came out, toy dealers around the country were all looking for a good value to promote. A sort of "loss leader" they could advertise to bring people into the stores. It had to be something that represented a great value for the money and that would be a popular toy. The Family Farm set fit their needs exactly. The toy dealers could afford to sell it for $9.95 (just under the magic figure of conventional wisdom), and at that price they wouldn't get hurt. It was obviously a good deal, and so thousands of dealers stocked up heavily and sold out over and over again. Instead of leveling off at 150,000 sales, as the research had predicted, Family Farm took off like a rocket and sold something like 700,000 units that first year. Fisher-Price had to scramble like mad to keep up with reorders, since they hadn't geared production for that kind of demand.

Every now and then professional research will get all tangled up in its own feet, too. At Sears, the product design staff went to work on a pecan sheller brought in by a doctor from Georgia. The doctor had forty acres of pecan trees and had been selling pecans for some years as a sort of cash-crop hobby. A tinkerer by inclination, the good doctor devised a little gadget that shelled the pecans mechanically. He used it on his own pecans because shelled nuts always bring a much higher price than unshelled ones. But it occurred to him that housewives could use the sheller to save money. They could buy the cheaper pecans, still in the shell, take them home and turn them into expensive shelled pecans with his gadget. It made a lot of sense, so the doctor set up a small factory in an old post office building near his home and began turning out the shellers. It was a pretty simple device, with a couple of moving parts and some rubber bands. It looked a little crude, but it sure did the job. Sales grew and the doctor turned the sales and distribution over to a sales outfit in the South where it began doing a brisk business. Finally, it became such a success that the doctor and his pecan sheller were discovered by Sears!

Sears liked the idea, but they felt the gadget was too crude looking for their market. So they assigned a top industrial designer to streamline the doctor's design, get rid of those hokey old rubber bands and generally do a cosmetic job on the gadget. Before it was over, five engineers had taken a shot at improving the doctor's design, and they all gave up. With a sigh Sears put it into the catalogue in its down-home, funky original form and proceeded to sell it at the rate of $100,000 a year.

No, that's not marketing research, so it's really a slightly different category than we've been talking about. But here's the interesting sidelight—Bob Clower took a gross of the shellers to a church bazaar to demonstrate it and see what kind of sales results he could get with it. He wanted to get some idea of how it might do in the catalogue. Now Bob is an old door-to-door salesman and he's no slouch when it comes to something like this. If anybody could sell that sheller, Bob was the man. He rolled up his sleeves and shelled the hell out of a bunch of pecans and worked the crowd like an experienced pitchman. Sales result: zero. Nobody bought it. Bob went home with a sinking feeling that he had a real loser on his hands, that the sheller was going to *die* in the catalogue. And it was already printed.

As we know, of course, it sold beautifully. Bob said, "What if that sheller had been professionally market tested before we put it into the catalogue? It would have failed before it ever had a chance to succeed. We would not have put it in the catalogue, and we would have missed $100,000 in sales per year."

The point of all this is that research is not infallible by a long shot. The research can err either way—it can give false indications, and at best it can only sort out the extremes. But for all of that, it's one of the few ways of measuring desirability. Desirability remains a pretty subjective question, no matter how much research you do, so it's nice to know that there are other things you can do to make sure you have a desirable product in mind.

For instance, nearly everyone I talked to in doing my research for this book told me the same thing? "We're not looking for something completely new, no total breaks with what's gone before. Rather, we're more interested in finding a variation on an existing theme, an *evolutionary* rather than a *revolutionary* development."

Bob Hicks told me, "Ninety per cent of all new ideas really consist of taking an old, basic idea and using new materials and styling." (For example, the Family Farm toy that took off so unexpectedly.)

WHAT'S A GOOD IDEA?

The Barbie Doll at Mattel is another classic example of that kind of product. Paper dolls you can dress up have been around for years. Barbie simply translated that idea into three dimensions. The kids enjoyed it more because it was more realistic to put a real dress on a three-dimensional doll. Mattel enhanced that realism by giving Barbie a boy friend, a family, a choice of careers and all the accoutrements of the modern "good life" as seen on TV. And, of course, Mattel enjoyed it more because it put paper dolls into a new, higher price category and created a complete aftermarket. (Having bought the doll, the kids would want to keep adding to the wardrobe and the collection of status symbols for Barbie, Ken, et al.) It was an evolutionary development, but it revolutionized toy marketing.

The Die-Hard battery at Sear, Roebuck is also a great example of evolutionary ideas being winners. The major difference about the Die-Hard is that the walls of the battery are much thinner and lighter than those of previous storage batteries. More of the battery is the part that makes electricity, instead of the part that holds the battery acid in.

Thus, you can get the same amount of power out of a smaller battery. Or you can get more power out of the same size. I imagine that the Die-Hard battery is the most successful invention of its kind in history. Sears must have sold a jillion of them.

So when you're thinking about your invention, see if it emulates the Barbie Doll and the Die-Hard battery approach. If so, you have made a good start. As Bob Hicks told me, "A successful idea needs to have some relevance and continuity with the past. The new idea ought to be the next logical step in a progression." In other words, evolutionize, don't revolutionize.

Another way to insure the desirability of your invention is something we touched on in the last chapter. Make sure your idea solves an existing problem. Logically enough, if the problem you solve is a common one and the solution you devise is really a good one, you've got a desirable invention. Measure your idea against this benchmark!

There's one final aspect of product desirability that you ought to bear in mind. You may have a perfectly desirable invention, but if it is only desirable to a very limited group of people, it may not be marketable. If the only people who can use your invention are left-handed lady pinochle players, you're going to have a devil of a time getting it on the market. That's just too limited an audience to bother with, in terms of profit. There's not enough money to be made in selling it.

Anyway, whether you use some form of research or testing, whether you try to think of problems to solve, however you go about it, the first consideration is whether or not your invention will be wanted by a sizable number of people. Once you're past that hurdle, you have to figure out if it can be made for the right price.

The exact steps you have to take in determining the selling price of your invention are covered in some detail in Chapter VI, "Doing Your Homework." For the moment, the point is that price has a lot to do with the success or failure of a new invention, no matter how many people would like to have one. It gets down to the question of how much people are willing to pay to own your product. And that's not quite as straightforward a proposition as you might think.

The price acceptability of a product actually varies, depending on where it's sold. You know yourself that you might see some product in a discount drugstore and be shocked by the price—but not bat an eyelash at seeing the same price in a swankier store. For that very reason, many manufacturers make the same product with a different brand name, different packaging and—of course—different price tag. The upper-crust brand name will be sold at Madame Fifi's Gifte Boutique while the plebeian version will be hanging on aisle racks at Cheapo Charlie's Discount Mart. They'll both sell like gangbusters, too. Same product. Different package and price.

Price acceptability works the other way around, too. It is actually possible to make a product to sell too cheaply. By doing so you obviously cheat yourself out of some profit. But what's less obvious is that you could also cheat yourself out of some sales. Your invention might be highly desirable, but if the price is too low, people may be unwilling to buy it. They may have qualms about how well made it is, or they may have feelings that it is somehow beneath them to buy something that inexpensive to do what your invention does.

Ultimately, the only way to find out if your price is right—once you've done your homework and calculated what you'll have to get for the product to make a profit—is to do some research. Check the stores to see what similar or related products are going for. Find out how much price variation is going on in the field your invention fits into. See whether higher- or lower-priced versions of products in your field are being marketed in different kinds of stores. In other words, get a fix on what the price range is for products like yours and figure out if you can play in that league. And if you do some of that supermarket parking-lot research we were talking about a while ago, be sure you ask some questions about price.

Finally, there's the question of whether your product will make a profit for all the people along the line of distribution—manufacturer, sales organization, wholesaler, retailer. Again, it's not as simple a question as you might imagine. What you consider fair and reasonable profit for a manufacturer might not be fair and reasonable at all to the manufacturer with whom you're dealing.

Suppose, for instance, you're hoping to make a royalty deal with a manufacturer of automotive accessories. You've calculated your projected retail price on the basis of allowing 50 per cent markup for the manufacturer. That might sound just fine to you. But it's possible that your manufacturer only works on items with a 100 per cent markup. Your deal isn't going to interest him.

What it boils down to is that you're going to have to do a little research into the markup structures involved in the industry where your invention fits. Needless to say, the profit structure along the way from manufacturer to retailer will have an effect on the price of your product, which will have—as I said—a lot to do with whether you have a bad idea or not.

If you find that your invention covers all three main bases—desirability, value and profitability—there's still no guarantee that you're going to make a lot of money with your new idea. As I pointed out earlier, there's just no way to tell whether your idea is a winner or not. All you can tell is whether or not it's a loser.

III
PATENT IT, FAST!

Getting legal protection for your idea. What it costs, what it does, how to do it.

I was standing in a line not long ago, and to pass the time, I struck up a conversation with a stranger. She was a motherly-looking woman, probably hard-working, certainly not very wealthy. And it turned out she had an idea for an invention. An idea that was going to put her on easy street.

She had no way of knowing that I was writing a book about that very subject, and I didn't tell her. I wanted to see if the thing I expected to happen would happen.

It happened. It always does.

The conversation went something like this:

"It's really a great idea," she said.

(So far, so good. I've never yet heard anyone say, "I've got this mediocre idea here . . .")

"It wouldn't cost much to buy and just about everybody would want one," she continued.

"What sort of invention is it?" I asked.

"Oh," she said, embarrassed. "I wouldn't want to talk about it yet. Not until I've sold the idea. Someone might steal it."

"Have you thought about getting a patent for the idea?" I pressed. "Then you'd be protected."

"Oh, no. They cost so-o-o much money, and my brother-in-law told me I don't need one. He said all I have to do is mail a registered letter to myself explaining the idea. That

PATENT IT, FAST! 33

gives me proof that I had the idea first, in case anyone tries to steal it and claim they thought of it."

And that was that. I never did find out what the idea was, of course, because she was convinced I'd steal it and run off to Acapulco with the fortune that rightfully belonged to her. I wonder how she plans to sell the idea to someone if she can't talk about it?

The point is that, like most people with an idea for an invention, she was terrified of having the idea stolen and equally terrified of getting the protection of a patent.

The important lesson you should learn now is this: the first thing—the *very* first thing—you should do with the invention you want to develop is apply for a patent.

Hardly anyone does, unfortunately. Like the lady in the line, most first-time inventors are full of misinformation and trepidations about getting legal protection for their ideas. They live in mortal fear of having their idea stolen. But they dread even more the thought of getting a patent. All the money they'd have to spend, all the legal rigmarole they'd have to go through! You may feel the same way yourself. So let's set a few things straight about patents.

1. Just about everything you think you know about patents is probably wrong.

2. Patents, while not exactly bargain-basement stuff, can cost a lot less than you think. They're certainly much easier to obtain than most people have been led to believe.

3. A patent is the *only* real protection there is for an invention.

You can forget that old gag about mailing yourself a registered letter. The letter-to-yourself trick does offer some protection, it's true, but it is only partial protection at best. At worst, it's a trap. If all you have is a letter to yourself proving that you had the idea first, someone else still can steal your idea and run with it. Worse still, he may even be able to get a patent on your idea! And you won't be able to stop him with your letter.

Why? Well, in the eyes of the law, there are two steps involved in the act of inventing something. First there is conception—having the idea. By mailing yourself the registered letter, you are establishing that you had the idea as of the date you mailed the letter. And as far as it goes, that's fine. It works. It's proof, all right, but it misses the crucial second step. The second step is called "reduction to practice"—putting your abstract idea into some concrete form. Your letter to yourself doesn't have a thing to do with this step. In fact, there are only two ways to reduce to practice: (1) You can make a model or example of the invention. This is called "actual reduction." (2) You can apply for a patent. This is called "constructive reduction."

Okay. So there you are with your letter. And you get word that some no-good creep has stolen your idea and has applied for a patent. If all you have is that registered letter, your chances of beating him aren't worth much. In all likelihood he gets the patent and you get the short end of the stick. Even if you actually made a model—that is, you achieved "actual reduction to practice"—you still have to prove to the satisfaction of the government that you did it before he did. You've gotten yourself hip deep into a messy, costly, time-consuming legal battle. And you could lose.

Suppose the other guy hasn't applied for a patent either. Suppose he's simply gone into business cranking out your invention and selling it. "Aha!" you say. "I'll soon put a stop to this by taking him to court and showing the judge my letter, proving I had the idea first." Wrong. It doesn't matter who had the idea first if you don't have a patent. Only a patent will stop him from producing your invention and marketing it. Only a patent will prevent him from selling it to some manufacturer for a royalty deal. You can't touch him with anything short of a patent, and that's what you'll have to get before you can shut down his machinery. In the meantime, he can sell as many as he wants, perfectly legally. He may even completely glut the market with your product before you can get him stopped. And there you'll sit—no market left for your product, wishing you'd applied for a patent before things got out of hand.

There's one more catch to the registered-letter gimmick. It is a piece of evidence. Maybe your *only* piece of evidence. But shortly before going to trial with it, the odds are that you'll destroy that evidence. That's right. The majority of people do. The reason you send the letter by registered mail is to have proof of the date it was sent and to have an official United States Postal Service seal on the letter flap. The seal proves that the letter hasn't been tampered with and that the contents are the same ones you originally mailed. So far, so good. Now it's getting close to your day in court. It probably has been more than a year since you mailed yourself the letter. Now panic and doubt set in. Your whole case is based on the contents of the envelope, and you begin to wonder if you really remember exactly what the letter says, all the details of the invention you described at the time. Are you sure? Nope. So what do you do?

You open the letter. You destroy the seal. You make the evidence worthless.

Sure you're smarter than that. But a surprising number of people aren't. I suppose the way to beat that particular problem is to make a carbon copy of the letter when you write it, then clip it to the sealed envelope when it comes back to you in the mailbox. But it still doesn't solve the essential problem of getting real protection for your idea.

There is no short cut to protection. Getting a patent is much easier and better than relying on some legal folk remedy like the registered letter to yourself. So let's take a look at what that real thing is, how you get it, what it costs and how long it takes.

To begin with, there really are a number of different kinds of protection available. I've been referring to them all loosely (if somewhat inaccurately) by the name "patent." In fact, the five different kinds of protection you can get are:

COPYRIGHT Copyrights are for works of artistic endeavor. Paintings, photographs, poems and this book all are examples of things that can be and are copyrighted. A copyright is, in effect, a patent for something that is published rather than manufactured.

TRADEMARK REGISTRATION Trademark registration protects a brand name you choose for your product, along with any distinctive design you may use in displaying that trademark. A certain cola manufacturer, which shall remain nameless, gets very huffy every time someone uses its brand name without proper capitalization. Rightfully so. As exclusive owner of that name, the company is legally entitled to prescribe how it may be used in public. The company spent millions of dollars and a lot of years making it a recognized brand name, and it deserves to benefit from the reputation built for that trademark. Registration of the name protects the company's rights. It also gives the owner of the trademark a means to prevent that name from becoming a generic label for all cola drinks. That's easier said than done, of course, because we have a tendency to turn a brand name for a popular product into a synonym for that kind of product. Think about it. For instance, what do you call cellophane tape? Facial tissue? What did your parents call a refrigerator? See what I mean?

Even patents themselves come in three different flavors. There are design patents, utility patents and—somewhat rarely—plant patents. Each one has a different job to do and a different kind of protection to offer.

PLANT PATENTS The plant patent covers most new strains or new varieties of growing things. New varieties of roses, for example, often are covered by plant patents. Orchids, camellias and hybrid corn are other fairly common subjects of plant patents. The rule of thumb (green, of course) is this: If you developed it, if it grows and if it's unique, it can be covered by a plant patent.

UTILITY PATENT The utility patent is the one most of us mean when we say the word "patent." It offers the strongest protection of all the patents you can apply for. It's only logical, then, that the utility patent also is the most complicated and expensive to apply for. The utility patent covers the mechanical design and functioning of a device, which is sort of what you thought patents were for all along, right?

DESIGN PATENT But the design patent is something else again. It covers only the surface aspects of an invention—the ornamental design as opposed to the mechanical functioning of an object. Any invention that is unique because of the way it looks rather than the way it works if rightfully the subject of a design patent.

Those, then, are the five different kinds of legal protection available to you. You can use them in just about any combination, depending on the nature of your idea. For instance, on the Rickie Tickie Stickies, I copyrighted all the material on the package and the display items I designed to merchandise the flowers. And I got a design patent on that illegible type face I designed for the trademark. Of course, I registered the trademark, too. I did *not* get a design patent, because I figured that it was too easy to beat, in the case of the flower. Any minor change in the design would be enough to beat that patent. As we'll see later, that may not have been the wisest decision I ever made. The theory is to give your product as many kinds of protection as possible.

But what, precisely, is it that these five things do for you? How do they protect you? They're no permits. You don't need a permit from anybody to manufacture and market your idea, work of art or brand name. What you *do* need is a way to prevent someone else from doing it and making money from your stroke of genius. That's what your legal protection does. It gives you the exclusive right to manufacture and market your idea, or to license the manufacture and marketing of it to someone else. The key word is "exclusive." You control the ball game. You own the license. If you choose to let someone else in on that license, you can charge money for it or you can charge a royalty on merchandise produced under it.

Getting the protection of a patent, a copyright or a trademark registration ranges all the way from ridiculously easy to fairly complicated and time-consuming. The cost varies from peanuts to a moderately large sum of money. It depends on what you're looking for and how complicated your invention or idea is. Let's take a look at patents, for openers.

The first thing to do when you decide you want a patent is, logically enough, to call a patent attorney and make an appointment. I'm lucky in that respect. I've known Warren Patton, a highly regarded patent attorney, since I first became involved in marketing inventions. In your case, you probably don't have the name of a patent attorney in your address book, so you'll have to do a little scouting around. Your banker may have a name or two for you. If you have a lawyer of your own, he may know the name of a good patent attorney in town. Maybe even the bar association of your county or state could help you out. One way or another, find one and tell him you'd like to meet with him to discuss a patent application.

The initial meeting is practically guaranteed to be easy and painless. Most patent attorneys charge only a very nominal fee—or sometimes no fee at all—for the first brief discussion of your invention. It usually lasts for about half an hour. And that painless half an hour may save you enormous amounts of blood, toil, tears, sweat and treasure.

I don't know how many times Warren has had to tell an inventor at that first meeting, "Sir, that's a fine idea you have there, but it's been done. The patent was issued several years ago." Or on other occasions, he's said something like, "I'm sorry, but there simply doesn't seem to be any way to patent that idea. It sounds workable and salable, but it's made up of a combination of things that already are in general use."

The wording of the federal statute on patents is worth quoting in regard to that last one. The law says, "A patent may not be obtained . . . if the difference between the subject matter sought to be patented and the prior art are such that the subject matter as a whole would have been obvious, at the time the invention was made, to a person having ordinary skill in the art to which said subject matter pertained."

In other words, if it's obvious—if it's simply a new combination of old, well-known objects or a new use of an old, well-known object—it's not an invention, and it can't be patented. There are any number of good ideas that fall into this category. Your patent attorney can tell you right up front if yours is one of them. Naturally, that doesn't mean you can't market it. But you won't be protected by a patent if you do, and you can expect competition to crop up fairly quickly after you get on the market with it. You also may have some trouble selling an unprotected idea to a manufacturer.

Sometimes the patent attorney might even break the news, as gently as possible, that the idea is a loser and the inventor probably is wasting his time. You don't have to take the attorney's word for it, of course, but most patent attorneys worth their salt have seen enough inventors come and go to be worth listening to.

When you see the patent attorney, you should be prepared to give a complete and fairly detailed explanation of your invention. Until he understands fully what your invention is and what it does, he can't start action on your patent application. Your presentation doesn't have to be elaborate. It might be nice to have some sketches or maybe even a model of the invention, but if you can talk and flap your arms well enough to get the idea across, that's fine. (If you have drawings, by the way, they don't have to be professional quality. Even if they were, they'd have to be redrawn for the patent application. The Patent and Trademark Office has its own carefully specified style of drawing and won't accept anything else. There are artists who specialize in those drawings, and your patent attorney will take care of all that for you.) In the case of a design patent, where the whole thing lies in what it looks like, you may have to have some sort of drawing or sketch to get the idea across to the attorney.

Once the attorney understands your invention, he'll open a file which sets your patent application into motion officially. That may not sound like a big deal, but it has one important benefit. It is legal proof that, on such and such date, you had the idea for your invention. This is proof of conception which will stand up in just about any court in the land. (For whatever it's worth, you can prove conception by explaining your idea to someone and getting him to sign a statement that you did so, that he understood it and that the date was so and so. This is at least as good as the old registered-letter routine.)

Having opened your file, the attorney's next step is to conduct a search. This is a very critical part of any patent application. What's involved is this: The attorney (or more likely an associate of his in Washington, D.C.) goes to the patent office and carefully checks out all the patents that seem to have some bearing on your invention. Any patents of particular interest are copied and sent back to your attorney.

Actually, you can do the same search in many public libraries across the country. A number of cities have libraries that are official patent repositories. But doing the search in the library will take longer and will almost certainly be less thorough than doing it at the patent office in Washington. The cross-indexing system in the library patent repositories is much less complete than the system used in Washington. Doing it at the library is doing it the hard way.

The object of the search is to make sure that no one has already obtained a patent on your invention or something pretty close to your invention. It also uncovers other inventions that may be able to do some of the things your invention does, which will have a bearing on the claims you can make for your invention in the patent application.

You may be able to skip the whole search, by the way. If the invention is in a very specialized area, an area in which you are very familiar, you may not need a search. You'll know all the products on the market and in use in your specialized field, and you'll know, for a fact, that your idea is unique. This sort of situation is rather rare, but it *does* happen once in a while.

The first page or so of your patent application is pretty much spelled out by the law. You must offer a detailed description of the invention and some background on the area of interest to which it applies. There must be a description of what the law calls its "best mode of operation"—how to use it. And there must be drawings of the invention, except in cases where that's impossible. A chemical process, for instance. This whole section is called the "specifications."

The next section is a series of numbered paragraphs called "claims." This is where you put forth your notion of the unique, exclusive features of your invention. The features that make it unlike anything covered by an existing patent. Here is where there is almost always a lot of haggling back and forth between your attorney and the patent office. The government is interested in keeping your claims as narrow as possible, limiting them to the most specific and least sweeping ones. You, of course, are interested in claiming as much as possible for your invention, and in the broadest possible terms so that you have more protection.

I'd better explain a little bit about broad versus narrow claims. Let's say, for the sake of illustration, that you're trying to patent your new process for turning base metals into gold. The patent office may well come back and say you can only claim to turn lead into gold, based on their interpretation of your specifications. Back and forth go the arguments, volley and thunder, until some mutually acceptable compromise statement is agreed upon. If you have to settle for a patent limited to the process of turning lead into gold, someone else may be able to patent a process for turning brass into gold. If, however, you've proved to the satisfaction of the patent office that your process will turn *any* base metal into gold, you're covered and the new guy loses. That's what I mean by narrow versus broad claims. The more you cram under the umbrella of your patent, the less there is left over for someone else to patent.

In putting forth your claims on the patent application, you put the broadest claims first, getting narrower as you get farther down the list. Why bother putting in the narrow claims, too? Because later on in your negotiations with the patent office it may turn out that your broad claim is not protectable. Then you can fall back on the narrower claim, and so on down the list.

The whole application, all the drawings, all the legal statements and the patent search will be handled by your patent attorney. All you have to do is sort of help out when he needs some additional information about your invention. And you have to pay the man.

As you might expect, the cost of a patent application varies all over the lot, depending on how complicated it gets and how long it takes.

You can figure on spending something like $300 to $400

PATENT IT, FAST!

for what is called a "preliminary novelty search" which is a search to determine whether or not your idea is novel, or, in other words, new and unique. For a little bit less you can have a "state of the art" search which will tell you, for instance, what patents are in effect regarding vacuum cleaners. Or lawn mowers. Or whatever. This sort of search is helpful if you're trying to come up with some sort of new idea in a specific area. It's no help for someone who already has invented something and wants to find out if it can be patented.

Filing the application is the next cost. A utility patent application for a relatively simple idea—one that can be shown in one page of patent office drawings and a relatively short set of specifications and claims—will cost anywhere from $700 to $1,500. Unless you have a pretty technical invention, this is about what you could expect to pay. Naturally, filing the application for a plant patent or a design patent costs less since there is less work and time involved.

Then there's the cost of all that negotiation between your attorney and the patent office over your list of claims. Depending on how hot the fight waxes and what the attorney has to go through to win for you, the fee may go from $250 to $1,000. About $500 is a reasonable figure to work with.

You can rest assured that the government wants some of your money, too. Fortunately, they don't seem to want very much of it. For a utility patent, the federal fee is around $150 depending on the length and complexity of the application, and the patent lasts for seventeen years. For a design patent, the fee is calculated in a strange and wondrous way. You have a choice of paying $10 or $20 or $30. For $10 you get a 3½-year patent. For $20 you get a 7-year patent and for $30 you get a 14-year patent. Why the government believes someone would choose a 3½-year patent instead of a 14-year patent just to save twenty bucks is beyond me. The only way to renew a patent is by an act of Congress, by the way, so don't count on it. Once the patent lapses, it's generally bye-bye for good.

As you can see, the real sweaty palms period of the patent application is during the negotiation with the patent office over your claims. Here's how that works:

After your patent attorney files the application, everybody sits back and waits nervously for the patent office to make its move. After a while the patent office replies, usually saying something terribly discouraging. Like, "No." They may ini-

42 HOW TO TURN YOUR IDEA INTO A MILLION DOLLARS

tially refuse to grant a patent at all, or they may grant only a very narrow claim. This letter is called an "office action," and it is just the opening gun in the battle that almost always ensues. Don't be distressed. Everybody (or just about everybody) has to go through this wrestling match. It's all part of the game.

The lawyer then sends back a thoughtful reply, pointing out to the patent office all the reasons you should be granted a patent after all. The patent office grudgingly reconsiders a few things, your attorney insists on a few more and so the battle goes until somehow a resolution is reached. The patent office bases its objections on patents already existing and on published material that seems to indicate your idea isn't new. Your attorney, naturally, puts forth arguments that those other inventions aren't anything at all like yours.

One disappointing fact is that the patent office generally will *not* cite conflicts between your application and other applications which are pending. If there is another patent in the works that conflicts partly or totally with yours, you have no way of knowing. And the patent office won't tell you. They're not being mean or unreasonable, by the way. It's just that they can't very well talk to you about a conflict with a patent that hasn't been issued. Without a patent, there is no infringement. The first time anybody normally finds out about such a conflict is when one of the pending patents is issued, at long last. Then the applicant whose patent has not yet been issued gets a letter from the patent office. The letter points out that the applicant's invention now is in conflict with the other, brand new patent.

Once in a great while two or more conflicting patents will near completion at almost the same time. When the patent officials see that kind of situation shaping up, they'll step in and tell all of the applicants involved that there is a problem. Each applicant then has the right to copy down all the claims on the other applications, study them and call for a federal "interference proceeding" aimed at parcelling out the claims among the conflicting patent applicants in as equitable a fashion as possible.

Getting a patent takes time, of course. Starting from the beginning, the search usually goes on for about six weeks. Then your attorney needs a month or so to prepare the patent application, including all those specifications, claims, drawings and so forth. Finally, there's all that haggling with the patent office. The government would dearly love to be able to complete this part of the process in eighteen or twenty-four months. So far, though, that's the wildest kind of wishful thinking. In real life, you'd better figure on something more like thirty to thirty-six months. Personally, the fastest I've ever been awarded a patent was twenty-seven months.

Trademark registration is a whole different process, although you'll still need the services of a patent attorney. As the law stands right now, you can't register a trademark unless it is currently in use in interstate commerce. (There's a feeling in the legal profession that someday you'll be able to register a trademark based on your intention to use it in commerce, but that day hasn't come yet.)

All your attorney has to do is file an application along with a drawing of your trademark in its least specific form—i.e. block letters with no punctuation except for hyphens. If you plan some distinctive way of displaying it—some tricky type face or with some sort of drawing built around it, for example—you have to furnish a sample of the name in that form, too. Finally, you'll need proof that the product is currently being sold both in and out of state. (You needn't send that proof along with your application, by the way. You just need to have it on hand in case there's a question.)

You bundle up your application, along with a check for $35, and that's it. In a few weeks you'll receive a filing receipt from the patent office, acknowledging that they got your application. Later, after a few months, you'll get a letter saying one of two things: (1) Your trademark seems to be allowable and will be published for opposition by anyone who thinks it conflicts with his trademark, or (2) your trademark is not allowable.

It might not be allowable because it's too close to an existing trademark. Or it might be in violation of some statute. Or it might be what the office calls "scandalous." (That covers not only obscenities, but also things repugnant to public morality, such as the use of the deity in your trademark.) The patent office will cite its specific reasons for not allowing your trademark, and you can argue back if you disagree.

If, after all is said and done, no one objects to your trademark and the patent office can't find any reason not to allow it, you will be permitted to use this symbol ® with your trademark, indicating that it is registered and, therefore, protected.

While the registration is still pending, you're entitled to use a "T.M." with your trademark. This indicates to the world that it is your trademark and, by inference, that you plan to register it. It does not mean that the trademark is protected. That T.M. is a statement of *your* intention, not the government's.

Once your trademark is registered, no one else can use it and trade on your product's reputation by stealing its good name. The actual degree of protection is a little subjective, though. For instance, it might be possible for someone to use a name very similar to yours, provided that the type face or means of displaying it are distinctly different from the one you use. By the same token, a similar type face or means of display might be used if the name is distinctly different from yours. It's all a matter of judgment, and if pushing comes to shoving, it has to be settled in court. Needless to say, the government won't register a trademark if there's one already registered with which it would clearly be in conflict. So, by registering your trademark, you also get some assurance that you are not in danger of looking too much like some other trademark on the market.

A trademark may be renewed every twenty years for as long as it is used in interstate commerce.

Copyrights used to confuse me. According to the old law, you had to publish something before you could copyright it. The question was, what constituted "publication"? If you wrote a poem and ran off some copies on the office copying machine, had you published it?

Worse, until you published, anyone could come along and steal your idea. (In theory, at least. In practice, the ancient "common law copyright" gave you protection of a sort by avowing that the creator of an idea owned the rights to it.)

The whole thing was a little murky for my taste. But as of January 1, 1978, a new copyright law went into effect in the United States and it clarified a lot of that murkiness. Here's what the new law says:

As soon as you write your poem or paint your picture or do whatever it is you want to protect, you can copyright it. You don't have to publish it first. As long as the material has been fixed in some tangible form, even if it's just a handwritten manuscript, you can get protection.

Better still, that protection now lasts for the lifetime of the creator, plus fifty years. (Under the old law, a copyright was good for twenty-eight years and could be renewed for another twenty-eight years. After that, it became part of the "public domain" and available for anyone to quote or reproduce.)

Copyright protection is the simplest of all to obtain. You simply file the official copyright application form with the Copyright Office in Washington. Not the Patent Office. The Copyright Office. There's nothing to it. And it costs only $10.00 for the copyright fee, plus a few dollars to the lawyer for filing it. No more than $100 on the average. In fact, you don't really have to have a lawyer in on the case, since it's no major undertaking to fill out the form yourself.

All through this whole chapter, I've been concentrating on the protection aspects of patents, copyrights and trademark registration. But there are some equally important, if less obvious, benefits to filing your application early in the game. By applying for a patent, you're telling the world that you're serious about your invention. You mean business and you're doing a full-bore, professional job of developing your idea and taking it to market. That can be very important to you. Millions of people have ideas, after all. Bright ideas, even. Most of them never bother to take that next step and apply for legal protection. Simply taking that step begins to separate you from the crowd of hazy dreamers and puts you in the much more select group of doers. Doers attract a great deal more attention—and money—than hazy dreamers.

Let's say, for example, you're approaching a manufacturer to whom you'd like to sell your idea for a royalty deal or a flat fee. If you have a patent in the works, you're way ahead of the inventor who doesn't. Your application for a patent is evidence that you've done your homework, that you're not just wasting the man's time with some half-baked scheme. It gives the manufacturer one more reason not to ignore you, and you stand that much better a chance of being considered seriously.

What's more, a reputable manufacturer will feel a good deal more comfortable talking to you about your invention if you have a patent application in the works. Strange as it may seem, that patent application protects *him*, too. Warren Patton, my patent attorney, explained it to me this way: "With a patent application, you, as the inventor, are relying on the patent laws of the United States to establish your rights. Here is something that's on file in the patent office. It's a matter of record, and if you get into a fight in the courts, it can be established as to what you had at that time and what you submitted to them."

It makes sense when you stop to think about it. One of the things any manufacturer dreads is that an inventor may come to him with some idea, then claim later on that the manufacturer stole it. Manufacturers are always developing ideas, and they may well have something already in the works that's related in some degree or other to your invention. But your patent application spells out completely, and in full detail, exactly what it was that you presented to the manufacturer for his consideration. It's all down in black and white with very little room for fudging. All you can prove talking about at your meeting is the invention you describe in your patent application. By the same token, you've got proof of what it was you presented in case the manufacturer *should* try to steal your idea. The end result is a much more comfortable meeting. He'll feel more secure. You'll feel more secure. Together you can get down to the business of discussing your invention without all those doubts casting a shadow.

Finally, your patent application tells the manufacturer a couple of other things he likes to hear: that there's pretty good reason to believe your invention really is unique; that you have some indication your idea can be protected. Those are two of the early questions you seek to answer in the process of applying for a patent. Your patent application tells the manufacturer that his investment in your idea will have some degree of protection.

The same kind of thinking applies when you make a pitch to get backing for your invention on your own. To a bank committee, perhaps. Maybe a group of investors. They're all impressed by the same kinds of things as the manufacturers. And for the same reasons. If they're going to sink money into your idea, they'd like to know that you're going about it professionally, and they'd like to believe that their investment has some protection. It's up to you to convince them.

I hope that the lady I met in the line reads this and follows up on it. I'd like to believe she will develop her idea, she will get protection and she will wind up in Acapulco with a fortune. I hope I've done a good enough job of convincing her—and you—that getting legal protection is one of the earliest things to think about when you're developing an idea. But I can't leave you without pointing out an important fact.

PATENT IT, FAST!

A patent, copyright and trademark registration are absolutely your only protection. But the protection is *not* absolute. There is a dark side to the coin, and I'll devote the next chapter to it.

IV
THE PLAINTIVE PLAINTIFF

Getting legal protection doesn't automatically mean you're protected.

A patent, as I see it, is nothing more than an invitation to a court case.

Joseph A. Iaia

Joseph A. Iaia is not a name you're likely to recognize right off the bat. He's not a world-renowned authority on how patents work. He is, however, rapidly becoming an authority on how patents sometimes don't work.

Joe is a bluff, up-front kind of guy who owns and operates a little manufacturing operation called Aero-Stat Company in Gardena, a small corner of the Los Angeles urban sprawl. Joe started it a few years after he got out of the Navy. He took some knowhow and some skills he developed in the service and, just as the recruiting posters say, turned them into a business for himself in civilian life.

But don't get the impression that Aero-Stat is a dinky little back-yard mom-and-pop business. Joe is right up to his eyebrows in the highly sophisticated, highly technical aerospace and electronics industry. A small piece of it, at least. He has a little something to be proud of every time an F-5E fighter takes off someplace in the world, every time he reads about the historic Apollo space shots. Joe even designed a componet for the new-fangled electronic wizardry with

THE PLAINTIVE PLAINTIFF 49

which our infantrymen are equipped these days. Right now he's working on an advanced new fighter evolved from the F-5 series, and he's designing a bit of the space shuttle that will be our next manned venture into space.

Joe is involved in all this because he invented a new kind of sealing system. He began working on it when he was an enlisted man in the Navy, coming up with sealing systems for fuel tanks in carrier aircraft. Later he perfected the system. Joe's special seals are used on a lot of planes and rockets and electronic gadgets. His customers are biggies, government contractors who probably spill more in a month than Joe's whole company cost.

Some of those biggies have ripped Joe off. They've taken his patented sealing system, manufactured it and sold it to the government—to you and me—without ever paying a cent of royalty to Joe. That brings us to our topic of patents.

Joe started out by doing what he thought was the right thing. As soon as he perfected his sealing system, he got a patent on it and on the special screw he designed to make it work. At the time, he was working as a salesman for a firm that dealt in aerospace components. So Joe made a royalty agreement with his employer and added the new sealing system to their bag of wares. For a couple of years or so, that was fine. But the time came when Joe decided to go into business for himself. The great American dream. He quit, set up his shop, started making sealing systems and promptly found himself in court.

The company for which Joe used to work sued him, claiming that the patent belonged to them, not to Joe. It took six years of court battling, plus uncounted thousands of dollars in legal fees and related expenses, for Joe finally to win. And that was just the beginning. While he was still in court with his first case, Joe learned that another company was making and selling his sealing screws to a manufacturer of civilian aircraft—without paying any royalties to Joe. Since he already had the legal machinery rolling, Joe took on the second manufacturer simultaneously. He won, of course. But it cost him several thousand more dollars.

The settlement was perfectly amicable. In fact, Joe was praised by the judge when, immediately after winning, he asked the judge for a meeting in chambers. There Joe offered his erstwhile opponents a good deal. He sold them a non-exclusive license to manufacture and market his sealing system, retaining the right to manufacture and sell it himself as well. As Joe put it, "Everybody got a little bit of what they wanted and that made the judge very happy." The deal was struck, the company went on selling the sealing system, Joe collected his royalties and everyone was pleased. For a while.

To understand Joe's next lesson, you have to understand a little of how his business works. We'll set up a hypothetical case to show you what has happened to Joe a number of times. The case is fictitious, but the pattern is drawn from real life.

Joe gets an order from Acme Amalgamated Aircraft. "Joe, whip us up a sealing system for the tracking radar unit on our new F-26 'Flying Farblundget' interceptor," they say. Joe solves the mathematics and physics of the problem, deals with all the tricky compound curves and comes up with the design. He provides Acme Amalgamated with the blueprints and specifications and knocks out a couple samples on his machinery for the test model of the plane. Acme Amalgamated installs the sealing system on the radar unit, the test flights are a success and somewhere in the darkest depths of the Pentagon, an admiral or a general signs an order for several hundred of the new Flying Farblundgets. So far, Joe hasn't made a dime. He has spent several months perfecting the new seal, adapting his system to the specifications of the new plane. He has spent money to make the prototype, for which he receives a nominal sum. But he doesn't start to make a profit until he begins collecting on those several hundred airplanes the government ordered. Ideally, Joe will get the contract to manufacture the seals himself. Less ideally, he would settle for a royalty on the seals made by someone else or by Acme Amalgamated in its own shops. That's the plum the law offers Joe or any other inventor as a reward for succeeding with an invention. But that plum often turns out to be a prune.

After a decent interval, Joe calls the company and asks what's going on with the contract for the radar seals. "Oh, thanks a lot for the design, but we won't be needing you to make those for us," the company replies airily. "We'll be making those ourselves right here in our own shops." Without, of course, paying any royalties on the seals.

The first few times it happened, Joe was incensed. Who wouldn't be? But he quickly found out that the only way to collect his royalties was to go to court. What's more, once the

THE PLAINTIVE PLAINTIFF

company went so far as to fight Joe in court, they would wait until the very last minute—until their defeat was absolutely imminent—before they'd offer any kind of settlement to him. The theory seems to be that they'll force Joe to go all the way to the mat and spend all his time and money, just to make sure he can't be bluffed out. Then, when Joe has a loaded gun pointed at their heads, they'll say, "Don't pull the trigger. We'll make a deal."

Joe has learned that to beat the predators, he has to go to court just about every time, spending a small fortune on every case. It doesn't matter that he wins.

"I just can't afford that again," he said. "Besides, if I spend all that time in court, I won't be working on new projects. That's what I really like to do."

He's not bitter. Just disappointed that the system set up to help inventors doesn't seem to be working for him. Sitting in his shop with me one afternoon, he mused aloud about the shortcomings of the patent laws.

"You can't protect yourself," he said. "That's where the laws really fall down. They say, 'Yes you can,' and if you've got a million dollars, yes you can. For a small company like this, you might just as well fold up. I would have to hock the whole place and then maybe I might lose it. So what's my alternative? I can sue 'em. Or I can keep my mouth shut."

He has chosen to keep his mouth shut. The risks are more than he cares to accept, so he takes his lumps and hopes to make a profit with the good guys who still are out there doing business. For every time he gets hustled and taken to the cleaners, Joe figures he'll get a couple of contracts that make money for him and for Aero-Stat.

I can sympathize with Joe. I've been there myself. A case in point involved a chain of clothing stores in Southern California which ripped me off a few years ago. I discovered one day that a copyrighted poster I had developed and was marketing was being printed on the front of T-shirts sold by the clothing chain. When I challenged them about it, the store operators were very apologetic. They said they'd bought the shirts in Mexico from some salesman who said they'd been made in Pakistan, and the store was sure sorry that the shirts were causing me a problem.

I don't know where the shirts actually were made or how the chain came by them. For all I know they could have been telling the truth. Anyway, the store promised to quit selling the T-shirts, since there were only a few left anyway. But when I tried to talk to the store operators about paying some sort of damages, they absolutely refused. Wouldn't hear of it. They'd gotten into the market and out of it, they'd made their money and as far as they were concerned, I'd have to sue them if I wanted to collect. I knew that, based on my estimate of their sales, the most I'd be able to collect would be five hundred or a thousand dollars in damages. It just didn't make sense to spend a lot of money to recover a few bucks. So what did I do? Like Joe, I kept my mouth shut and took my lumps, even though I was sorely tempted at the time to go ahead and sue them.

Just what *is* involved if you decide to defend your patent, copyright or registered trademark?

Let's assume that you've found out that somebody's stealing your idea. Maybe you saw it in a store, maybe a friend told you about it. One way or another, you'll soon get the word if you've been knocked off. Obviously, your first move is to write a letter telling the guy to stop. You will demand that he cease and desist from manufacturing your invention and that he pay for your share of the profits he's made from it. Often as not he will either ignore your letter completely or reply to it by refusing your demands. Then you've got to make up your mind if you want to pursue it all the way to court. It's your only remaining recourse.

If you've made up your mind to haul the rascal to court, you file a federal suit. (Patents are covered by federal, not state, laws.) Your goal is twofold: First, you want to make him stop manufacturing and selling your invention. Second, you want to collect from him the money you would have made on royalties if he had been playing fair and square with your patent. If this is the first time you've defended this particular patent, the judge is not likely to grant you a temporary restraining order or preliminary injunction to stop your opponent from making and selling the product while the case is being settled. After all, it's a fundamental principle of our legal system that one is considered innocent until proved guilty. So your opponent is presumed to be pure as the driven snow until the court rules otherwise. He will be permitted to continue on his merry way with your invention while the case is pending and in court. As we know from Joe Iaia's experience, that can go on for years. Not a very happy prospect.

On the other hand, getting an injunction is not all hearts

and flowers, either. If you've already won an earlier case with the patent in question, the judge may decide to grant you the restraining order, all right. But it isn't cheap. In order to get it, you'll have to post a bond. A substantial bond. It has to be big enough to pay your opponent for all the profits he would have made if you hadn't churlishly restrained him from doing business with your product. If you lose the case, he gets to keep the money you put up for the bond. If you win the case, you get it back. Meanwhile, you have a sizable piece of change tied up.

Why a bond? Well, the court still must consider your opponent innocent until proved guilty. But the court is entitled to feel that he might not be quite as innocent as the next guy, since your patent has been upheld before. So he compromises by granting you the injunction, but making you post a bond in case you're wrong.

Naturally, your opponent is going to claim that he would have made a fortune if you hadn't enjoined him. He wants you to put up a great, big bond. (That might force you to reconsider the case, or at least the injunction. And if he happens to win, he'll have a handsome profit for his time in court.) You, on the other hand, will disagree. You'll argue that he wouldn't have made a whole lot of money anyway and that you can cover his potential profits with a very small bond. The judge, trying to be as fair as possible, will determine the size of the bond, and that will be that.

While all this is going on, you'll be spending other money. For an attorney, to begin with. Probably your patent attorney, since that's his specialty. He'll be conducting the case for you, laying out the legal strategy, putting together the information he needs and the briefs he'll submit. You'll probably be spending quite a bit of your own time conferring with your attorney, appearing in court and so forth. That costs money, too, since your time is as valuable as the next guy's.

The big day finally arrives. The judge finds that your patent has been infringed and he orders your opponent to quit it. He then orders your opponent to account to you for all his profits on the invention and to pay you the amount the court feels you are entitled to for royalties. Big deal. It usually turns out that most of the money you collect goes to pay your expenses for the lawsuit. Maybe even more than you collect, if the case has been long and difficult. Even in the rare cases where the judge orders your opponent to pay additional damages and costs to you, it still rarely makes the suit profitable. Purely in terms of profit, you would have been better off digging ditches than winning your lawsuit.

But profit may be the last thing on your mind when you file suit. You may very well be more interested in setting an example for others who might think of stealing your ideas. You may simply be angry and looking for revenge. You may even be planning to use the court decision as leverage on your opponent to make a royalty deal with you for the future. There are a lot of pros and cons to be balanced, and you are the only person who can make the final decision on whether or not to go to court.

So you shouldn't feel totally depressed, I ought to point out that there are a few other tricks you can have up your sleeve to fight the knock-offs. I nailed a Canadian outfit early in the Rickie Tickie Stickies adventure and I never once had to say the word "patent." In a way, it was amusing, although it sure didn't seem so at the time. The theft was so blatant, I couldn't believe it. To print their package they simply photographed a Rickie Tickie Stickies package and made plates from the picture. It was such a quick and dirty job that they didn't even bother to opaque the negative and blot out the staple holes they left when they opened the package to get the flowers out. Every package they sold had a lovely picture of two little staple holes printed on it. For their brand name, they used a photocopy of my brand name, with the letters rearranged to spell "Stick 'em Ups." Aside from being an appropriate name, under the circumstances, it meant that they only had to draw three letters of their own in my type style.

Now I had no patent on the flowers in the U.S., much less in Canada. And, although I did have a U.S. design patent on the type face, that was no help north of the border. But I got the rascals anyway. When they photocopied my package, they included some pictures of people using Rickie Tickie Stickies. That was part of my package design. I had signed releases from all of the models on file, and I knew all of them personally. (Being an impoverished inventor when I did the package, I used friends and relatives instead of professionals for my models.) So I called the company in Canada and pointed out that the unauthorized use of those people on their package constituted an invasion of privacy and that the models would be happy to sue them for every dime in the company

THE PLAINTIVE PLAINTIFF

treasury if they didn't cease and desist right away. There was a short silence and then a loud "gulp" from the other end of the line. That was the last we ever heard of "Stick 'em Ups."

There was another occasion, later on, when I was able to stop a Japanese company from copying the Stickies. I did it with my type face patent and my copyright on the package. They had photocopied the instructions on the back of our package—instructions Margaret wrote when we first began marketing the Stickies. The only thing that was changed was the name. Every time Margaret had written "Rickie Tickie Stickies" in the instructions, the Japanese had blanked it out and inserted their own name. (Knock-offs seem to have a penchant for dreaming up appropriate names. These were called "Tackies.") They also copied my weird type face for the label identification on the front of the package. Now this was a different deal altogether from the Canadian affair. These flowers were being sold in the United States. I was protected here by my design patent on the type face and by my copyright of the package. That copyright was the best six bucks I've spent in a long time. When I pointed these violations out to the U.S. distributor, he quickly and quietly took the Japanese flowers off the market. For him, the item was a pretty small piece of business. It wasn't worth the hassle of going to court. I guess the flowers continued to be sold in Japan, but that was really no skin off my back since I wasn't doing much business in the Japanese market anyway.

You may wonder, by the way, why I never patented or copyrighted the design of the flowers. Well you're right, in a way. But a design patent on something like a plastic flower really isn't worth the effort. By changing the design ever so slightly, someone could market his own stick-on flowers without violating my patent. There *are* some products that can be very effectively protected by a design patent, but on the whole it is an easy patent to beat. What about a copyright? Fine. It offers excellent protection, which is why I copyrighted my package. But if you're copyrighted, you have to put a copyright symbol on the thing that's protected. In my case, that would mean putting © R.T.I. on the front of every flower, which would have made a mess of the way it looked. (R.T.I. is a name I registered for copyright purposes. It's neater than printing out "Rickie-Tickie, Inc." which was the official name of my company.) Putting the symbol on the package was no strain, so I did it. These are all considerations for you to bear in mind when you think about protection for your invention, too.

There is one, final, ultimate protection you have for your invention. It's saturation. If you can get distribution with your product—have it out all over the country quickly in lots of outlets—you can corner the lion's share of the market. By the time someone else gets the machinery cranked up to start copying you, all he'll have left is a small fraction of the market. But saturation isn't easy to get. Unless you can sell the product to a manufacturer who can distribute it through his own major sales organization, or through a major national chain like J.C. Penney or Sears, you'll have a tough time getting massive distribution quickly enough to saturate the market.

Quick saturation, by the way, doesn't mean just a few weeks. In business terms, six months is lightning quick and a year is plenty fast. In the case of the Rickie-Tickie-Stickies, I dawdled around too long selling them myself before I got major distribution through a national network of manufacturer's reps. My guess is that something like twenty million dollars' worth of the flowers were sold over a period of about four years. I sold about 3 million dollars' worth of those. Knock-offs accounted for the rest. If I could have gotten out there quickly enough and massively enough right at the start, a lot more of the money generated by my idea would have gone into my pocket. But that's hindsight.

As long as we're in the neighborhood, we might as well go over some of the other shortcomings of the laws that protect your idea or invention. For one thing, they tend to protect you only in the United States. Once your idea crosses the border, your protection generally evaporates. If you plan to market your invention in, say, Finland or England or France, you'll have to apply for patents in those countries, just as you did in the United States. Every country has its own peculiarities of the law, but your patent attorney ought to be able to deal with them all. In every case, the basic theory is pretty close to the U.S. theory.

One exception to the above is a copyright, which protects you over most of the world. An international agreement among publishers—even Russian publishers, lately—enforces copyrights beyond the borders of the country in which the copyrighted material was published. If you're copyrighted in the United States, you're pretty well covered anywhere in the world. Who knows? Maybe someday patents will work the same way.

In the case of trademark registration, things are a little slipperier. On the one hand, you ought to register your trademark in all the countries where you plan to market your product. It's your only real protection in those countries. On the other hand, there have been cases where a trademark was protected in countires where it had never been registered. The courts in those countries held that unauthorized use of the trademark represented an unfair trade practice.

You should also know that until your patent is actually issued—until you have it in your hand—there is no protection. Someone can be cranking out your invention like mad for all those months while the patent is pending and you won't be able to stop him. Without a patent, there is no infringement. You won't be able to collect retroactive royalties, either, once the patent is issued. Obviously, though, the fact that you have a patent pending makes your product a good deal less attractive to a thief.

Your choice of how to make your protection work for you is going to be determined largely by the kind of product you have and the nature of the attack you suffer. All I'm trying to say is that there *are* limitations to your protection and there *are* drawbacks to the laws. To quote Joe Iaia one last time, "A patent isn't worth the paper it's printed on until it is adjudicated."

On the other hand, without a patent, or a copyright, you're fair game for any idea pirate who comes down the road to buckle your swash.

V
RESEARCH AND RIP-OFFS

Those "Inventors Wanted" ads may be selling real help or just a scam. Here's how to tell the difference.

In the olden days, robbers stood by the roadside rattling their pistols and waving their sabers, yelling "Stand and deliver!" These days you'll find them back among the aspirin ads in your daily newspaper, saying "Inventors Wanted."

Most inventors are wary enough of the "stealers." But many new inventors don't realize that there are other kinds of scoundrels out there who may be even more dangerous. These varmints don't even bother to run off with your idea. That's too much trouble. They go straight for the wallet.

In case you haven't run across this particular scam yet, let me fill you in on a couple of variations of the "Inventors Wanted" rip-off.

The first variation is the "don't worry about a thing" gambit. You submit your idea, and if it meets their standards for a marketable invention (I've never yet heard of one that didn't. Your idea *always* meets their standards, no matter what the invention is), they'll "market" it for you. The unspoken promise is that they'll do all the dirty work for you and lead you through the business jungle to vast wealth and eternal bliss in the invention business.

What really happens is that the rip-off company mimeographs a sheet of the latest batch of inventions they've accumulated and sends it out to a few manufacturers and marketers.

RESEARCH AND RIP-OFFS

In the first place, there's only the briefest kind of description of the product. In the second place, I wonder who gets the fliers, since I've rarely met anyone in the idea business who has seen one. And in the third place, you can imagine the kind of reception that mimeo sheet gets when it arrives at some company. If you can't, let me give you a few quotes from people I talked to in the process of researching this book. They're instructive.

Bob Clower, Housewares Buyer, Sears, Roebuck and Co.—"I have never in fifteen years in housewares and shoes even *heard* of a manufacturer who has been contacted by one of these businesses, and I've dealt with hundreds of manufacturers over the years."

George Parker, Vice-President, Creative Services, Hallmark Cards—"I've never been approached by a new-product development company."

My own question is, who *has* been contacted by these rip-off artists, if two of the biggest idea users in the world have been skipped? But the question is academic, based on the response of some people who have received the fliers:

Bob Hicks, Vice-President/New Products, Fisher-Price Toys—"In my twenty-five years at this company, we have not been approached on a professional level by any 'Inventors Wanted' organization. They send form letters from time to time, but I throw them in the wastepaper basket."

I've never yet run across a single instance of an "Inventors Wanted" company *ever* making a sale of an idea to some manufacturer or marketer. To be fair, I'm sure there are some. I've never yet seen one of them even try hard. The most concerted effort at selling I've ever seen them try is that tired old mimeographed flier. There may be some reputable company out there doing this kind of thing, but I'd sure like to see one. In fact, I'd like to hear from one so I could recommend them when the question comes up.

That's one version of the old rip-off game. It's fairly transparent, although it may get past the inventor's defenses by making him feel really wanted. (These companies always profess to be impressed by the invention, firmly convinced they'll make a sale, ready to go to the mat for *this* idea—sign here, please.) Oh yes, there's *always* a fee! Usually a few hundred dollars.

60 HOW TO TURN YOUR IDEA INTO A MILLION DOLLARS

Another variation of this scam is a little less transparent. In fact, until you take a close look, it even seems like a reasonably decent deal. Here's how it works:

A "marketing" company looks at your idea, gets excited, offers you a marketing survey and analysis of your idea. It sounds like good stuff. They promise to give you a complete breakdown of the market for your idea, full background information on your product category, professional drawings of your product, cost analysis—all the things you'll need to make a sale to some manufacturer.

That's the theory. The practice is a little less impressive. At best, you'll pay a stiff fee to get a handsomely bound document that purports to be a complete analysis of your product and its prospects in the marketplace. The document will be fat and impressive, chock full of genuine numbers and, in several places, will actually mention your product by name. The drawings will be bound into the volume so that they fold out dramatically. Hot stuff! But what does it all mean?

What it usually means is that if you sign up, you've been ripped off. Most of the information is totally irrelevant to your product. Anyway, you could find it with a quick trip to the library. There may be page after page of non-essential information lifted directly from the last census report and having nothing whatever to do with your product. An analysis of your product category may be nothing more than a long-winded rehash of someone else's research on the number of stores selling that kind of product.

Worst of all, these reports invariably pump up the inventor's ego by telling him what a swell idea he has and by predicting success (in carefully circuitous language) no matter what the product is or what the real odds of success. On the basis of this impressive, expensive and meaningless report, an inventor may be moved to throw away thousands of dollars and months of effort in pursuit of a phantom. The idea may not have a whisper of a chance on the market, but in guarded language, this report will lead the inventor to believe he has a real winner. It's criminal! Or it ought to be.

When I was planning this book, I had a fantasy of sending my worst idea to one of these companies and publishing the results of their report, just to point up how absurd this rip-off is. As it turned out, I didn't have to. A couple of guys I know

RESEARCH AND RIP-OFFS 61

did it for me. To keep me out of court and them from possibly being harassed, let's call them Fig and Newton. Fig and Newton worked for months developing an electronic game we'll call "Spots." Now, new games are *poison* in the new idea marketplace. Toy and game manufacturers have so many new ones going all the time that they don't need any outsiders' ideas. And any outsider who tries to beat them in the marketplace on his own is likely to get cut into little tiny pieces (and then diced again) by the intense competition. Trying to market a new game on your own is the nearest thing I can imagine to financial suicide.

Worse still for Fig and Newton, this particular game would have to go at retail for more than $40—a kiss of death for a game. The two inventors, being new to the business of inventions, had no idea of all this, nor any way of knowing. They just went about their business, developing their new game. (As a matter of fact, it's a pretty good game, too.) Then they answered one of those ads. Sure enough, for a fee of nearly $2,500, they could get "the complete market analysis" of their game. They wrote the check and, in due time, received the report. It's a lulu.

It's handsomely bound in a hard cover with the marketing company's name embossed on the cover. Very uptown looking, until you look closer and realize it was done on one of those desk-top office bookbinding machines. It has 149 pages—including several blank filler pages. It has neatly tabbed sections with headings like "Product Definition" and "Market Evaluation" plus *five* appendices. And it has numbers, numbers, numbers. From time to time it even says "Spots" in the copy.

As you may know, there are automatic typing machines which will insert any given name from time to time as it goes through a predetermined piece of copy. You've probably received letters typed that way from land developers, dance studios and contests that say "You may already be a winner, Mr. Smith." That's how the report was done. Somebody put together a bunch of standard sections, plugged in the product name in a few places, did some drawings and a dab of real research, bound it up in a hard cover and shipped it off to Fig and Newton.

To show how bad it really is, let's be specific. Of the 149 pieces of paper between the two covers, 133 are meaningless in relation to the actual product under consideration. There are eleven pages devoted expressly to "Spots," including three pages of drawings which are professional, but which are also very vague. You could have them done for about $50 apiece.

In addition, there are five pages on which the name "Spots" is inserted into totally generalized material. I think it would be safe to conclude that the really pertinent part of the report could have been typed out on not more than sixteen pages of typing paper. If it weren't double spaced (and the entire report is double spaced, with generous white areas between sections and paragraphs) the report could have been done on less than eight pages. My first conclusion has to be that this is a lot of money to spend for eight pages of information.

For instance, there are three pages devoted to an analysis of the market for outdoor play equipment. Outdoor play equipment! What has *that* got to do with an indoor electronic game? It looks to me as if the clerk who pulled together the pre-written sections to make up the report simply went down a shelf pulling out every section that could remotely be connected with games. A report on any other toy or game would have contained substantially the identical material. And it would be as consistently bad!

Another example of filler in the report is the six pages of blank paper stuck into one of the appendices, just to pad it out a bit and make it seem impressive. On closer examination of the whole report, though, I'm inclined to believe that these blank pages do less harm than some of the ones that have typing on them.

Where the information pertains to the product at all, most of it is extremely misleading. For instance there's a fairly workmanlike breakdown of manufacturing costs. But the tooling cost is spread out over 200,000 units of the game. The poor inventors, looking at that bit of information, can only conclude that they're working on a game with a selling potential of at least 200,000 units or more than 8 million dollars' worth at retail! Holy cow, Fig—we're gonna sell 8 million dollars' worth! Now that's possible. Anything's possible. But it's not the kind of assumption you would want to bet your life's savings on.

And there's another, worse part to the report. By its *apparent* heft and completeness, Fig and Newton were con-

RESEARCH AND RIP-OFFS

vinced they had a valuable sales tool to take to toy manufacturers along with their model and plans. Had it been a professional analysis they would have been right. Since it wasn't, they were wrong. If they tried to take that report to some manufacturer to make a royalty deal, they'd probably never get past the receptionist.

At one place in the report, the development company makes the following marvelous statement: "Games have a healthy future predicted for them by industry representatives. Inevitably, game prices will increase due to rising costs of materials and an estimated 10% boost in operational costs for game manufacturers. But the increase in business should counter this."

Are they saying that there will be a loss on every unit, but we'll make it up in volume? What, exactly, *are* they saying?

Elsewhere there is a statement that " 'Spots' seems to have appeal for this market and *should do well*, once manufactured and distributed." (The italics are mine.) Well you'd better believe this is what any inventor wants to hear. No one wants to be told that his children are ugly! Especially when he's paying so much money for an opinion.

You and I know—and so do the two inventors of "Spots" now—that the odds against success by any game are fantastic. But here's this company blithely giving the impression that this game is practically a surefire winner. (Notice how carefully they avoid making any concrete promise, by the way.)

There's one more quote in the report that's just too good to pass up. In the "conclusions" section of the book, the rip-off company says, "This item seems to be well conceived and of good design."

Well now, in the first place, "this item" doesn't even deserve the robot typewriter treatment of plugging in the name "Spots," apparently. It's so far into the report that the compiler probably figured the reader would already be asleep.

Next is *"seems* to be well conceived." No chance of being sued for that ambiguous statement. Ben Franklin built a solid reputation on his judicious use of the word "perhaps."

For the money this report cost, I would have demanded some positive (or negative) statements about my product based on the best research available at the time of its preparation. Instead what the inventors got was a lot of warmed over census reports and some generalizing about the marketplace. No discussion of the odds against such an idea, no guidance as to what steps to take next, nothing of any substance at all. After reading through the whole report, I can only come to the following conclusion:

The product development and marketing services company that prepared the report didn't care about anything other than making a profit on the time spent with the inventors. That they did, handsomely. Just for ducks, I analyzed the report and tried to come up with an estimate of what costs actually were involved in producing the $2,500 report. Here's where I came out:

1. One hard cover with imprint (ordered in quantities of 1,000, I assumed) $ 2.50
2. Fifteen different plastic-tabbed divider sheets (ordered in quantities of 1,000) $ 1.50
3. Collation of 149 individual pages for one report $ 4.00
4. Typing 8 pages of special copy $ 12.00
5. Three professionally done drawings $150.00
6. Typing five pages of insert copy $ 6.00
7. Conference time for total report including writing and signing a one-page, personal cover letter. (6 hours at $100 per hour) $600.00
8. Printing six copies each of sixteen pages with specific product reference $ 9.60
9. 20 per cent for overhead and coffee $157.12

TOTAL $942.72

As you can see, the company made more than a nice profit . . . for themselves. But that's not really what bothers me. Rather, I'm concerned about the misleading information. Such companies ought to be held responsible for the inaccuracies of their conclusions (even though they were carefully phrased to avoid making any commitment). Inventors who are encouraged by such reckless suggestions can wind up wasting untold amounts of sweat, toil, tears and treasure chasing a will-o'-the-wisp they'll never capture. Or recapture.

I'm not trying to talk anyone out of marketing his idea, believe me. Not even a toy or electronic game idea, although

RESEARCH AND RIP-OFFS

you know by now how I feel about the odds against success in that area. My only concern here is that inventors who fall into the clutches of these rip-off artists may never be apprised of the odds against them until they find out the hard way. In the example we just saw, it is a gross injustice to the two inventors to tell them that "Spots seems to have appeal for this market and should do well."

If you're tempted to go with some company that offers to market your invention, be careful. One way to be sure of their intent is to insist that they take their fee as a percentage of what *you* make. It may cool their enthusiasm considerably to be told that they won't make any money until you make money. Otherwise, do a very careful check of just what it is they plan to do for your fee. Find out *specifically* what they plan to research for you. (Don't let them get away with generalities like "Oh, we'll look into the marketing picture.") Take a look at some samples of the research they've done for others and see if it's just a lot of junk or meaningful information. If they claim they're going to market your product for you, find out where they're going to do that. And when and how they're going to do that. Exactly.

Better still, spend the money on a sample production run or a patent attorney or some valid research or something else that will help your product along in a realistic way. Inventions never have enough backing anyway. So why waste what finances you have on some outfit that claims it will take the drudgery out of being a successful inventor? I know a lot of successful inventors—I've been one myself—and I've never yet heard of an easy way to go about it. Drudgery goes with the territory, and no rip-off artist is going to be able to change that, no matter what he claims.

Since I've just destroyed a $2,500 report on the grounds that the information was shabby, I thought it only fair to show you an example of a $2,500 report I feel was worth the price.

Several months ago I was introduced to a couple of guys who (you guessed it) had a "great, new, million dollar idea." They wondered if I could help them market their product. Unfortunately, the product is an automotive sound system—something about which I know less than the reproductive progressions of a Crossopterygian.

Having disqualified myself as any kind of authority on

their subject, I then proceeded to tell them something I've already told you: Apply for a patent. They had. Good.

"Now, go sell the idea," I suggested. "Don't try to make and sell the product on your own."

"Why?" they asked.

"Because," I guessed, "you're looking at extensive tooling costs—somewhere around $40,000 for openers."

"Actually, we checked that all out and the figure is $32,500," they shot back.

I obviously didn't have a Fig or a Newton on my hands this time. That figure didn't deter them, so I laid on additional cost estimates. I pointed out our fee for naming the product, designing the packaging, creating the necessary marketing support tools, and helping establish a distribution network would be around $35,000. They had figured around $40,000. Nothing spooked these guys. Real Riverboat Gamblers.

"The miscellaneous stuff will probably run your initial investment up to $100,000," I added. "And at that you will have no assurance of success. Worse yet, if you're successful, some giants in the electronics world will jump on your concept and kill you in the marketplace with a 'variation on your theme.' "

The $100,000 they had thought of. Being knocked off was a new concept. After we discussed the Plaintive Plaintiff chapter in detail they started to reconsider their position. At that point they left.

Then they came back. They had decided to become manufacturers after all, and wanted to know how soon we could come up with a catchy name. At this point, Don-the-wet-blanket stepped in again with, "You're not ready to spend money with me, yet. How much have you budgeted for market research?"

"None." They wondered if they needed it. I pointed out that if I were contemplating a $100,000 initial investment in a brand new concept, I would certainly want at least a few more bits of information to help me decide GO or NO-GO.

It pained me that I was sitting there doing my best to boot away a $35,000 marketing project, but I gave them my lecture on research. First, I said, there is no better research in the world than putting a prototype run of a product on a store shelf and watching what happens to it. Anything south

RESEARCH AND RIP-OFFS

of that is educated guessing. When the cost of good research is about the same as doing a prototype run and actually selling the product, I'll go for the sales experience every time.

In the case of the Riverboat Gamblers and their automotive sound system, however, the cost of going into a limited market was much higher than the cost of research. I figured—correctly, as it turned out—that they could buy a good preliminary research report for around $2,500. I suggested that they go to a reputable firm and commission them to do a market study. The Riverboat Gamblers took my advice.

What they got was worth every penny they spent. There were no absolutes in the research report. There never are, not for $2,500; nor for $25,000,000. But there was some sound, fundamental information about the market for their product and how best to approach it. The very first words of the report were heartwarming to me. "Purchase interest for the product is quite low based on the concept description of it."

No phony hype about what a wonderful product you have there, Mr. Inventor. No glowing, and unsupported, predictions for sales success. Just hard facts, some encouraging ones and some discouraging ones.

The researchers didn't fill up their report with a lot of canned statistics. Instead, they took a handmade sample of the sound system out to some shopping centers and talked to potential customers about it. They demonstrated the sound system and probed reactions to it both before and after hearing the demonstration. And the questions they asked were meaningful.

As the researchers said in their report, they had a specific set of objectives in mind when they questioned their market sample. "The purpose of this investigation," the report said, "was to determine the market viability of the product, to identify its strengths and weaknesses in the eyes of potential consumers, and to identify the target market. Specifically, the objectives of the study were:

1. To define the prime prospect in terms of its demography—age, income, type of vehicle owned, education, type of sound equipment owned in auto and home.
2. To determine what is liked and disliked about the sound system.

3. To determine how the sound system compares to alternative systems.
4. To determine at what price individuals feel the system should sell.
5. To obtain a measure of purchase interest in the system.
6. To determine at which type of retail outlet consumers would expect to purchase the system.
7. To rate the system on a variety of attributes:
   —sound reproduction compared to other speakers only
   —design attractiveness
   —ease of installation
   —sound separation
8. To obtain consumers' perceptions of products to which the new sound system is most analogous."

It's apparent that the researchers were out to give the inventors of the system some basic knowledge about who to sell to, how to sell, where to sell, at what price to sell and even how to improve the product's marketability. The researchers may have laid it out in dry-as-dust prose, but it's poetry to the ears of anyone who's about to sink $100,000 into a gamble on his new idea.

The guts of the report takes up about thirty pages and contains more useful information than a dozen 149-page rip-offs like the one Fig and Newton bought. Just to give you an idea of the difference between the reports, here are a few examples of what the good one had to say:

After pointing out that the test subjects expressed much more interest in the product after hearing it demonstrated, the report went one step farther and probed the importance of that fact in terms of retail price. "The expected price for the product increases substantially after listening to it . . . The expected price is about $33 before listening and $39 after listening. The greatest interest occurs among monaural owners.* Stereo owners tend to hold to the expected price before and after listening."

That gives my friends, the Riverboat Gamblers, a pretty

---

* I assume that means owners of monaural sound equipment, not one-eared music lovers.

RESEARCH AND RIP-OFFS

fair notion of how to position their product in the marketplace and how to sell it most effectively.

The researchers chose only people who told them they would like to improve their automotive sound system—in other words, the most likely customers for the product. Then they analyzed just who it was who expressed that interest. "The individuals who qualified for this study . . . are definitely younger, more likely to be single, to be students and to have lower personal incomes. Stereo owners are more likely to exhibit these characteristics than monaural owners . . . Although (younger singles and students) have low personal incomes, the price of the unit is not a problem because they have a great deal of discretionary income they can spend on things that are personally gratifying and enjoyable to them. Life style is more important than income in defining the target market."

With that piece of information in hand, the Riverboat Gamblers know who they'll have to reach with their advertising and promotion for the product.

Another important observation about the good research is that the researchers laid all their cards on the table for their clients. In a section entitled "Methodology," the researchers explained where they set up their interview project, who they talked to, how many people they interviewed, what questions they asked, how they went about it all and how they analyzed the data. Needless to say, the people who did Fig and Newton's "research" gave out no such information.

There's one last thought about research to consider. Since this chapter is about a con and a pro, let's see how the right kind of research can be used to con the pros. We'll presume for a moment that both Fig/Newton and Riverboat Gamblers, Inc. have decided to try selling their ideas to a manufacturer. Fig and Newton's $2,500 investment in research will be laughed right out of any board room because it's bad, slippery stuff. The Riverboat Gamblers, on the other hand, will have a valuable supplementary tool that will help convince a manufacturer that the idea they have is worth further exploration. When push gets to shove, the Gamblers will be able to tack an additional $2,500 onto their deal to cover the cost of their research because it's good stuff which the manufacturer can use.

The Riverboat Gamblers will be repaid for spending

money to help make a sale. Good for them. Bad for me. Undoubtedly, the manufacturer will have his own marketing group which will be eager to use the $35,000 for naming, packaging and the like.

But that's my problem, not yours. Your problem is how to tell rip-offs from research. I hope that by now you've developed a healthy skepticism about those people who promise you success and deliver a census report.

VI
DOING YOUR HOMEWORK

Calculating wholesale and retail price, including manufacturing, packaging, selling and shipping.

Somewhere along the line, I seem to recall promising you that you were going to have to work like a dog and spend real money before you turned your idea into a success. Well now's the time to start.

The little bit of effort and money we talked about in the chapter on patents was just the beginning. You see, there are still many unknown quantities about your idea at this point. It doesn't matter whether you plan to sell the idea to some manufacturer for a royalty, and make or sell your invention on your own. One way or another you'll have to turn all those unknowns into knowns before you reach the shelves of the stores.

You'll have to find out if your idea actually can be manufactured. You'll have to figure out how much it will cost—including materials, manufacturing, packaging, shipping, sales commissions, overhead and, of course, profit. You'll have to get some kind of handle on whether or not it will sell. And how well. And for what price. In short, you'll have to do some running, digging and spending.

Let's tackle those questions one at a time, please. I confuse easily.

Can it be made? The answer to that, logically enough, is to make it. A sample production run, perhaps. Or some prototypes. Maybe just a model. It depends mostly on the kind of idea you have. If it calls for tooling up with thousands of dollars worth of special dies or something, it's a pretty good bet you're not going to be making any sample production runs. But in that case you can make a model of your invention—or have someone make it for you. On the other hand, in the case of Rickie Tickie Stickies the idea was simple enough and the production was inexpensive enough that running off a sample batch of 3,000 was no big thing.

In between the two extremes, there's the possibility of making a prototype. That's a real, working example of your product in the same shape, size and detail as the production version will be. If possible, it ought to be made of the same material, too.

Until you do one of the three things—a production run, a model or a prototype—your idea is a pig in a poke. It's a figment of somebody's imagination. Your imagination. Nobody has proved it will work. Nobody knows if it actually can be manufactured.

But once you have a sample, you don't have to wave your arms and say "imagine, if you will . . ." to explain your invention. You can just hold it up for people to look at and touch. It exists in living, three-dimensional full-color splendor. It's the real thing.

Now, that may strike you as a lot more trouble than it's worth. But it's an important phase in the life of any new product. It comes under the general heading of getting that pig out of that poke. It begins to solve some of the problems of manufacture. No matter what your idea is, little details you wouldn't have anticipated in a million years on paper will leap out at you when you have to translate your idea into a three-dimensionl object.

Sooner or later, these snags are going to have to be dealt with. Much better you should say "Oooooops!" now, when there's time to work out a solution, than later on, when you may be up to your fiduciary nerve in production deadlines. If you're going to manufacture and sell the product yourself, it's just one more step bringing you closer to success. If you're planning to sell your idea to a manufacturer, he'll be very happy to have those problems already solved. It shortens the time he has to spend between buying your idea and getting it on the market. And it's in the marketplace that your idea will generate money, not in the production planner's office.

Another critical question has to be answered now. In fact,

DOING YOUR HOMEWORK

it's really a fiendishly complex, interlocking series of questions. The series begins innocently enough. How much will your invention cost to manufacture? That question quickly leads to the question of how much your invention will have to sell for at retail. That, of course, leads directly to the ultimate question: Will anybody want to buy it?

Let's take a look at all the costs involved in manufacturing your invention. You *have* to find out what it will cost before you can talk intelligently about your invention. Many beginning inventors regularly ignore a number of real costs they'll have to face, and it's a trap. By doing so, they con themselves into thinking they've got a much more attractive proposition on their hands than they really have. The costs to calculate are these:

1. *The cost of materials.* You can't just say—as one inventor recently told me—that this is negligible. "Oh," she said, "there's nothing to it at all. Just a piece of wood and some paint and stuff. Less than a penny apiece." But when you multiply "less than a penny" by a hundred thousand or so, it becomes a substantial cost. Calculate it as closely as you can. Think in terms of mills . . . tenths of a cent . . . as the pros do. Call up or go see some suppliers and find out from them what they'll charge for a supply of the materials. Get quotes from several suppliers. And get them to quote on the quantity you'll need for a small production run, then for a larger run, finally for the biggest production run you could realistically expect. Make sure they understand exactly what grade of material you're looking for. (You may not know, youself, at this point. But the suppliers can help you figure it out, often as not. After all, they're looking to make a sale, so they have a vested interest in being helpful.)

2. *Production cost.* I'm talking about the physical activity of making your goods. If you're going to hire an assembler to do it for you in his shop or factory, you'll have to go around getting bids—the same as you did when you were pricing materials. If you're planning to make the goods yourself, you'll have to calculate the cost of the space you'll use as your factory, the cost of the equipment you'll have to buy, and the cost of labor in the manufacturing process.

By now, you may be wondering how you—probably not the world's foremost model maker, certainly no manufacturing expert—are going to do all the things I'm talking about: make a prototype or a model of your invention, calculate production costs, figure out what materials you'll be using and so forth. The answer is easy. Don't do it yourself, hire an expert. Get out your Yellow Pages and look up "industrial engineers" or "industrial designers." These people make their living by working out the proper materials, the best processes and the least expensive techniques for manufacturing things. They can also make your model, or put you in touch with someone who can do it. These people know all the ins and outs of manufacturing and can find ways to cut your costs substantially, so the money you spend on their services will probably pay big dividends. (You may be able to obtain their services without putting out any cash, by the way. More about that in a later chapter.)

While you're wrestling with production costs, there's a nasty word you'll have to learn. It's "Amortization." It's a word that turns a solid, upright, hard-working businessman into a hollow-eyed crapshooter. Amortization means laying off the cost of your capital investment (your manufacturing equipment and factory investment, in this case) against the number of products you'll make with that investment. In other words, you have to guess how many units of your invention you're going to sell. Of course you can't. That's why it's a gamble.

The best you can do is make an estimate based on how many stores you think you'll be selling in, how many products like yours they sell every year, how long you think you'll be manufacturing the product. Based on all that, you close your eyes, grit your teeth and take a stab at some logical sounding number. Be careful! If you try to write off the whole investment against the first few orders for your product, you'll jack your per-unit cost up so high that you'll price yourself out of business. On the other hand, you can't just airily figure on making a zillion pieces, either. You may never make that many units and you'll be stuck with an expense that was never truly reflected in your cost of goods.

3. *Packaging.* Hardly anything is sold without packaging, so somebody's going to have to design a package for your product. That's going to cost some money. How much money depends in part on what kind of package you choose—a blister pack to hang on a "J" hook rack, a box, a bag or whatever. Unless you are an accomplished writer/art director/designer, you'd better figure on paying somebody to do it for you. As a starting point for your calculations, you

can use $2,000. That should bring you right up to the point of being ready to print the boxes. It ought to cover artwork, layout, copy, typesetting and mechanicals. You can get it done for less. You can spend a lot more. Two thousand is just a nice, round, rough starting point. Later we'll also discuss ways of getting this kind of work done without putting out hard, cold cash. But the expense still has to be reflected in your cost of goods, one way or another. In other words, you have to—excuse the expression—amortize it.

Once you have the design, you have to get some estimates from printers on how much it will cost to print the packages. There's no way an amateur can calculate this cost on his own. It involves mystical subjects like color processes, stock weights, coated vs. uncoated stock and a hundred other things you don't even *want* to understand unless you're a printer.

Finally, somebody has to take the product off the assembly line and stick it into a package. It was at this stage of the game that we made a marvelous discovery with Rickie Tickie Stickies. We were dealing with vinyl decals, you'll recall, approximately nine inches in diameter, which were being shipped to us in cartons of about 3,000. That's a lot of slippery little pieces to handle. With some friends and neighborhood teen-agers, we packaged the first batch in their plastic bags, working around folding tables in the garage. But very quickly we were swamped. Where to turn? Where else! We got out the Yellow Pages again and looked up companies that do packaging.

But what looked like a monstrous job to us was really too small to interest the professionals. Oh, they'd do it all right. But in order to make our little job worth their while, they'd have to charge a lot more than normal per package. Then we had a brainstorm. We knew that certain organizations around the country hire handicapped or mentally retarded people for packaging work that was not too demanding. So we called around and we ended up working with Goodwill Industries in Long Beach, an easy thirty-minute drive from our house.

They'd handle a small job at rates competitive to what the professionals would charge on the basis of a big job. For several years it was a perfect blend of product and labor force. What was just as important, the relationship provided us with many touching, funny, wonderful experiences. All the kids who worked for Rube Goakes, manager of the shop, had

76   HOW TO TURN YOUR IDEA INTO A MILLION DOLLARS

a fierce determination to do a successful job for us. No overload seemed to bother them, nothing got in the way of doing a first-class job for us.

For one thing, of course, Ruby and her kids were happy to have the business. Most of their work came from machine shops. Having a chance to work on something clean and bright like our flowers was a treat for them. Depending on their ability, some of the workers could only count out three flowers of the same color. Others could count out up to nine assorted colors. Some learned to work with the heat-sealing equipment we brought into the shop. All of them loved their work and were pleased to be able to take home an occasional bright "reject" from their day's work.

The point is, you can do yourself and the world around you a very good turn if your product can be packaged, or even manufactured, by one of these "sheltered" workshops like Goodwill Industries. You'll be pleased with the quality of work, you'll get a competitive price and some deserving people will get a chance to participate in society. That's a pretty fair parlay!

The cost of this packaging operation must be included in your cost of manufacture, naturally. And while we're on the subject of packages, don't forget that you have to ship your products. That probably means buying corrugated cardboard shipping cartons, each big enough to hold a quantity of your exquisitely designed, beautifully printed packages and strong enough to protect them from the ravages of the shippers. These boxes come in standard sizes, or you can have them specially made for your product. Here again, figure out exactly what you need, then get bids from several suppliers, based on different levels of production. After you've found your cost per box, divide that price by the number of units you'll ship in each box and you'll arrive at your cost per unit.

The total of all these fixed costs is called your cost of goods or C.O.G. But that doesn't mean you're done, yet. It simple means you're through with the easy part. Now you have to get involved in an area of sliding costs, costs based on a percentage of your selling price. First I'll explain the costs. Then we'll figure out how to go about calculating them.

4. *Sales cost*. Somebody has to sell your products for you, unless you're going to spend the rest of your business life working out of the back of a station wagon. These salesmen are paid a commission, or a percentage of the price they get.

Later on we'll get into the whole question of reps and commissions. For right now, just figure on paying 20 per cent of the price of your products to the salesmen. (It may be less than that, in real life, depending on the type of distribution you choose. But 20 per cent is a good safe starting point.) That commission is based on the price *you* get, not the price the retailer gets when he sells your product in his store.

5. *G.&A.* That's technical talk. It stands for "general and administrative" costs, but most businessmen like you and me refer to it by the initials. It's also called "overhead." Or both. It includes a mixed bag of costs, things like salaries, advertising and marketing, your own office overhead (as opposed to the manufacturing overhead), all of the little niggling, miscellaneous costs of being in business. Like insurance for fire. Theft. Liability. Earthquake. Hindenburg. How much is the G.&A. cost? The only way to calculate it exactly is by amortization. But as a general rule, you should allow no less than 20 per cent of the wholesale price of your product as G.&A. expense.

That may sound astronomically high when you're working out your cost of goods right now, but later on when some of the bills start rolling in, you'll understand that it's pretty realistic. Even if you're planning to start on a shoestring and work out of your home, allow for this expense. Sooner or later, if you're successful, you'll be expanding into a real office, just like the big kids. When you do, you won't have to jack up the price of your product to pay for your new prosperity if you've already included it in your costs.

6. *Shipping.* Shipping cost is determined by how big the box, how heavy the product and how far the journey. Normally, you expect your customer to pay for the shipping, but for a number of reasons you may find that you'll wind up paying at least a portion of the cost yourself. Therefore, you ought to know what it is.

When we first got involved with shipping, it didn't take us long to realize how much we take for granted the fact that parcels leave one place and arrive, magically, at another. Once we passed the stage of handy home delivery, however, we suddenly found we were in another new arena of which we were supremely ignorant.

We first learned that you have to be careful about the carton you use for shipping, because practically every company has some restrictions on what it will handle. I remember having a length of chain in the shipping room that established the allowed measurement of girth-plus-length of our orders. We also found that we could buy a shipping scale that had destinations coded by distance and made computing of charges much easier.

While we were learning about shipping—under the tutelage of all the companies that were after our shipping business— we discovered something of the psychology of shopkeepers. Shopkeepers, it turns out, never place an order for your product until the last one in inventory has just been sold. Then they leap to the telephone in a blue panic and beg you to ship immediately because they have a line at the counter waiting for your product to arrive. That means you're going to have to learn all the fastest ways of getting an order out, as well as the cheapest. (We also found that shopkeepers never change the size of their order. If they bought a dozen the first time, they'll always order a dozen. Even if they're reordering every twenty minutes, it never seems to occur to them to place a bigger order. Why? Damned if I know!)

This led us to the discovery of air freight. At first, we worried that the cost would be prohibitive. But it was clear that we were losing quite a few sales by not having our product on the shelves of stores that ran out. So we did what had by then become our custom. We called air freight companies and got the story on what we would have to spend for their services.

You'll probably find, as we did, that you'll use a combination of shipping processes. We finally settled on a combination of U.P.S. air service, regular U.P.S., general air freight and sometimes surface trucking for practically all of our shipping. We avoided the U.S. Post Office whenever possible. A few experiences convinced us that each post office branch keeps a truck on hand specifically for the purpose of running over all the boxes at least once on departure and again on arrival. This did not please our customers at all, and they usually let us know.

I mentioned that you might find yourself paying at least part of the shipping cost yourself. One of the most important reasons for doing that is to use a shipping allowance as a sales incentive. You offer to pay part of the cost for a customer if he'll place an order for some minimum quantity of your product—more than he would have ordered without the incentive. Customers with well-oiled financial management like that because they can turn it into a real savings for themselves. You'll like it because it leads to bigger orders. There's no real set figure, but as a rule you'll allow 3 per cent of the price of an order as a shipping allowance.

There are some customers who jam freight allowances down your throat. These are some of the big, corporate-style customers who write their own freight contracts and you like it or lump it. It can lead to some soul searching on your part to see if that huge, exciting order from that huge, exciting chain of stores is really worth it. By the time some of these customers automatically refuse to pay freight, automatically take a 2 per cent discount for cash payment even though they don't pay for 60 or 90 days, and automatically return unsold goods for credit even though you never agreed to it, their orders become a little less exciting and a little more not-worth-it.

No, they don't all behave that way. But you ought to be a little cautious and do some checking when the demands start going beyond the bounds of common decency.

While shipping is a headache at times, it is one of the most important aspects of a manufacturing company. Someone in your organization had better make it his business to learn all the ins and outs. The freight business is a highly regulated one with rigid policies. You have to keep informed not only about rates but about the whole question of liabilities and damages. You also may find that you have to educate some of your customers, too.

Once we had a particularly knotty bit of education to do. We had worked out a system whereby we air-freighted a bulk shipment to each of several cities. Once it was unloaded from the plane, the shipment was broken down into individual orders and delivered to our customers by U.P.S. The problem arose from the fact that our invoice made separate note of the shipping charges for the order.

That was all well and good, except that U.P.S. put their own stamps on each order for the amount it charged to deliver from the airport to the customer. There was nothing on the package to denote the additional cost of the air shipment to the point where U.P.S. took over. So a customer would get an invoice charging him $3.00 for shipping and a package that said $1.62. We got some pretty heated phone calls about how we were gouging people on shipping. It finally got so bad that U.P.S. had to print up a batch of fliers explaining the situation. One of the fliers was delivered with each order and after a while the howls of protest finally subsided. But it was pretty ugly for a while.

7. *Profit.* Ah yes, profit. Profit is like one of those optical illusions that keep changing perspective while you look at it. On one hand, it seems a pretty puny return for this idea of yours. (That's when you're looking at the few pennies you'll get for every product you sell.) On the other hand, when you're trying to shave your cost of goods to arrive at a competitive price, it seems like an inordinately huge hunk of cost. You're right on both counts. Profit is simultaneously way too high and nowhere near enough. For whatever it's worth, most companies are happy to make between 10 and 20 per cent of the factory selling price of their product as profit, before taxes.

Don't get the idea that you're limited to that, though. Some products can be "value priced." That is, the apparent, perceived value of the product is very high in relation to the cost of making it. For years, kids' toys with endorsements by the reigning cowboy stars fit into that definition. A more modern example is Gary Dahl's Pet Rock. You can plug in any number you want as profit, so long as the retail price of the product still makes sense to the consumer. If it works out that you're making 300 per cent profit, that's your good luck—as long as it sells.

And that's it. Those are all the costs that go into making your wholesale price. As I mentioned, some of those costs have to be arrived at backwards. You've got some hard, fixed costs: materials, production, packaging and so on. Then you have some costs which are figured as a percentage on your selling price. But how can you do that if those are the figures you have to use in calculating that price? Sounds like Catch-22. Since this is starting to get confusing, let's see if an example can help clarify this whole process.

We'll start with a hypothetical retail price. That's the price the ultimate customer will pay for the product. How you zero in on that figure is covered a bit later in this chapter. For now let's say the retail price is $2.00. The first thing we do is subtract the markup for the retail store. On average, that amounts to about 50 per cent of the retail price, or $1.00 in this example. So now you're down to $1.00. That's your wholesale price. From that we subtract the sales or distribution and shipping costs which average about 20 per cent or $.20. Your $2.00 retail item brings your company about $.80.

DOING YOUR HOMEWORK

From that you subtract your cost of goods. Let's say your product costs you $.40 to make. We now have $.40 left to split between G.&A. and profit. Figuring 20 per cent of wholesale for G.&A. we come up with $.20. That leaves you $.20 before-tax profit, which on a $2.00 retail item is about right. Here's how that should look on your notes when you're doing your first financial review:

	$2.00	Retail
—	$1.00	50% to store
	$1.00	Wholesale Price
—	.20	20% to Sales and/or Distribution and Shipping
	$ .80	Factory Selling Price
—	.40	C.O.G.
	$ .40	
—	.20	20% of Wholesale allotted to G.&A.
	$ .20	Before-tax Profit.

It's that simple to do when you're using a hypothetical example. In real life, there's a little more to it. For one thing, you have to do some refining of the cost figures you'll plug into your calculations. So don't break out the scratch pad just yet. You've got some legwork to do.

What you want to find out now is the best way to distribute your product when you go to market. The distribution system you choose will tell you what percentage figures to plug into your calculations for things like markup from wholesale to retail, sales commission, shipping costs and other factors.

There are quite a number of different distribution systems and they all have their own peculiar effect on those calculations of yours. The next chapter in this book deals with all that in some detail. You'll need to read and reread that chapter before you can actually refine your wholesale price, but for right now you just need to track down a little information.*

---

* As a matter of fact, you really ought to finish reading this whole book before you actually set out to market your invention. I've tried to put things in some sort of logical order, but there's a lot of information to cover and much of it interlocks. To help you organize it all, I've included an inventor's "Checklist" at the back of the book as Appendix I. It puts all your chores down in order, letting you check them off as you go along.

In order to figure out your best method of distribution, you'll have to go to the kind of stores that will be likely to sell your product when you get it on the market. Let's say you've got some kind of automotive accessory in mind. You go to your friendly local accessory store and buttonhole the manager. Don't be shy. After all, how many times a day does the owner or manager of a small store have a chance to become a marketing expert and pass out learned advice? He'll usually be happy to spend more time with you than you're interested in spending with him. But then, most things in life are a trade-off.

What you want to learn from the retailer is where his store gets products like the one you have in mind. It couldn't hurt to find out how much he marks up products of that type, either, although his distribution system will probably define that markup. If you're nervous about letting people know precisely what your idea is at this point, find something in the store to use as an example. Something in the same general price range, aimed at the same general type of buyer as your product. Level with the guy and tell him you can't reveal exactly what the product is yet, but you're going to be marketing a new product and you need some help.

Once you know where he gets things of that nature and what his markup is, you can go to *his* source—a wholesaler or distributor, manufacturers' rep or whatever. Find out what the wholesaler's markup is, what the distribution system is, whether or not there are other means of distributing the same sort of product. Find out what the advantages and disadvantages of any alternate methods are and figure out which of them makes the most sense for your product. Do it all more than once, just to be sure you're not getting funny information from any of your marketing experts.

Now you've got the means to refine your product costs and arrive at a fairly solid wholesale price. You know the markup structure you'll be working with, and you have a pretty fair notion of the other costs involved in the distribution system (if you've read the next chapter, that is). You've got a number you can rely on, more or less. You'll still find that you may have to use some Kentucky windage in some of your calculations, so don't get panicky if you can't pin down a rock-solid figure. When you err, try to err a little on the high side. I once made a horrible mistake at this point in the de-

DOING YOUR HOMEWORK

velopment of a new product. It cost me more of my own personal, private dollars than I care to remember.

The product was a doll, made of felt and called (for reasons that seemed to make sense at the time) "Little Lumpsie." I went out and collected bids from fabric suppliers, from sewing factories, accessory suppliers, the whole bit. I was really proud of myself. "Nothing to it for a professional like you, Kracke," I said to myself. I didn't realize that my experience in printing didn't necessarily make me a genius in the field of soft goods.

Anyway, the doll costed out beautifully. I ran off a couple of samples and it was presented to F. A. O. Schwarz, the ritzy toy store in New York. They loved it. Placed an order. Hot damn, I was in the doll business!

Boy, was I in the doll business! All those suppliers who gave me firm bids turned out to have been doing a little fibbing. When I went into production, they doubled their prices. All of them. Every last one. It was like a giant conspiracy to drive me to the wall.

But I was committed to fill the order, so I paid the price. I didn't want to renege on a deal with F. A. O. Schwarz because I'd like to be able to come back to them again sometime with another idea. I'd rather take my beating than lose a good contact. I lost money on every last one of those damned dolls. Worse yet, it was a success. Schwarz reordered again and again. At that price, I didn't need the volume.

Ultimately I sold the idea to Fisher-Price Toys for a royalty. They were able to scale the idea down a little, cut their costs and sell the toy at a profit. They sold a lot of dolls and I got back my loss (at $.05 each, royalty). I chalked up another lesson.

The lesson was this: When you're getting bids from suppliers, don't be afraid to ask them for a contract. Put in penalties they have to pay if they don't deliver on time or at the price they quoted. I'd guess something like 10 per cent is enough leeway to allow them in their price. They won't be overjoyed, but it will make them think twice about shooting you a lowball bid.

As a beginner with a new idea, you may feel you have to go around to suppliers with your hat in your hand, especially when you're talking about fairly small orders. Don't worry about it. It's *your* neck that's being risked. It's *your* money they're playing with. You deserve all the protection you can get. And if the supplier is a smart businessman, he'll be willing to invest a little understanding at the beginning in order to reap a little loyalty later on. We had a perfect example of that kind of thinking when we first ordered some small plastic bags for our packages of Rickie Tickie Stickies.

Margaret called a number of companies and asked them about sizes in stock and how we might do business. With one exception, the companies were just not too interested in dealing with a suburban housewife who wanted a tiny order of small bags. Their prices reflected their reluctance.

One man, however, whose business was miles and miles from our home, was amazingly co-operative. His company was one of the biggest, we later found out, so he wasn't exactly desperate for business. It's just that he was decent and smart. He listened patiently to our needs and, most surprising of all, shipped our order out to the house with nothing more than a promise to pay when the bill arrived.

As it turned out, his trusting response to that first order paid off for him and his company. As our operation grew we kept ordering all our bags from him. At first the orders were pretty puny. Later they became respectable enough to attract attention from his competitors. Suddenly the bag makers who didn't have time for our silly little company began dropping by to see us, offering special deals. Weighing the one-time special deal against the benefits of a long-term relationship with a conscientious supplier, we stayed with our original source. We never regretted it and neither did he. Altogether we'd bought several million bags from him by the time we got out of the flower business. And the next time I need bags, I know the first number I'm going to call.

Anyway, don't be afraid to act like a real businessman when you're getting bids. Even with a contract, you have no guarantee you won't be hustled by some unscrupulous supplier. But giving yourself at least that much protection lets people know you mean business. Better that than to go blithely off to market on the basis of a loose verbal quote. That way could be disaster. And insolvency.

So now you've got a wholesale price and you know the distribution system you'll probably be using. Put them together and, *voilà*, the magic number emerges: your retail price.

It's probably too high.

It almost always is. So now you've got to go back into your costs and find ways to cut them. Find different suppliers.

Find less expensive ways of manufacturing and packaging. Rethink your design. Bring your wholesale price down to a point where it leaves you with a viable retail price.

But how can you tell what's viable and what's not? There are ways, ranging from the ridiculous—our efforts at the beginning of the Rickie Tickie Stickies adventure—to the sublime—the kind of market research done by the industrial giants. Somewhere between those extremes lies your answer.

In our case, with the Stickies, we sort of held up a wet finger and decided that $.25 a Stickie was about right. It fit our estimates of manufacturing cost and left us a decent profit. Then, when the neighborhood kids came around asking to buy the flowers, they confirmed the fact that we were correct in figuring on two bits as the retail price.

Another way is to go around to the stores and see what similar products are selling for. Even if there's nothing similar on the market, you can get some sort of feeling for where your product will fit into the general scheme of things in that line of goods.

Finally, there's a somewhat more sophisticated, although still fairly straightforward, way to find out if your product will sell at your price: try selling it. On a small scale, of course. There are a number of advantages to doing this. First, of course, it will tell you what you want to know about your price. More important, in the long run, is the fact that it gives your product a sales track record in the real world. That's extremely important to you as a means of attracting attention when you try to sell your idea to some manufacturer. It's equally important to you in getting into new, bigger, more lucrative markets with your product. If you can prove you have a winner in a limited but projectable market sample, you have a powerful argument in your favor. Needless to say, it could help you when you have to go looking for financial backing.

When we were able to attract the attention of an industrial giant who wanted to buy the rights to produce our Stickies, it was our solid, real-world sales figures that opened the door. Those numbers made it possible for our little gnat of a business to be noticed by the great, powerful moose of industry. We were manufacturing the product. People were buying it, stores were reordering it. The gnat bit and the moose scratched. It was a triumph of market research.

At the time, of course, we didn't think of it as market

research. We were just out there selling the Stickies the best way we knew how. Margaret was hitting the neighborhood stores and a few department stores, order book in hand. We had run off that short sample run which became our opening inventory. From there on, we just kept half a jump ahead of the orders as we went along. Well, maybe sometimes we were half a jump behind. But the theory was correct. We simply spent as little as we felt we could get by with to keep up with sales in our rather limited sort of market area. And as reorders climbed, our number of stores expanded.

Reorders, by the way, are called "turns at retail" (a little something to liven up your cocktail party chatter). A product is said to "turn" at retail when it is reordered by a store. The measure of a product's ability to perform is the number of turns in a given period of time. In our case, it didn't take a mathematical genius to project our sales potential.

Sales in the five hundred Southern California stores we finally reached had been going briskly through October, November and December of 1967. (We were happily unaware, at the time, that nobody buys at wholesale in November and nobody, but *nobody* ever places a wholesale order in December. We merely noticed a worrisome little lag in sales those two months. Blissful ignorance.)

There were approximately 24,500 similar stores in the United States, according to some high-powered research we did at the local library branch. An "average" product in those stores turned at retail about four times a year. Rickie Tickie Stickies were not just turning, they were positively revolving. Something between twelve and eighteen times a year.

In making our sales projection, we ground in one more factor. Southern California is considerably more receptive to new ideas than most parts of the country. People here are a lot more likely to buy something new and strange, which is maybe a commentary on Southern California. Therefore, we arbitrarily cut the national sales projection in half. Simple arithmetic, based on a fair sales test in a California sample, indicated an $18 million potential at wholesale for 1968 across the country. I settled for $9 million in my presentations. As it turned out, the number was over $10 million.

You ought to be able to do pretty much the same sort of calculation with your product. Figure out what kind of sample market you can deal with (bigger is better, more pro-

DOING YOUR HOMEWORK

jectable), crank up limited production, then get out there and sell. And keep track of your turns at retail. Once you have a reasonably fair idea of how the sales are going, you've got a powerful attention getter for your product. You'll also know whether or not your price is right.

You might even be able to get some stores to co-operate with you in a little market research gimmick. Try selling the product in one store at a low price, while some distance away you're selling the product at a high price. Meanwhile, sell your product somewhere else at the regular price. Try to match the stores as closely as possible and try to make sure they're far enough apart that they won't have any of the same customers. Watch what happens to your sales at those stores. If your rate of sales at the high price is about the same as the rate at the regular price, you can obviously afford to charge more for your product and make more of a profit for yourself and for the stores that carry your product. If sales surge markedly at the low price, well—better find a way to cut costs.

One hidden advantage of test marketing a product is that you may be able to use your successful sales efforts as a lever to force distribution. I'm involved right now in a classic example of that.

The product is a book called *The International Handbook of Jockstraps*. (I didn't say it was a high-tone product, did I?) It's a gag book, a whole series of cartoons of different kinds of jockstraps. The "Jock Cousteau," for example, is a picture of a jockstrap with a diving mask on it. Some of the cartoons are funnier than others, but by and large it's a fairly good example of the sort of gag gift item you'll find in a lot of stores.

When I took it around to publishers, however, the silence was deafening. None of them believed in it. I couldn't get it sold anywhere. So what to do? I didn't want to spend a lot of my own money getting it published. And I didn't want to give up on it. What I *did* want to do was prove to some publisher that the book would sell and would be a profitable item.

So I did something that I've done before. I co-ventured the book. I made a deal with a printer giving him a percentage of the book in return for printing it free. I'm out nothing but my time and the time of my fellow authors. The printer has run off the book during down-time on his presses, so he's out essentially nothing. And we are at the moment into our second printing. We've sold over 26,000 books in a limited number of stores, distributing the book through gift and stationery reps.

We're just about at the point now where I feel confident about going to a publisher, showing him my sales figures and asking again if he's interested in publishing the book. I think he'll do it this time.

Those, then, are the main areas that come under the general heading of doing your homework. You'll find plenty of other jobs to be done as you develop your idea, of course. You're going to work very hard before you reach your goal. And you'll find that doing your homework is such a recurring theme in this book that you'll be tired of hearing it. But I have to tell you it is awfully important to you.

Yes, it *is* possible to sell an idea without doing your homework. It is also possible to fill an inside straight.

But I wouldn't bet on either one of 'em.

VII
WHICH WAY TO GO

Many roads lead to the marketplace, but some are better than others.

It's time to start thinking about making money. The question before the house is this: How will you go to market with your product? It's a question you can't put off any longer. You *must* get out into the marketplace one way or another if you want to make money. And there is an endless variety of ways to go. So which will it be?

Will you make it and sell it yourself? Sell the idea to a manufacturer for a royalty on his output? Build a mail-order business operating out of your home? Sell the product to a major catalogue marketer like Sears, Penney, Spiegel or Montgomery Ward? Sell it to one of the specialty catalogue outfits like Sunset House or the Horchow Collection? Maybe form a company to make the product, then sell the company? Turn the product into a premium or sales-incentive item for some company like a fast-food chain or a soft-drink bottler? Or what?

Before this chapter is over, we'll have a good, hard look at all the options. We'll find out the ins and outs, the advantages and disadvantages of all the main routes to the retail market—and a couple of sneaky back roads, too. But let's get one thing straight right up front. There's only one way you *want* to go.

What you want to do—desperately—is to sell your idea to a manufacturer for a royalty deal. Anything else is second best. A fall-back position. Collecting royalties is the cleanest, neatest, most profitable, simplest way for you to make your fortune in the inventing game. Naturally, it works out that the most difficult and frustrating task you'll face in this business is making this type of sale to a manufacturer. You're probably going to have a lot of doors slammed in your face. However, all it takes is one "yes" to make it all worthwhile.

Usually at about this point, people begin to wonder if it could possibly be worth all that aggravation. The answer is yes. Unequivocally yes. Absolutely yes.

"Well, yeah, but isn't that giving away a big piece of the profit on your product?" people aften ask. "Wouldn't you make more money if you manufactured and sold it yourself?"

Theoretically, yes. In practice, no. To sort out the objections, let's take a look at what's involved in going it all on your own. As a matter of fact, you may have to do that for a while anyway, to establish enough credibility in the marketplace to make a royalty deal. It can be good for you in limited quantities, as it gives you a feel for your market, points up some of your problems while there's still some hope of solving them, tells you how successful your product is likely to be. And as I said earlier, a little successful sales history is a strong point in your favor when you're negotiating with a manufacturer later on. So you might as well know what going it alone is all about.

In its simplest form (a misnomer if I ever heard one), going it alone starts with devising a way to manufacture the product, then working out packaging, pricing and merchandising. The next step is to manufacture a quantity of the product, load up the family car and start schlepping your product around to a lot of stores, making sales calls and delivering orders. Later, after you've established a little headway, the smart move is to get a sales rep or a network of sales reps and expand to a regional operation. Maybe eventually to a national operation, if it comes to that.

In a way this is all kind of appealing. With you as honcho of the operation, all the profit there is to be made rolls merrily into your bank account. As top banana of the business, you have total control over how the product is made, how it's merchandised, how it's distributed, where it's sold, how much it sells for. The whole works.

However, being the boss isn't all hearts and flowers and deposit slips. I soon discovered, when I started out with the

Stickies, that getting all the control and all the profit means you get all the headaches, too. It's a package deal. And some of those headaches can be real migraines.

For instance, picture yourself doing the old soft-shoe routine for some irate customer whose order won't be filled on time (the guy who makes the boxes for you missed his delivery deadline). I got to be a regular Fred Astaire when I was selling the Stickies.

Or how about conjuring up a mental image of your living room or garage, all stacked to the rafters with a few hundred gross of big cardboard cartons full of your product, due to a slight misunderstanding with the shipper.

Imagine you and your banker on a first-name basis—yours, not his—because your loans are so big that if you go, he goes. You begin to get the picture.

And that brings us to the question of who pays for all this manufacturing and merchandising activity. Somebody has to scrape up the money for tooling, for the design and printing of packages and store display units, and money for shipping. Somebody has to buy the raw materials, cash up front. Somebody has to pay the help and absorb all the costs of being in business—everything from phone bills to typewriter repairs. Somebody's got to spend some big money.

Guess who.

Okay, so there's a lot of work, expense and worry involved in manufacturing and distributing your own product. But that's not the end of your problems. There's an even more insidious danger you face when you go it on your own. You could be setting up your idea to be stolen.

You are limited in the number of outlets you can reach. (How many stores can you call on with the family station wagon?) But there are companies out there with big, efficient, nationwide sales and distribution organizations just shopping around for new ideas to steal. Yours, for instance.

So there you are, selling briskly, making a nice profit out of the back of your car as you call on your handful of stores. Maybe you've even built up a nice regional business with the beginnings of a fairly decent distribution system. Then along comes the big, unscrupulous manufacturer and notices you. He makes a few discreet inquiries. Yep, your product looks like a winner, all right. And while you're trying to figure out how to reach another half dozen stores, he's cranking up the factory, filling the distribution pipeline with a copy of your idea. Before you know what hit you, he's saturated the market with a well-oiled national blitz.

You're left with the remains of your back-room business and your headaches while he's off scouting up another new idea to knock off. After all the legal niceties are over, after all is said and done, the guy who gets there biggest and fastest in the national market is the guy who gets most of the marbles. I've told hundreds of inventors. Now I'm telling you:

An idea is *some*thing.

But distribution is *every*thing.

The way to avoid this problem if you're going it alone, then, is to get maximum distribution rolling just as fast as you can. That means getting a manufacturers' rep or a network of reps. A manufacturers' rep is a salesman who calls on a regular list of retail outlets and/or distributors in his territory and sells them the product of the various manufacturers he represents. Hence the term. The rep goes out and sells an order for a couple dozen gross of your product to a store or distributor and sends the order on to you. You ship it out to his customer from the warehouse or from your garage or wherever you're storing the goods. And you enclose an invoice. Simple as that.

You may connect with a rep who has national coverage. If not, have him help you put together a national network of similar regional reps. He'll know who the good ones are and be able to supply arcane bits of knowledge like the fact that whatsisname in Atlanta sells like gangbusters for the first six months with a new product, then fades in the stretch. Or whatever.

Needless to say there's more to it than just picking a rep out of the Yellow Pages, calling him up and signing on. He's in business to make money, the same as you are. So you're going to have to convince him that you will be a profitable addition to his list of clients. Sales figures can help, if you've been out peddling the product on your own for a while. It's great to be able to show him where you've been selling, how much you've been selling and how often your customers have been reordering. If you haven't been selling yet, you'll have to make a pretty convincing case for your sales estimates and projections. Bad reps jump at fantasy. Good ones react to facts.

The rep will be interested in other things, too. For in-

WHICH WAY TO GO

stance, he'll want to be sure you will keep a big enough inventory on hand to fill his orders when they come in and that your rate of manufacture can keep up with his rate of sales. Finally, you'll have to convince him that you're solid—that you're going to be in business for a while, especially under the pressure of growing national sales. (That sounded absurd to me when I first heard it, but I soon learned that keeping up with a spurt of sales can put awesome strains on your finances. Prosperity can be a killer.)

There's one more thing he's going to want to see: a production sample of your product. Not a handmade model. Not a picture. Not a glowing, animated description with arm waving and fast talking. A real, honest-to-God production sample, just like the ones he'll be selling for you. There are times when you can get away with a model or a picture, as I mentioned earlier in this book, but not when you get to this stage. Besides, he's probably going to be displaying your product in his showrooms and in various trade shows around the country where his customers come to order their wares for the upcoming season. If he doesn't have the product, he's not going to get many orders.

So much for what the rep expects from you. You have a right to expect a few things from him, too. Like Will Rogers, I've never met a rep I didn't like. But I have to point out that they're all a little optimistic when it comes to the territories they claim to cover. Make sure the ones you use really do cover the territory they claim or you could miss out on important sales.

When negotiating with any manufacturers' reps, start out with the premise that they need an office and/or showroom space and at least one salesman and a secretary in each major metropolitan area in each state in which they want to represent you. If they lack coverage in some areas, find reps who do cover these places and give them that part of the territory. The first rep will kick and scream, but you're the boss. And you'll be right.

For your information, there are twenty-one major metropolitan marketing areas in the United States. You should be represented by real, living people—preferably with showrooms—in each one of those areas.

Normally you'll assign territories to a rep on the basis of geographical regions, usually divided along state lines. They'll ask for exclusive rights to sell your product within the agreed boundaries, and that's fair. Up to a point. And that point is, you may lose some good sales if you don't limit your reps to "vertical" lines of distribution. To illustrate:

Ever stop to consider how many things are sold in military P.X. and commissary stores? Jillions! And how about school bookstores—high schools, junior colleges, colleges, universities. Now you're beginning to catch on. Who sells to those places? Reps. The same reps we have been talking about? Normally not. These guys are specialists. Have you ever tried to figure out a government form on anything? You should see their order forms! It takes a specialist, believe me, to understand them. So keep that in mind when you're assigning reps. You're perfectly within your rights to limit your reps both geographically *and* vertically.

How do you find school reps and military reps? Call your local college bookstore and ask for names. Call your favorite military base, ask for the P.X. (or B.X. in the Air Force, Navy and Marine Corps) and do the same thing. Once you've selected a rep in your area, he or she will lead you to other such specialist reps around the country.

One last word of caution. You'll be approached, if you're successful in a regional or local test, by someone claiming that the only way to go is with a national distribution organization. He may be right. There are a lot of advantages. Just remember to find out if he has people and showrooms in all of the twenty-one major metropolitan areas of the country.

Foreign sales can be a very important part of your success story, and they're not as hard to get as you might think. The biggest order we ever got for the Stickies was $52,000 worth at one time. I've still got a photostat of the check on my wall. Wish I still had the real check. The buyer? Ahlens department store in Stockholm, Sweden. And when those Swedes make up their mind to sell something, they don't fool around. They built a whole special promotion around the Rickie Tickie Stickies and sold out all $52,000 worth in one month. That was $104,000 at retail!

Breaking into the Swedish market was easy, too. In the first place, when we first started out and I was patenting and registering and copyrighting and things like that, I registered the trademark in a whole bunch of likely sounding countries, including Sweden. When things were moving nicely here, I called Scandinavian Air Service and asked for some informa-

WHICH WAY TO GO

tion about marketing in Sweden. The SAS lady came to see me and gave me all kinds of detailed information about the Swedish market, how to enter it, what regulations there were, what the marketing setup was and so forth. She had it all down, chapter and verse, and she knew what she was talking about.

By contacting someone like SAS or various countries' trade attachés or their industrial development offices, you can find out just about everything you need to know to market your product in foreign countries. They will also lead you to foreign reps or brokers.

There are more advantages than meet the eye, too. For instance, even as the enormous enthusiasm for Stickies was wearing down here in the U.S., new countries were just discovering it. By rolling out into new countries, you can keep a momentum going for your product and keep your manufacturing operation at a relatively steady level, keep your sales curve more like a curve than an alpine range. And, of course, checking up on your sales overseas is a pretty snappy excuse to do a little world traveling. 'Ah, yes. Off to Rio to check up on business."

As you can see, going out there on your own can be difficult. That's not to say it can't be done, though, if you conclude it's the best way for you to reach the retail market. Before you come to that conclusion, let's take a look at some of the alternatives. Which brings us back, after all our digression, to the ideal way to go: selling your idea to a manufacturer for a royalty.

The biggest advantage of going this way is that it puts your product on the market through the manufacturer's distribution system—hopefully a big, complex, efficient, nationwide one. Where you would have had to sweat and strain to work your way up to national sales and distribution, the manufacturer can jump right into the market with his best shot immediately. It gives him—and your product—a thumping big start on the knock-off artists.

For another thing, it puts the responsibility for financing the business on the manufacturer's shoulders, not yours. You don't have to spend any of your money for tooling. You don't have to bear the expense of being in business. Best of all, you can dump all the worries on someone else's desk.

The first step to take is to pick out a likely manufacturer.

That's not as simple as it sounds. One of the commonest mistakes made by inventors at this stage of the game is choosing the wrong manufacturer. Far too many inventors try to sell their idea to a company whose production capabilities don't match the product, whose market is totally wrong for the product or who simply is not prepared for one reason or another to deal with the inventor's idea.

Bob Hicks at Fisher-Price told me that outside inventors bring him some 2,000 ideas a year. He has to reject about 1,400 of them out of hand because they don't match his product line—they can't be made by the equipment in Fisher-Price's factory, they don't fit into their product categories, or they are totally unsuited to Fisher-Price's market. All 1,400 of those poor inventors could have saved themselves a lot of trouble by simply going to a toy store and looking around for fifteen minutes.

So the cardinal rule in choosing a manufacturer is to find one that makes and sells products compatible with yours. Look on the shelves of the stores where you expect your product to be sold. See where the manufacturer you have in mind fits into the picture. If you have an idea for a product made out of wood, there's no point in approaching a company that makes everything out of plastic. If you have a product that ought to be sold in hardware stores, don't go to a manufacturer who sells most of his stuff in department stores. Check the price, materials and market of your product against the price, materials and market of the company you're planning to approach. If they don't match, don't bother.

Something else to bear in mind is that you can get into an immature, unsophisticated industry much more easily than into a mature one. The classic example is toys. Toys are a very, very difficult market to break into with a new idea. The industry is dominated by a few highly sophisticated, extremely rich companies. The competition is intense. Cutthroat, even. Almost *no* outsider ever makes it with a new toy idea. My own experience of selling my Little Lumpsie doll to Fisher-Price a few years ago was an incredible exception. Bob Hicks, who bought the idea from me, told me that he has seen 50,000 new product ideas from outsiders in his twenty-five years with the company. In all that time, out of all those ideas, he's bought five, counting Little Lumpsie.

On the other hand, the gift and stationery field is imma-

WHICH WAY TO GO

ture. An outsider has as good a chance as anybody in cracking the gift and stationery market with a new idea—and Rickie Tickie Stickies is the proof of that particular pudding. Pet Rock is another. There's no single, big dominant manufacturer in the field, nor any group of dominant manufacturers. Gift and stationery stores themselves tend toward "mom and pop" operations, small stores where the owner waits on customers. There are few big chains. So a neat, marketable idea—even something as off-the-wall as Gary Dahl's Pet Rock—has a good chance of making it.

Part of the reason for the difficulty of cracking a mature industry is that the biggies have such a heavy investment in their own idea-generating organizations that they don't *need* any outsiders. In fact, after seven months of politely trying, I couldn't get into Whamo (Hula-Hoop-Frisbee) Corporation to discuss this book. They were *that* busy. Or something. A vice-president at Mattel explained to me that a development group of fifty people will be involved in coming up with a new idea within the company. And that's just to get it to the point where it's ready to be refined by another development group of from 200 to 250 people. With that kind of high-powered idea organization, it's small wonder that fewer than .05 per cent of the ideas Mattel carries to some stage of development come from outside the company. And most, by far, of those outside ideas come from a few professional inventors with whom Mattel regularly deals. The odds against you or me getting to first base in that kind of situation are astronomical.

In addition, the biggies in a mature industry have researched the field so intensely and have gained so much experience that they know more than any outsider could possibly hope to know about their market. Fisher-Price, for instance, won't hesitate a moment to mount a $50,000 research program for a single toy idea they plan to market. Granted, as Bob Hicks points out, that research is far from a science, but it sure beats holding up a wet finger and making a wild guess.

Most important of all, an idea has to be capable of generating *enormous* sales before it's worth bothering with by one of the giants in a mature industry. It has to support 250-person development teams and $50,000 research projects. At Fisher-Price, I'd guess that an idea would have to look like 2 to 5 million dollars in sales a year at wholesale before Bob would be interested. Anything less than that wouldn't be worth the time, effort and investment that would go into it. It could be a swell idea. A perfectly salable idea. It could tickle the fancies of Fisher-Price and Mattel, but unless it can generate big, big money, they won't buy it.

All of this boils down to a couple of rules for you to bear in mind when you're setting out to sell your idea to a manufacturer: Make sure your product matches the company's need and capabilities. And try to stay away from the ideas in mature, sophisticated industries like toys or games or clothing, to name a few. (Don't throw away a good idea, just because it happens to be a toy, mind you. Just be aware of the odds. Don't be discouraged if Mattel doesn't snap it up like a hungry trout leaping for a gray hackle fly.)

Every route to the marketplace involves its own special distribution system. Since every distribution system has its own peculiar set of costs, you ought to understand the markup structure inherent in each. You'll need that information to arrive at your wholesale and retail price, as we discussed in the last chapter. To simplify matters, we'll use a hypothetical product that sells at retail for $2.00 to explain each distribution system. Every time we come to a major distribution system in this chapter, we'll stop and take a look at what happens to that $2.00 item so you have a benchmark to work with.

Whether you go it on your own or sell your idea to a manufacturer, you'll probably be involved in one of the two most basic distribution systems: the distributor/wholesaler system, or the factory-direct-to-retailer system. Here's how that $2.00 is spread around in each of these two distribution systems:

At this point you're probably wondering why in the world everything isn't distributed on a factory-direct-to-the-retailer basis rather than through a distributor. After all, the manufacturer gets more money going direct. Good question. Fortunately, I have a good answer.

A good Class-A distributor earns his money. He warehouses the product. He sells the product using *and* paying his own sales force. He bills and collects the money. He handles the problems of damage, returns and the like for the manufacturer. And probably the most important thing he does is to pay the manufacturer promptly. Not because he's just nice. That 2 per cent discount for prompt payment does add up.

A good distributor network can save a manufacturer other

BASIC DISTRIBUTOR/WHOLESALER SYSTEM

CONSUMER

RETAILER

REGIONAL OR NATIONAL
DISTRIBUTOR/WHOLESALER

MANUFACTURER'S SALES
REPS OR OWN SALES FORCE

MANUFACTURER

Who gets how much on a typical $2.00 retail item with this form of distribution?

The consumer pays the retailer (plus tax)	$2.00
The retailer pays the distributor	1.20
The distributor pays the manufacturer	.90
The manufacturer pays his sales force	.07
The manufacturer allows cash discounts and freight credits amounting to about	.05
The manufacturer's factory gross is	.78

FACTORY DIRECT TO RETAILER

CONSUMER

RETAILER

MANUFACTURER'S SALES
REPS OR OWN SALES FORCE

MANUFACTURER

Who gets how much on a typical $2.00 retail item with this form of distribution?

The consumer pays the retailer (plus tax)	$2.00
The retailer pays the manufacturer	1.00
Hhe manufacturer pays his sales force (This will vary from $.05 to $.20 depending on the industry. An average of $.10 is fair.)	.10
The manufacturer allows cash discounts and freight credits amounting to about	.05
The manufacturer's factory gross is	.85

problems, too. Fifty Class-A regional distributors can cover the United States for just about any product you could invent, regardless of what kind of store the consumer finds it in. Those distributors will be reaching upwards of ten thousand separate accounts, with all the attendant problems of billing, hand holding and collecting. The manufacturer has only fifty. Fifty bills at the end of the month instead of ten thousand. That's a good beginning.

Unfortunately, all industries don't have good national distributor networks. Gift and stationery, for example, is one. In the heyday of Rickie Tickie Stickies, I would have been happier to have had fifty large accounts instead of the 6,200 little ones we ended up with. And the bottom line would have come out the same. It costs money to do it yourself in the distributing business.

If you haven't been able to sell your idea to a manufacturer, and you don't want to mess around with making sales calls, and you're not yet ready to sign up with a manufacturers' rep, there's another way to go. It has some impressive advantages. It's called mail order.

By setting up your own mail-order business, you give yourself broad market penetration immediately. You can reach anywhere in the country—anywhere in the world, for that matter—with your ads. You can become an instant national or international company, not limited by the number of stores you call on in person. Your customers are everywhere.

You can even do a mail-order business while simultaneously doing retail business in stores. Be careful, though. Quite a few retailers—and quite a few reps, too—don't take kindly to competing with mail-order sales of the same product. It works the other way around, too. Retail sales can kill off a mail-order business. A customer may feel better about getting the product immediately at the store than waiting around for the mailman to deliver it. And some products simply aren't as good in mail-order business as they are in a store.

Anyway, if you decide to go mail order, you have to decide where to place your ads. The trick is to go where you reach the most potential customers for the least amount of money—and that doesn't necessarily mean going to the cheapest medium. The first step is to figure out who it is you're trying to reach. Make up a composite outline of your most likely customer, how old, male or female, probable interests, income and education level and so forth. For instance, if you're trying to sell a new kind of fishing rod, you're probably going to be selling to men, probably in the 18 to 49 age range, with an interest in outdoor activities. If your fishing rod is an expensive one, you're probably looking for relatively affluent customers. Now you look around for the kinds of media most likely to reach that imaginary average customer. Forget *Redbook* and *Newsweek*. *Redbook* aims at women, *Newsweek*'s readers are so varied you'd be reaching a lot of people who couldn't care less about a fishing rod. You'd be better off in *Field & Stream*, for example. Possibly the sports section of daily newspapers around the country could be a good buy. Maybe even the classified ads, under such headings as "sporting goods" and so forth.

There are people, called media buyers, who make their whole living working out problems like this, but you're probably not at a level where you can afford their services. You'll have to do it on your own. Every publication, in the masthead, lists its advertising representatives. Call them and find out about the cost of advertising. (They'll quote prices "per line," which is technically called an "agate line." There are fourteen agate lines to an inch, so a 14-line ad is one column wide and one inch long.)

Once you've figured out where you want to advertise, place your ads and wait for the checks to roll in.

Until a couple of years ago, it was possible to let those checks finance most of your manufacturing operation. The "smart guys" wouldn't begin to manufacture the product until enough orders accumulated to pay for their raw materials, labor and so forth. Quite a few small mail-order businesses operated that way. But the customers out there waited for six to eight weeks, sometimes even longer, before receiving what they'd paid for.

Now there's a law that says you have to fulfill the order within four weeks, or else. It makes life a little more difficult for the mail-order companies—even some of the biggies have to scramble to meet the four-week deadline—but it gives some badly needed protection to the poor customer.

Although mail order is a nice, clean way to extend your reach, it's not entirely without problems. For one thing, all those ads not only increase the size of your up-front investment, but the cost of all that advertising will have to be borne ultimately by the price of your product. More advertising makes for a more expensive item. Sure, the ads are relatively small and inexpensive. But three hundred dollars here, a hundred fifty there, a couple hundred more someplace else add up quickly to a sizable hunk of money tied up in advertising space. That's not counting the cost of producing the ads that go into the space, either. It's a continuing expense. You don't just hit 'em once with a bunch of ads, then forget about it. You have to keep on going back again and again with advertising to keep the sales moving.

Shipping is more expensive for a mail-order business, too. Filling a retail order for one hundred pieces can be handled in one bulk shipment fairly inexpensively. Shipping the same hundred pieces one at a time by mail or through some parcel or express service costs more. Lots more. These higher shipping figures, like the advertising costs, show up in the price of your product. (Most mail-order outfits quote a sales price "plus shipping," but that doesn't fool anybody. The cash outlay is the sum of those two costs, no matter how you try to disguise it.)

The danger in adding costs to your product is that you could price yourself right out of the market. An item that just walks out the door at $2.49 could become a slow mover at $2.98 and a complete and utter failure at $3.50.

Of course, selling by mail gives you more maneuvering room in your price. But you'll find that you can easily spend enough on advertising and added shipping costs to make up for all the slack you thought you had in your price structure.

There isn't any nice, clean way to show what happens to our hypothetical $2.00 item in this distribution system. That's because there are some variables involved. It works this way:

CONSUMER
/
MANUFACTURER

The consumer pays the manufacturer direct $2.00

But before the manufacturer can arrive at his factory gross, he has to deduct the cost of advertising and shipping involved in that $2.00 sale. Amortization, in other words. He has to total up all the advertising expense that led to a given batch of sales, then divide it by the number of sales those ads led to. (If he spent $500 on ads and generated 1,000 sales, his advertising expense is $.50 per sale.) Then the manufacturer deducts the cost of shipping the order. The result, after all this is done, is the factory gross.

Getting into the mail-order market doesn't necessarily mean you have to do it yourself, though. There's another way to sell by mail. A much better way, which eliminates most of the drawbacks we just discussed. You sell your product to a catalogue marketer. If your product is something that interests Spiegel or Montgomery Ward, you could have a one-way ticket to fat city. You'll be plugged right into their national catalogue sales and distribution system, to say nothing of all their retail outlets. That's better than having the hottest rep in the country, believe me.

It's easier said than done, naturally. You don't just stroll in and make your sale to one of the biggies just like that. You have to convince them that your product will make a nice profit for them.

If that's beginning to sound like a recurring theme, you're right. And so is the routine you have to go through to make the sale. You have to do the same things you do if you want to convince a rep to take on your product. Show sales figures, if you have them. Show solvency and reliability. Show the ability to keep up your supply with their demand. And you have to show a production sample, not a model or a drawing.

In many ways, selling your product to one of the major catalogue marketers is almost as good as making a royalty deal with some manufacturer. For one thing, it lightens the burden of doing business, because making one big sale is a lot more profitable and painless than making a dozen small sales. Even shipping will be cheaper, since you'll be sending a big batch at one time to the marketer's warehouses. All that adds up to a more profitable and lower-priced product, which means more money in your pocket.

One more thing, before we leave the topic. Often you will be asked to give the catalogue house an exclusive right to carry your product. That is, they will ask that you not sell it through any other outlets, at least for a period of time. That's to give them the chance to establish the market for the product, skim the easy sales and take the position as the innovator—the company that brought this great new item to the

WHICH WAY TO GO 105

consumer. Later, when they may no longer have an exclusive, they hope that the public will still think of them first when they think of the product.

Naturally it's to your advantage to avoid giving anyone an exclusive. It just cuts down on the number of places you could be making sales. But you may have no choice in the final negotiations. It's worth holding out for, but it's not worth losing the big sale for.

Oddly enough, sometimes a Sears or a Ward will do a complete about-face and actually help you market the product someplace else rather than ask for an exclusive. A case in point was a new kind of spillproof ice cube tray that Sears decided to develop. Now, nobody gets rich selling ice cube trays. Every refrigerator comes with a couple of them and there's just not that much of a market for replacements. Still, it was a good item and if someone else could stir up an awareness of the need for spillproof ice cube trays, Sears could sell quite a few of them. So Sears helped the manufacturer sell the tray idea to a big appliance company. The company advertised the clever trays as a product advantage in their line of refrigerators, making the spillproof trays well known. Then Sears advertised the trays in their catalogue, saying that you could have this new product feature for your old refrigerator. They sold a lot of ice cube trays, Sears got what it wanted and the appliance company had a new benefit to advertise. Everybody won, with a little help from Sears.

Sears and J. C. Penney and the like do not control the entire catalogue sales game, by a long shot. There's a whole world of specialty catalogue companies out there, reaching a completely different spectrum of consumers with a completely different kind of product. They represent another way for you, as manufacturer of your product, to get at your market. We're talking about companies like Sunset House, Hanover House, Greenland Studios, Ambassador-Leviter and so forth. As a general rule, the products they sell are novelty items, usually of fairly low price (although the Horchow Collection is an example of a specialty house with three- and four-figure price tags in the catalogue). The pieces are usually relatively compact and easy to ship.

The big catalogue marketers we were discussing earlier car engines and kitchen stoves. They're prepared to deal with have a tradition of carrying big, bulky items like complete the shipping problems involved. The specialty catalogue people aren't fascinated by that kind of challenge.

To get the inside information on this market, I talked to Lewis Halper who was for many years a buyer and product director for Sunset House, the Big Kahuna of the specialty outfits. He knows whereof he speaks. One of the things I asked about was the feeling that specialty catalogues are sort of "court of last resorts" for the inventor who hasn't succeeded anywhere else. Not so, said Lew. The specialty catalogues are a very distinct market with a set of characteristics all their own. They're not a dumping ground for losers, because a loser wouldn't last very long in the intense competition for space in the catalogue. What's more, some items that would absolutely die in ordinary retail outlets can become enormously successful in the specialty catalogues. We discussed an example.

"Suppose you have designed a little plastic gadget," Lew said. "You press it down on the end of a radish and it makes an instant radish rosebud for a salad tray. Now, you figure you can sell it for about 39 cents, retail. You put that thing in a store, you'll be lucky to move maybe five or ten a week. Nothing! But that same item might get as many as 100,000 orders in a catalogue."

How come? Well, in a housewares department or someplace that sells cooking items, your little radish cutter would be lost in the shuffle. And without some kind of detailed explanation displayed at the point of purchase, not one person in ten would know what the gadget is supposed to do. (How many times have you found some fascinating, but totally incomprehensible little doodad among the pots and pans? Did you buy one? Probably not.)

In a specialty catalogue, on the other hand, there's room for a picture of the cutter in action, plus an explanation of its inner mysteries and some sales copy. Anyone thumbing through the catalogue can be stopped by the item, understand it instantly and—if it meets a need—order it.

What makes an item especially suited for this specialized market? "Uniqueness for one thing," Lew said. "That's very important. No me-too products here. Also there has to be a high degree of utility or usefulness that the consumer can relate to. Then it should have low price, low weight, ease of shipping and ease of packing." Obviously, the radish cutter makes it on all counts.

WHICH WAY TO GO

In many ways, the specialty catalogue is tailor-made for inventors like you and me. So many of the things we come up with seem to be the type of thing you find in these books. More important, the people who put out those catalogues are constantly searching for people like us—people with novel new ideas they want to develop. The big, traditional catalogue marketers are interested in new ideas, too, but they also lean heavily on regular run-of-the-mill merchandise for their sales. The specialty marketer depends entirely on unique products, special new ideas. Hence, the term specialty catalogue.

Lew had some tips for people who are trying to develop a product for this market. "Bring your sky-high thinking down to earth," he said. "Sure, you start out with this magnificent big idea. But before you market it, you have to scale that thinking down into line with the realities." Cost consciousness is part of it. A big part of it.

You have to be sure you've figured out the cheapest possible way to manufacture it. That includes simplifying the design wherever possible. Maybe using thinner or lighter material, as long as it doesn't detract from the value of the product. Make sure you've shopped carefully for a factory to make your product and that you've gotten the best possible price on your raw materials.

Shipping is a good place to save money, too. Call a few shippers to find out their requirements for package size and weight. If your package is too big to meet those specifications, you're going to have a lot of shipping expense on your hands. Think about shipping your product unassembled or knocked down. (In the trade it's called a "K.D. item." That ought to liven up your conversation at the next coffeeklatch.) That could save money on shipping. Also, think about ways to make the product smaller while fulfilling the same function. For that matter, maybe by making it just a little bigger you can make it a lot more useful at no great increase of shipping cost.

The same kind of cost-consciousness applies to the packaging itself. The basic requirement is to give the product adequate protection during shipment. The more cheaply you can meet that basic requirement, the better off you are likely to be.

Anything you can do to lower your cost of manufacture without hurting the product will increase your chances of making the sale.

The specialty houses are even able to do a type of market

testing if they think they like your product, but they're not sure. The traditional way, which works pretty well, is for the specialty house to purchase a small quantity of your product and allocate just a little bit of space to it in their next main catalogue or one of the sub-catalogues they occasionally issue. Experience tells them what results to expect in a given price range with a given size of ad. If your product matches up to their expectations, they'll probably give it a bigger ad the next time around and you'll be in business. If not, you'll be out. The golden rule of the catalogue marketer is, "If it doesn't perform, out it goes." There's no room in the catalogue for a slow mover.

Recently, though, there has been a new development in catalogue testing. It's a little complicated, but here's how it works:

Let's assume you have a new product and the catalogue house says, "Sure, let's give it a test." They will ask that you pay them a fee—something like $1,000. For that fee, they will print 100,000 fliers, usually in full color and in a format approximating a listing in their catalogue. They put one of those fliers inside the package when they fill an order from their catalogue. So Mrs. Smith, out in East Gymshirt, Texas, goes to the mailbox and finds that the radish cutter she ordered has arrived. She opens the package and there, along with the cutter is your flier. (In fact, there may be a couple of fliers in there, advertising different products they're testing.) She reads the flier, likes the product and sends in her order. You've made a sale.

The advantage of this system to the mail-order house is that they're only buying from you on consignment. They'll stock a quantity of your product to fulfill the orders, but they only pay you as the orders come in. They don't pay for the stock in advance, the usual way. Your $1,000 fee pays all their printing costs for those fliers, so they haven't spent any of their own money at all. For them, it's a good deal.

It's a good deal for you, too. For a relatively small sum, you've obtained an excellent market test of your product. You know how many fliers went out, you know how many orders came in. You can make very accurate projections from that. So can the catalogue house. If they like what they see, they'll probably sign you up on a regular basis and start doing business cash up front. You also can take the results of that test someplace else, if you'd rather, and use them to get into a different catalogue. Take your pick.

WHICH WAY TO GO

Two things you'll want to check up on, in one of these tests. First, you'll be wise to insist on some sort of guarantee that the fliers were actually printed, that they, in fact, went out to the number of people you were promised. Second, you'll want to know *who* the people were, on what basis they were selected for the mailing. If you have a product that's designed for outdoors, then ladies who buy radish cutters aren't going to be very representative of your market. Likewise, you can't get a very valid test of the salability of your new kitchen aid if the flier goes out to everyone who bought a duck call.

Let's run our $2.00 example through a catalogue distribution system and see what happens to it. We'll have to use two different charts on the factory selling price because there's usually a difference between a deal with a major catalogue house, like Ward, and a specialty catalogue house like Sunset House. This confused me at first. But after being counseled by experts, the reasons finally sunk in. The majors normally deal in higher ticket items and can pro-rate their printing and production costs against a larger sales and distribution volume. Let's start with a "major."

MAJOR CATALOGUE SALES

CONSUMER

CATALOGUE
DISTRIBUTOR

MANUFACTURER*

The consumer pays the catalogue distributor	$2.00
The catalogue distributor pays the manufacturer	1.00
The manufacturer's factory gross is	1.00

*This type of sale is normally a "house" account in which a principal of the manufacturing company is the sales contact. It's that important. There are reps specializing in chain sales. When involved, they usually get around 10 per cent.

110 HOW TO TURN YOUR IDEA INTO A MILLION DOLLARS

The factory gross will vary up to plus or minus 10 per cent because of two important factors. Chains normally represent large-volume sales and, therefore, they qualify for large-quantity discounts. They will also normally receive the maximum freight allowances (like for free) and will take advantage of all cash discounts.

When I noted "qualifying for large-quantity discounts," it reminded me to remind you of a very important fact if you end up being a manufacturer. Decide *before you go to market* if you will be offering quantity discounts.

Also, anticipate discounts for *foreign* brokers before you finalize your numbers. Double check these quantity discounts, then check them again to make sure large sales don't fall into the "feeding the monkey to watch him crap" category. If you're satisfied that you can make a profit while offering quantity discounts, then *publish* the fact. Even if it's only a few carbon copies. Have some copies in your files. And be sure you offer the *same* terms to everyone. *All the time.* The Feds take a dim view of your offering different strokes to different folks, especially if you end up selling overseas at different prices than here. They call that "dumping," and if you can't prove it is a consistent sales policy, they can really dump on you!

Now we'll look at a "specialty" deal. The same distribution chart applies:

'SPECIALTY' CATALOGUE SALES

CONSUMER

CATALOGUE
DISTRIBUTOR

MANUFACTURER

Here's where we get a variation on the theme:

The consumer pays the catalogue distributor	$2.00
The catalogue distributor pays the manufacturer	.50
The manufacturer's factory gross is	.50

WHICH WAY TO GO 111

Why? As we said, the specialty catalogue has basically the same start-up costs of a major catalogue. Prorated against much less dollar volume per item, the difference has to come from somewhere. That somewhere is the hide of the manufacturer!

There's one way to sell your product I'll bet you never thought of. You could sell it to some company as a premium item, the kind of thing that's given away or sold at a low price when you buy the jumbo-juicyburger and fries at your local hamburger hustler. The kind of thing you send a box top and a buck for. That may strike you as a kind of goofy way to get sales, but quite a few products get to the public that way. It could be either a jumping off place for you—a way to get some exposure before you go to retail—or it could be the natural market for your product.

You don't actually have to be the manufacturer to sell your product as a premium (although you make more money if you are). If you can meet the heavy production demands of the premium user, fine. But if not, most companies who buy premiums have a regular stable of manufacturers with whom they work. They'd be happy to buy your idea from you, either for a straight cash buy-out or—more rarely—on a royalty basis.

The price range of premium items varies vastly. Some of the cigarette companies, for instance, have sold everything from sailboats to binoculars as premium items.

The big-ticket or moderate-ticket items used by cigarette companies represent one end of the premium spectrum. The other end is represented by the little inexpensive gimcracks that are handed out with a purchase of the promoter's product. In between, there's a vast area of premium users who should also be considered as possible markets for your product. Sunkist, the citrus giant, uses some extremely interesting ones. Recently they offered a kit of recipes for lemons and lemon juice along with a little plastic thing that makes juicing the lemon a snap. It's a nice idea and somebody, somewhere, had to invent that little plastic spigot. Look on the back of the next box of Kleenex you buy, and you'll probably find some kind of premium offer—anything from a potted plant (somebody had to invent the pot and mailer combination) to tiny needlepoint kits (somebody had to come up with the idea for the miniature needlepoint design). Cereal companies,

112 HOW TO TURN YOUR IDEA INTO A MILLION DOLLARS

soft-drink bottlers, canners and even coffee makers are also good premium users.

Basically, there are two different kinds of premium. The first, and most common kind, is called "self-liquidating." With this kind, the customer who orders the special burger deal pays another two bits, let's say, and gets a hand puppet or a genuine Moldavian police whistle or whatever the current premium is. The hamburger hustler bought the premium himself for two bits, so he breaks even on the deal. The premiums liquidate (pay for) themselves. The promoter can work the same trick with a "send one box top . . ." offer, except that the price of the premium also has to cover mailing expense and handling charge.

The second, less common, kind of premium actually costs the promoter money. For instance, the same hand puppet or Moldavian police whistle might be given away free with the purchase of the jumbo-juicyburger combination plate. Usually this sort of premium is only used in case of a big event (maybe the opening of a new store), in the case of some special celebration (the puppets are handed out to kids from the hamburger hustler's float in the Christmas parade), or in the case of desperation (so far this month, nobody has bought the jumbo-juicyburger combination plate and the regional manager's ulcer is starting to act up again).

In the case of premiums, the needs of the company and the mechanics of the operation are a little different from the usual retail setup, but you'll find that the ground rules for making the sale are about the same. When you make your pitch to the promoter, you'll have to do pretty much all the same things you would do to pitch Sears or Sunset House or a manufacturer's representative. You're especially going to have to prove your business stability and your ability to make enough of the product to meet their needs. They simply cannot afford to have you punk out on them in mid-promotion. Hell hath no fury like a kid who didn't get his Moldavian police whistle.

One of the people I talked to when I was researching this chapter was Richard Williams, director of promotions and public relations for Foodmaker, the company that owns Jack-in-the-Box restaurants. It's a chain of fast-food outlets that is well-known in many parts of the country. Dick buys a lot of premium items, because that's an important part of the marketing strategy at Jack-in-the-Box. A lot of what he has to say applies to premiums in general.

Like most premium buyers, Dick knows exactly what he is looking for. He knows his price range—usually around $.69 or $.79, almost never over a dollar. Jack-in-the-Box premiums should be compact, because of shipping considerations and because none of the eight hundred stores have much storage space to spare. Dick, like almost all of his compatriots, wants something unique, something you won't find at every other fast-food place or every two-bit store in town. Dick also has some needs that aren't necessarily universal in the premium business. He insists that any premium items he uses be readily identifiable as a Jack-in-the-Box item. (It is, after all, an advertising device.) He also insists on what he calls "instant play value." That is, you should be able to do whatever it is the product does right then and there, while you're still eating your burger or taco. Needless to say, most of the premium items Dick considers are aimed at children—a crucial factor in the fast-food business. (For whatever it's worth, though, he's had some great success with adult-type premiums. Collections of glasses, for one thing. First there was an imitation Tiffany glass, which went like the proverbial flapjacks. Later, at the beginning of the bicentennial madness, he did a premium offer of bicentennial mugs with patriotic emblems cast in the sides. Any premium that leads to a collection is good stuff, as far as Dick is concerned, because it brings customers back again and again to complete their collections.)

The mail-order or box-top premiums are another whole kettle of eels. Here, shipping considerations are even more important, since the orders are going to be fulfilled by mail. But low price is a less important consideration than the kind of premium Dick Williams buys at Jack-in-the-Box. If the item seems like a good value at the price, the actual price is hardly important at all. The classic example is the sailboat Kool cigarettes offered some time back. For a couple of cigarette packs (or a facsimile thereof) plus eight-eight bucks, you could get a complete, workable sailboat, with mast, rigging and sail. Now *that's* a premium! Naturally, every premium user has his own rules about how expensive or inexpensive the premium can be. More than anything else, uniqueness and value are the things to look for in this type of premium. Uniqueness to catch the eye, value to generate the order.

Every premium user has his own peculiar set of problems to deal with. Dick, for instance, is lucky in that all the Jack-in-the-Box outlets are company owned. When he buys a premium, everybody carries it. McDonald's stores are largely owned by independent businessmen-franchise holders. So when McDonald's wants to do a premium promotion they have to call a meeting and sell the businessmen on the idea. Also, most of the ideas that come to Dick are screened first by his advertising agency, Doyle, Dane, Bernbach, Inc. Other users do the preliminary screening themselves or turn the whole thing over to one of the agencies who specialize in premiums. You'll have to do a little research to find out how the company you've got in mind handles premiums.

How do you find the name of the premium user who might be interested in your product? Look around. Figure out who is using what kinds of premiums. Match them up with your idea and call the company that seems logical. Contact the sales promotion manager or the advertising manager directly for an appointment. Or write to the National Premium Sales Executives Organization, Union City, New Jersey 07087, for a complete list of sales promotion agencies that sell premiums to companies.

Premiums can be a fantastic market for you. Even though the time span is limited, you can sell a lot of product. A good promotion by Dick Williams will move 800,000 units in about four to six weeks! (That's a thousand each at the chain's eight hundred stores.) So, even though a marketer will rarely repeat the same promotion, the one shot you get is in the megaton range.

The concentrated nature of these premium promotions means they have to be scheduled well in advance, to give the manufacturer time to make and stockpile the product. In the case of Jack-in-the-Box, the promotions are scheduled anywhere from six to nine months in advance. They usually do three or four major national promotions a year, in addition to a number of local extravaganzas for special events. Dick also tests eight or ten ideas a year in groups of twenty to fifty markets, just to see if they're good enough to go national. And within that small group of restaurants, he'll play some variations to get a better feel of how the premium performs. In some towns they'll back the offer with a lot of advertising

WHICH WAY TO GO

support. In others, they'll do it cold, with no advertising at all. They'll pick test markets from widely different areas all over the country, too.

The most important thing for you to keep in mind if you decide to go the premium route is to match your product up with the right company. It could be a very lucrative and satisfying experience. And once you're done with the promotion, there's nothing to prevent you from going retail with the product. Sure, you will have killed off a lot of sales by using the piece as a premium. But you will also have gained a lot of exposure, which could turn out to be the best possible advertising for your product.

If you sell your product to some company as a premium, here's what the distribution system does to that hypothetical $2.00 item:

PREMIUM SALES

(A)	(B)
CONSUMER	CONSUMER
PREMIUM BUYER	PREMIUM BUYER
PREMIUM REP	MANUFACTURER
MANUFACTURER	

(A) SELF-LIQUIDATING

The consumer pays the company involved	$1.00
The company pays the manufacturer	.90
The manufacturer's factory gross is	.90

(B) GIVE-AWAY

The consumer receives the item free.

The company involved pays the manufacturer, usually about $.90

When there's a premium rep involved in the sale, he'll normally receive about 10 per cent of factory gross.

116 HOW TO TURN YOUR IDEA INTO A MILLION DOLLARS

There's another way to turn your product into a premium. An even easier way. A "fulfillment house" might sound like some kind of group psychotherapy operation—or worse—but it's really a kind of distributor, specializing in premium items. Someone sends in a box top and an order, the fulfillment house fulfills the order.

These firms have their own sales forces to do all the contact work with the premium users like soft-drink bottlers, cigarette companies and so forth. They sell one of these users on your product as a premium, handle the shipping, maybe even the manufacturing, and do all the dirty work for you.

Your job is to sell the fulfillment house your idea. Then you can just lean back and collect your money—either a royalty or a flat fee for the idea.

The profit structure in this distribution system is about the same as in the distributor/wholesaler system I talked about earlier. Here's what happens to our hypothetical $2.00 item in this distribution system:

COUPON OFFERS

CONSUMER (Through the
company making the
offer)

FULFILLMENT HOUSE

MANUFACTURER

The consumer sends in the coupon, boxtop (or whatever) $1.00
(plus postage and handling)
The fulfillment house or offering company
pays the manufacturer anywhere from $.10 to $.70

How come? Many of the coupon items you see offered are one-time purchases of factory close-outs. The prices get a little slippery. However, the reverse also happens. A manufacturer may use a coupon offer sale as an introductory opportunity for a new product. The item, if it's successful in a coupon offer, will then be rolled out as a consumer item through normal distribution channels.

WHICH WAY TO GO

Keep this in mind if you can't find any other way of underwriting your project. I personally have used this approach successfully twice. You'll be hard-put to get any giant-number guarantees from a fulfillment house or any offering company. However, if it's a national program, you can expect at least 10,000 responses. From there, my experience indicates an average of 40,000 responses can be expected. And really successful offers can run into hundreds of thousands.

Another interesting, and profitable, way to reach the marketplace with your product is through private-label sales, either exclusively or as plus-business if you end up being a manufacturer.

I am writing this at the office. It's a Sunday, the Number One Son and Janitor, David, just came in with our executive lunch—chicken from Colonel Sanders. I was lickin' my fingers and trying to find a good example of private labeling to make it easy for you to understand.

Nothing came immediately to mind until I got to the mopping up stage of lunch. I opened the little Wash 'n' Dry package, used it, and was about to throw it away when I realized it wasn't Wash 'n' Dry at all. Don't they come in a blue package? This one was red and white and had the Colonel's smiling face on it. It was a Wet-Nap ® "Folded Fingerbowl" ® and was manufactured by Nice-Pak Prods, Mt. Vernon, New York 10550, and distributed by KFC Corporation, Louisville, Kentucky 40213.

Now, I don't know if Nice-Pak also makes Wash 'n' Dry. It doesn't matter for this example. The point is that they are undoubtedly selling millions of their ® "Folded Fingerbowls" ® every year to KFC. It's undoubtedly highly competitive, but also probably profitable as well. Their product is getting to me, the consumer, through private labeling. I'm paying for it in the $1.49 lunch cost. It's probably also getting to me under a different brand name when my wife buys them at the market. Same product, different package.

One of my clients sells about $1,000,000 worth of an item every year using his own brand name, his own package, and his normal distributor/wholesaler pattern. He sells an additional $2,000,000 each year to Sears using an exclusive Sears brand name. Same product, different packages. I know. I designed both of them.

Another of my clients does the same thing with a different kind of product for Montgomery Ward. The same item is sold in two different packages. Again, I know, because I designed both.

Private labeling could be a way for you to go if the idea of manufacturing your idea appeals to you and the idea of marketing it doesn't. A toy I designed for an Eastern manufacturer will probably be introduced as an "exclusive," private label item with a major national chain. Why? Because the manufacturer is not in the toy business. He happened to have certain manufacturing capabilities, purchasing power, and some down time in his production area. I matched a toy item to those capabilities. Rather than start a whole new sales effort and develop a whole new distribution network, the manufacturer has opted to private label the item. In his case, it seems to be the best way to go, especially for the first year or so while the consumer's response to a new product is being measured.

There's one last way to go which we should discuss. It's a combination plan, where you start out building a company to make and sell the product (presumably with manufacturers' reps doing the selling, maybe even making a deal with one or another of the catalogue marketers). Then, having built up the company and established a name for yourself, you sell the company: The whole thing—inventory, equipment, name and "good will."

That's what I did with Rickie-Tickie-Stickies, Inc. Why did I sell Stickies? Because somebody made me an offer I couldn't refuse. Just for background, the company that bought me was trying to market something along the same lines as my plastic stick-on flowers. But every place they went, they found that I was already there, solidly entrenched and doing very well. Being smart businessmen, they figured that they might as well buy me, since they weren't doing all that well trying to sidestep me. They came, negotiated the deal, gave me a management contract for a predetermined period of time and paid me a good price for the company and its "good will."

Now, you may not be convinced of the value of that good will, but it really does make a difference. I suppose it's bragging, but I had been doing very well with—and by—my customers, and they had a good deal of respect for my organization. I didn't do anything all that spectacular. I just ran a pretty good business, and they appreciated it. They were interested in continuing to do business with Rickie-

Tickie-Stickies, Inc. That interest was worth a lot of money to the people who made me the offer.

The point of all this is that you can do the same thing. By building up your company and making a success of it, you'll be gaining an added dividend of good will which is a very valuable commodity on the market. Selling the company doesn't mean you have to get out of the idea business. It just means you have to come up with some new ideas. But you were planning on that all along, weren't you?

As you can see, there are a lot of things for you to consider before you make your try for the retail market with your product. There's only one thing you must keep in mind: everybody is in business to make money. Your aim is to handle your product so that everybody does just that.

Including you.

VIII
IMAGINE, IF YOU WILL...

A professional presentation can help sell your idea. Here's how to make one.

You are about to delve into the innermost mysteries of that indispensable skill called "making the presentation." There's no getting round it. By the time you've had your run with your big idea, you're going to be a master of the arcane art of presenting your idea in all its wonder and all its ramifications to a lot of different kinds of people. It doesn't matter whether you end up selling your idea to a manufacturer, doing a small run of product to generate some sales history or forming a company of your own to make and sell the product. One way or another you're going to make a lot of presentations...

to manufacturers
to bankers
to investors
to suppliers
to reps, distributors, retailers, consumers, patent attorneys and, of course, to your own family.

The fine art of turning people on to your idea is going to become one of your most important skills. So it follows that you ought to have at least a basic understanding of how to prepare a presentation that will make the most of the bolt of lightning when it strikes. Maybe even help the lightning along, a little.

The first and most important thing to bear in mind is that

IMAGINE, IF YOU WILL . . .

your presentation ought to be as complete as you possibly can make it. It ought to answer *all* the questions anyone might ask—and some they haven't thought of.

Another primary consideration is the physical format. How it looks. What's in it. There are a couple of schools of thought on this one. For one, there's the old "back-of-the-envelope" approach. A couple of rough sketches, some written notes, all stuffed into a dime-store folder represents the farthest reaches of complexity in this approach. You rely totally on the power of the idea itself to blow people's minds, hoping that the humility of the approach will help things along.

Nick Underhill, vice-president and national sales manager at Entex Toys (one of the giants of the toy-model business) told me, "All I need to see is a rough sketch and a simple outline of the features. We know everything else about manufacturing and marketing an idea our way, so anything else would be extraneous."

On the other hand, a Mattel executive said, "We're all human and tend to react in our profession the same way we do in the rest of our lives. Therefore, the more complete and handsome the presentation, the more attention we seem to give it." As you remember, at Mattel that won't help much (if at all) considering how few outside ideas make it there. But the point is well taken.

Which leads us into the alternate approach to the physical form of your presentation. Let's call it the "put-it-on-velvet" approach. Think of an $.89 ring. On cardboard, it looks overpriced. On velvet, it looks like a real value.

Of the two options, I favor the Velvet School. Regardless of what your idea is or to whom you're presenting it, if it's worth the time and money to make a presentation, it's worth the additional time and money to make as professional a presentation as you can. I know that the quality of the presentation made a sale for me once.

A few years ago, I created a gift item for the man who had everything. It was a paperweight in the form of a giant headache tablet. But which one . . . Bayer, Anacin, Excedrin? At the time, Excedrin had the most ambitious advertising campaign so it followed that theirs was the best coattail to grab. We wrote them a formal letter requesting permission to reproduce their E on the tablet and also use the name EXCEDRIN® in packaging and promotion material.

We received a prompt reply. "Absolutely not. Ours is a

top-quality proprietary pharmaceutical product which cannot be associated with a piece of novelty junk."

This reply irked me. It was so arbitrary. We were not, in my opinion, in the junk business. Novel, yes. Junk, no. So I gathered together samples of all our existing products, along with reprints of our national publicity and our full-color catalogues, wrote another letter pointing out the quality of *our* products and put the whole enchilada in a box measuring about 18"×30"×6". After wrapping it in white shipping paper, we covered the box with our vinyl flowers. The box fairly sparkled. A few days later I got a call from the Excedrin brand manager who said, "I had no idea what good stuff you're making and selling. Of course, we'd be happy to be associated with your new paperweight." I'm convinced the flower-covered box did the job.

What makes up a "velvet" presentation? A lot of simple things, beautifully presented. We've talked earlier about the value of getting good photography. You'll use it over and over again. One place is in your presentations. But before you take pictures, you have to have a subject to photograph. (Oh, the complexity of it all!) I always prefer photographs of prototype models to using drawings of an idea. It proves you've carried your homework one step farther.

If you do set up a photography session for your product, remember to do one simple thing. Make that four simple things. Shoot each setup:

1. In 4"×5" color transparency.
2. In 4"×5" negative film (for color prints).
3. In 4"×5" black and white.
4. In Polaroid (for your own file reference).

If you do this all at once, it won't cost you much more than doing any one way by itself. And if your idea takes off, you'll save a lot of photo money later on. Incidentally, I favor 4"×5" film. Your photographer may like 2¼"×2¼" or 35 mm. (If he *insists* on 8"×10" film, get another photographer.) It won't ultimately make much difference, although some printers insist that bigger is better, when it comes to reproduction quality. It's just that most of us take 4"×5" a little more seriously. And this part of your job is very serious.

If you find yourself having to send several presentations to various groups at the same time, you should consider using slides to copy the originals. I've usually found them the sim-

IMAGINE, IF YOU WILL . . .

plest and least expensive way to duplicate a presentation. Slides also command a certain amount of respect.

You might consider hiring a professional art director or an advanced advertising art student to help you develop your presentation if you choose the "velvet" approach. People in that line of work deal with presentations all the time.

So much for the graphic or picture side of your presentation. The words and numbers probably are more important. Especially the numbers. Exactly what you say in your presentation depends in part on whom you are trying to reach and what you want from them. But there are a few common elements to any presentation, whether you are using it to scare up some financial backing, trying to sell your idea to a manufacturer, wooing a sales rep or whatever.

The first common element is sales performance—projected from a small market sample, from a research study you've done or simply guessed at on the basis of typical sales patterns for products of the type you're discussing. Obviously, the more solidly based your sales projections are, the more weight they are likely to carry. But one way or another, you'll want to show that your product has a glowing future in the market.

If you have real sales experience to back you up, spell it out in detail: how many units sold, how many retail outlets sold to, how many turns at retail, what time period is covered by the sales history.

Then, using that sample as the basis of your projection, state what sort of sales prediction you make for your product. No need to give a long-winded explanation of the logic you used to arrive at your sales projection. Give the person the background information and let him draw his own conclusions about the soundness of your thinking. (He will anyway, whether you like it or not.)

The second common element is your cost-of-goods calculations. Obviously, you've done these calculations fairly early in the game or you wouldn't be making presentations. All you have to do is spell out neatly and concisely all of the various costs involved in making and marketing your product, as we discussed in Chapter VI. In addition to the obvious function of giving information on the cost of your product, this part of the presentation gives people an idea of just how realistic and professional you really are in dealing with the product.

Any patent applications, copyrights, etc. should also be

noted and explained in your presentation. What did you apply for, when did you apply, what's the current status of your application? This gives people a feeling for what sort of protection your idea is likely to have, and how professional you have been in your quest for glory.

Depending on whom you are presenting to, you may want to include cash-flow charts. If you are an accountant, you probably are familiar with cash-flow charts. If you are not, this book isn't long enough to explain what they are and how to make them. In general terms, a cash-flow chart is a graphic means of showing the income and outgo of money as you make and sell your product. Manufacturing costs money, selling makes money, but the crucial factor is this: *When* does the money come in and *when* does it go out? Ideally, there's always enough income to cover the outgo, of course, but at the beginning of a product's life that's rarely the case. You're always finding yourself one cycle behind on the cash-flow chart, needing to find funds to take care of the outgo long before it can be repaid by the inflow.

Other parts of the presentation will be dictated by the audience you are addressing. But in all cases, the objective to keep in mind is to present yourself as a professional, realistic businessman, and to present your product as a potentially successful and profitable one.

One good place to look early in the process of building your presentation is a bank. Get together with one of the loan officers and find out the kinds of information he would want to see in a presentation. You may not be interested in making your presentation to a bank at all, but the kinds of questions a banker has about your product will be indicative of the kinds of questions other people will be asking. If you can put together a presentation that satisfies a loan officer at a bank, you can probably satisfy anybody. Think of it as a dry run. (In my experience, that's how conversations with bankers usually turn out anyway.)

An accountant is another excellent source of information on what to include in your presentation. In fact, it would be well worth your while to hire an accountant to help you put the presentation together, especially if you are a little shaky on topics like cash flow.

Frankly, the whole question of presentations could fill an entire book by itself. I don't claim that this short treatment is exhaustive. All I'm interested in doing is convincing you that

IMAGINE, IF YOU WILL . . .

a professional presentation, even for the simplest of ideas, is important. If you can do it yourself, fine. If you have to hire professionals to help you, do it. One way or another, get a good, solid, well-turned-out presentation because it can mean the difference between success and failure. If I had to bet on a terrific idea with a lousy presentation, versus a mediocre idea with a terrific presentation—I'd bet on the great presentation every time.

There's one last subject to be covered under this general heading of presentations. It's the "idea submission form." This is the old light-under-a-bushel problem that ultimately confronts every inventor who wants to sell his idea but is afraid of having it stolen. And that's *everyone* on his first time out. You *and* me.

Applying for a patent ought to alleviate some of your fears, but not all of them. And what if you haven't applied for a patent, or you can't get one? You could become the screwee, or at least you could worry about it. (If you are presenting your idea to a well-established company, the odds against that danger are really quite long. But that doesn't stop those nightmares.)

Well, the submission form many companies ask you to sign isn't going to help you feel any better. Alcoa has permitted me to quote from their form here. It will give you an idea of the sort of thing you'll encounter. I like the way Alcoa goes about it. Their forms are just about the same as any you'll ever see for idea submissions. But Alcoa goes to the trouble to accompany the form with a thoughtful booklet explaining their position on new ideas from inventors. Still, what the form says is hardly reassuring:

_____, 19____

New Ideas Section
Aluminum Company of America
1501 Alcoa Building
Pittsburgh 19, Pennsylvania
Gentlemen:
  I have an idea relating to _____

which is fully described in the attached material or in material which I have already sent you. Although you have not asked me to submit this idea, I would like to have you examine it to determine whether it may be of some value to you.

I realize that, to avoid misunderstanding, ideas must be submitted under certain terms and conditions before they will be considered. Accordingly, I am submitting this idea to you on the following terms and conditions which shall apply to this idea, including all related material, and any supplemental ideas and material which I may subsequently submit.

(1) I am not submitting this idea in confidence. I agree that my submission of this idea and your consideration of it shall not create a confidential relationship between us, express or implied, and that you have no obligation to keep this idea a secret.

(2) I understand that you will consider this idea only to the extent that you believe it is deserving of consideration; if you decide that you are interested in the idea, I would appreciate your informing me of that fact.

(3) If you choose to do so, you may enter into a formal written agreement with me relating to this idea which may, among other terms, provide for the payment of compensation to me. However, I agree that you will be under no obligation to me with respect to this idea unless and until we enter into such a written agreement, and then only in accordance with the terms of that agreement. I further agree that neither your consideration of this idea nor any discussions we may have concerning it shall be construed in any way prejudicial to you.

(4) If you decide that you are not interested in this idea, I understand that you will inform me of that fact, but I agree that you will have no obligation to advise me of the reasons for your lack of interest, nor will you be obligated to return any of the material which I have submitted, reveal any of your activities in connection with your consideration of this idea, or to reveal any information pertaining to your research or other activities in any field of technology or business relating to this idea.

(5) I agree that the consideration you give to this idea shall not constitute a waiver of your right to contest the validity of any patent which has been or may hereafter be issued on it. Should I contend that you are infringing on such a patent, my sole remedy will be that available to me under the patent laws.

(6) I agree that these terms and conditions cannot be

IMAGINE, IF YOU WILL . . .

modified or waived except in writing signed by an officer of Aluminum Company of America.

Very truly yours,

The first time you read one of these "Idea Submission Forms," you'll probably react as I did. You'll shout and scream a lot. Things like "Rape!" But think about it a bit, and you'll realize that your idea is probably one of thousands presented in any given year. And whatever the company, they are developing ideas every day of the year themselves. They, too, must be protected from the proved psychological phenomenon called "Concurrent Development." Ideas somehow find their moment in history. All over the country, in fact, all over the world, several people can be working on the same idea simultaneously and never know it. So the form you are asked to sign protects the company from your later coming back and claiming they stole your idea. Believe me, their records or ideas are a lot more complete than yours will ever be. So what to do? All I can tell you for sure is what I do.

I sign on the dotted line.

There is one gambit you can counter with, however. It's called an "Agreement to Review Idea" form. Here's an example:

AGREEMENT TO REVIEW IDEA

We, the undersigned, agree to receive in confidence full details about an idea for a new product to be submitted for our consideration by Billy Smith.

It is further understood that we assume no responsibility whatever with respect to features which can be demonstrated to be already known to us. We also agree not to divulge any details of the idea submitted without permission of Billy Smith or to make use of any feature or information of which the said Billy Smith is the originator, without payment of compensation to be fixed by negotiation with the said Billy Smith or his lawful representative.

It is specifically understood that, in receiving the idea of Billy Smith, the idea is being received and will be reviewed in confidence and that, within a period of 30 days, we will report to Billy Smith the results of our findings and will advise whether or not we are interested in negotiating for the purchase of the right to use said idea.

128 HOW TO TURN YOUR IDEA INTO A MILLION DOLLARS

```
Company _____
Street & Number _____
City _____ State _____ Zip Code _____
Official to receive disclosures (please type)
_____ Title _____
Date _____ Signature _____
Accepted _____
```
Billy Smith, Inventor

The purpose of sending the company this form, instead of the one they'd like to have you sign, is this: Your submission form gives you a little more protection and restricts the company a little more than their form. You'll notice that this one requires the company to keep your idea confidential, it puts a time limit on them to review your idea, it requires them to report to you in writing on the outcome of their review, it even requires them to pay you for your idea.

From the inventor's standpoint, that's wonderful. But, frankly, I don't think much of these forms. Maybe I'm a little old-fashioned, but I still feel that the buyer has a stronger hand than the seller. If somebody wants to sell an idea, he ought to be the one who does the signing of forms. He needs the buyer much more than the buyer needs him.

The form I've reproduced here resulted in a perfect example of the reaction these forms usually get. I signed this one recently, mostly to get a current example of this kind of form. Billy Smith, the inventor, came to me with an idea and wouldn't reveal it to me until I signed the form. I sighed. And signed.

The idea turned out to be another spin-off of the Pet Rock idea. Around here we've taken to calling those spin-off ideas "Rock Offs." (Since you haven't signed Billy's form, I won't tell you what the idea is, exactly. I don't think you'd like it anyway.) I suggested to Billy that if Gary Dahl, the father of the Pet Rock, wasn't interested in developing Billy's idea, he ought to try getting into some company that has mass distribution in a market line where Pet Rock hasn't really penetrated. I gave him the name of one such company in Chicago.

Billy sent his idea to Chicago, along with one of his idea review forms. I told him I didn't think that was a very good idea, since the company was certainly reputable and might not take kindly to that kind of treatment. But Billy insisted,

IMAGINE, IF YOU WILL . . . 129

The day after the forms arrived in Chicago, the man in charge of new ideas at the company called back. He had a brief, succinct, gravelly voiced suggestion on how Billy might best dispose of his idea. And his submission form.

IX
A MIRACLE. JUST A LITTLE ONE

Turning a major marketer's interest into a lot of free help. It's called leverage.

Sometimes in this strange and wonderful business of chasing rainbows, it seems that the only thing that will help you survive is a miracle. Just a little one, but a miracle nonetheless. Okay. Here's a small miracle for you. Here is how to find a big, influential helper who can:

- put you in touch with the right manufacturers.
- help you find materials to make your product at a good price.
- get technical help for you.
- carry enough weight in business to open some sticky doors.
- give you a hand in hacking your way through the brambles of business.
- do it all for free.

The key to this miracle is simple. It's called the profit motive. If your idea looks as if it could make a lot of money for some major marketer, he'll be your friend. If a buyer for Sears or somebody of that ilk thinks your product can be a hot seller in his stores or catalogues, he's going to be on your side. He's going to *want* you to succeed so that he can make a lot of money selling your product. In order to help you get your idea off the ground and onto his shelves, he'll do what-

A MIRACLE. JUST A LITTLE ONE

ever he can to smooth your path. It's simply good business on his part.

The amount of help you get, of course, will be proportional to the amount of excitement your idea generates. Regardless of the degree of help you get, however, there's nothing unusual about it. I call it "leverage" and I run into it all the time. I'll give you an example of how it worked recently for an inventor.

The subject of our example is garbage. Specifically, a new way of dealing with garbage. That may not be a big turn-on for you, but garbage is important stuff these days. As we become increasingly aware that we run the risk of trashing ourselves off the face of the earth, we become more and more interested in garbage. It has become one of the big issues of our time.

For years, garbage has been just sort of indiscriminately tossed out with no real effort to sort it. On the whole, garbage has been treated like—well, like garbage. But today, there's a whole industry springing up around the job of reclaiming paper, glass and metal and putting them back to work.

A number of communities around the country now have laws requiring that trash be sorted, separating the various reclaimables from the coffee grounds and egg shells before they get the old heave-ho. More communities are passing such laws every year. Even where it isn't required by law, some conscientious people are sorting the trash anyway. They're doing their civic duty—and making money, too—by sorting out the cans, bottles and paper and selling them to recycling centers.

But sorting garbage is a drag. Either you have a whole bunch of separate containers cluttering up the kitchen or you have to go digging around in the garbage after the can is full. Yukkkhhh! There has to be a better way, right?

Well, Bob Clower certainly thought so. As the ecology thing began developing into an important factor in our lives, Bob was already looking at it from the marketing standpoint. A trash sorter was one of the things that sprang to his mind as a potential product. He asked the Sears research staff to run down some numbers for him on how many people out there were separating their garbage into the various reclaimable categories. The answer was mind-boggling.

Fully 15 per cent of the people who match the typical Sears customers profile are sorting their garbage! That works out to something like 12 million customers and a $150 million market for a neat, easy-to-use inexpensive gadget to sort trash, according to Bob's projections.

Frankly, that sounds kind of high to me. But Bob seems to know what he's talking about when it comes to those things, so I'll take his word for it. Either way, there's obviously one huge market out there for a trash sorter.

Needless to say, Bob had very little trouble cranking up a design project to develop a sorter. For three years, the Sears heavy-thinking-and-design types wrestled with the problem and got practically nowhere. Nothing. Then, in the middle of that frustration, Bob got a phone call that changed everything.

The caller was a bright, attractive woman named Suellen McDonough. She's a mother of four, part-time nurse and the wife of a manufacturer's rep in Durham, New Hampshire. Mrs. McDonough had this invention she hoped Mr. Clower might be interested in.

"What was it?" he asked.

"Oh, it's a sort of trash separator," Mrs. McDonough replied. "You know, for sorting out bottles and cans and stuff."

A few minutes later, she had spelled it all out. It was so simple. The whole thing, which she called a "Recycl-it Basket"[TM] is nothing more elaborate than a three-hole wastebasket. It's a one-piece plastic molding with three big pockets in a row, just the right size for the standard grocery bag. (It's ecologically sound in that respect, too, since most grocery bags nowadays are made of recycled paper.) It doesn't take up much more room than a regular ol' one-holer and it makes the whole process of sorting trash so simple you could do it in your sleep. No big technological breakthrough, no transistorized frammistats and microcircuitry, no devilishly complicated machinery. A plain old three-hole waste-basket. And nobody had ever thought of it before!

It was an ideal example of the little miracle I promised you. We had a major marketer interested in an inventor's product. And we had an inventor, Mrs. McDonough, who knew exactly what she was doing. She had covered all the right bases, done all of her homework along the way—just as I keep nagging at you to do yours. There were no dangling loose ends to disconcert anyone. It's worth stopping for a moment just to see how she went about it, because she's a perfect paradigm of how to give your product its best shot at the marketplace.

Back when her invention was still an idea on a piece of paper, Mrs. McDonough went to the local office of the New England Industrial Development Resources Center where she got first-class advice and counsel. (There are a number of similar governmental and quasi-governmental organizations around the country.) The center put Mrs. McDonough in touch with an industrial engineer who explained that there were two radically different ways to go about manufacturing her basket.

On one hand, she could spend the relatively modest sum of $2,000 or $3,000 to get a set of molds for a process called rotocasting. Rotocasting, he explained, is fine for small production runs. The only drawback is that it is a slow way to make plastic objects, which means that the price per unit is quite high.

On the other hand, the engineer continued, she could invest somewhere in the neighborhood of $40,000 to $50,000 for a set of high-speed injection molds, just like the big kids use.

That didn't sound like her kind of neighborhood, so Mrs. McDonough had a set of the cheaper rotocasting molds made. Then she ran off a sample batch of baskets and took them to Jordan-Marsh department stores in Boston where she made a sale. Shortly, it became apparent that the basket was creating a stir in her rather limited market, but the rotocasting process was totally unsatisfactory. It wasn't just the cost. The process simply didn't do a good job of making her rather large baskets.

Still, how could she afford to tool up for a more sophisticated manufacturing process? She decided to reach out for more stores and wider distribution so she could make the heavy investment in molds feasible. She went to New York to talk to buyers and manufacturers' representatives. Nothing much came of those visits, but the trip to New York wasn't a total loss. As long as she was in the Big Apple, she decided she might as well have a go at Sears.

There was a moment of chagrin when she discovered that Sears doesn't believe in the Big Apple. Their headquarters are out in the Midwest, like God intended. Nothing daunted, she dialed long distance information in Chicago, got in touch with the Sears switchboard and asked who bought trash containers. She was connected with Bob Clower who, up to that moment, didn't know her from Adam's house cat.

You might say it was all a lucky fluke. But as a matter of fact, there wasn't any luck involved. Mrs. McDonough was taking all the correct steps, and they led her unerringly to the man who wanted exactly what she had to sell.

If you do your homework—the golden rule of the idea business—you can be every bit as "lucky" as Mrs. McDonough.

Now we get into how Bob Clower helped her. Sears, like many major marketers, is not a manufacturer. They don't make many of the things they sell. Instead, they contract with manufacturers all around the country—big ones, little ones, middle-sized ones—to make the products for Sears. So in order to sell to Sears, Mrs. McDonough would either have to become a manufacturer herself on a large scale, or she would have to make a contract with an existing manufacturer to make the baskets for her. Obviously, her little rotocasting setup wasn't going to be up to the job of filling the orders Bob was thinking of. Equally obviously, she didn't have $40,000 or $50,000 lying around in the sugar bowl at home to buy high-speed injection molds.

So Bob gave her the names of three plastics manufacturers in her part of the country, all of whom had done business with Sears before and all of whom were capable of doing the job for Mrs. McDonough. Bob told Mrs. McDonough to let them know that he was definitely interested in her product and that he would be happy to confirm that for them.

Now *that's* a valuable piece of leverage! Anytime you can walk in and tell some manufacturer that Sears is waiting in the wings with an order book, you are going to have a whole lot of undivided attention. Notice that there was no concrete order at this time. Just an indication of interest. That's all you can usually expect, and that's all it takes, most of the time.

It's no guarantee of success, however. In the case of Mrs. McDonough, two or three manufacturers said they just weren't in a position to take on the project at the moment. The third was interested, but wanted Mrs. McDonough to pay for the high-speed injection molds herself, then let them manufacture the separators and pay her a royalty.

That's a bad deal. After she's borrowed the money to pay for the molds, she's still on the outside looking in. All she gets is a royalty, but no control over the operation. She'd have to sell an awful lot of trash separators just to break even. (You can argue that the manufacturer has the same problem, and you'd be right. But amortization—spreading the cost of the tooling over a predetermined number of products in the production run—is part of the manufacturing business. It's one of the costs they would normally calculate in determining their price. Mrs. McDonough shouldn't have to pay that cost for them.)

Bob felt she could do better than that, although Mrs. McDonough was ready to go out and borrow the money to pay for the molds. He was convinced that they could find a manufacturer who would invest in the molds himself, then make the separators under contract to Mrs. McDonough.

It took quite a bit longer than anyone anticipated, but eventually Bob found the right manufacturer. A company in North Carolina has agreed to make the baskets for Mrs. McDonough under a royalty arrangement. If you look in the Spring 1977 Sears, Roebuck catalogue, you'll see the maiden appearance of this successful invention.

As you can see from the example of the trash sorter, a big marketer is in a position to do you a great deal of good if the marketer is considering carrying your product. In the first place, any manufacturer has to be interested in making your product for you if he knows that a major outfit is willing to carry it. It indicates to the manufacturer that there's an existing market for the product. It takes a lot of the risk potential out of his tooling up for the project.

Second, it indicates to the manufacturer that the inventor is not just some kook with a hare-brained scheme. If you have stirred up some interest at Sears, you might be onto something pretty substantial. A big outfit like that doesn't fool around with weirdos and dingbats.

Also, with an expression of interest from a big marketer, financial backing for your idea becomes much easier to find. Few bankers or investors feel very secure about their personal understanding of the retail marketplace. An expression of interest from a major marketer gives them a lot more confidence about your idea. It takes some of the guesswork out of it for them.

Finally, with a handle on a big marketer, you can make

better buys on materials for your product, and you can get a better price of manufacturing. The bigger the order, the lower the price per unit, usually. And when you're selling to a J. C. Penney or a Montgomery Ward, you're talking in big, round numbers. With a lower cost of goods, you can make more profit, and you can sell at a more attractive price, which in turn ought to increase your sales.

You may be thinking that the marketer who helps you could just as easily knock you off. There is *no* guarantee of security anywhere in this book, nor anywhere in my experience. You always run the risk of having your idea stolen. The only real protection you can give yourself, at this point in development is—you guessed it—careful, complete homework. Here's what I mean:

There you are, showing your product to the buyer for some major marketer, and he's interested. Then he looks at your cost of manufacture and knows he can beat that price substantially. If he's a truly fine person, he'll point that out to you and probably help you find ways to bring down the cost. But there *are* people out there who are not so fine. They may simply turn you down, then get on the phone to a couple of suppliers and be out on the market with the same product— your product—only cheaper.

If you had done your homework, you would already have found out how to make it cheaper. If your price is pretty close to the best price he could get, he'd just as soon buy the product from you. It's a lot simpler that way. So do your homework thoroughly and protect yourself.

There are times when the kind of leverage I'm talking about here could make the difference between getting on the market at all and simply packing it in as a lost cause. My case in point is an invention I'm currently developing. It's a modular, prefabricated system of interlocking storage cabinets for home garages. I call it Neat Garage™.

Just a bit of background on the product, before we get into the details of how I'm going to go about getting it sold. All you have to do to establish the need for Neat Garage is to take a look at your own garage. If it's like most, there are rakes and shovels and garden hoses and bikes and woodworking tools and a Christmas tree stand and Lord knows what all scattered all over the place. You're lucky if there's room for a car in there at all, among all the accumulated oddments.

What to do about it? Well, you could call in a carpenter at fifteen or twenty dollars an hour and have him build you some storage cabinets and lockers around the garage. Or you could have him build a storage room as an addition to your garage. You might even put up one of those corrugated metal storage sheds in the back yard—the sort of pre-fab building you can buy at hardware departments.

Or you could use Neat Garage. The cabinets hang on the walls, interlocking with each other, taking up very little of your garage space. With built-in shelves and hanging hooks, they allow you to organize that incredible mess of junk and tools so that you can find it when you need it and keep it out of the way when you don't. Being prefabricated, the storage is a good deal less expensive than custom-made storage units. And putting it up is so simple, you can do it yourself.

It's a natural for some big cabinetmaking company or some big plastic molding company or some big aluminum company. It is definitely *not* a natural for someone like me to manufacture and market on my own. Tooling up for this one would cost something like the Bolivian national debt. I'm not about to spend that kind of money, even on the arrantly nonsensical assumption that I *had* that kind of money to spend.

Now, I've done my homework on this one. I've made some pretty realistic market projections, based on the number of new homes being built. (A natural market for Neat Garage is the company that builds those new homes. Another natural market is the guy who buys a new home and instantly discovers he has no place to store all that junk he's accumulated.) I've worked out my cost of manufacture as closely as I can. I've worked out all the bugs in the design. I've even built full-scale models (which explains why my garage doesn't look as messy as the average garage anymore). And I've put together a very uptown presentation portfolio, complete with 8"×10" before-and-after color glossies, sales forecasts, statistics and such. I'm loaded for bear.

But for quite a while I couldn't find the right bear. Boise-Cascade took an option on it for two months and did their own market research. They assigned a team of experts and spent weeks coming to all the very same conclusions I had come to. Yes, there is a market. Yes, they would sell a whole bunch of Neat Garage units. No, they weren't interested. At that time, they were looking for new products that would give them a 50 per cent return on investment, and they figured Neat Garage would return only 30 per cent. Now, in *my* book a 30 per cent return ain't all bad. But they were shooting for the big stuff, so they turned my idea down.

Another company I presented it to just wasn't turned on by the idea. As simple as that. So there I was with what is unquestionably a solid, marketable idea. Only I couldn't get any manufacturer interested in buying it from me. And I'm in no position to market it myself.

As you will discover later on in the book, a manufacturer has turned up with an interest in my idea. It's beginning to look as if I'll sell Neat Garage.

But suppose I'd never met that particular manufacturer? Or suppose, after pondering the idea, he turns me down? Then there would be nothing left but Plan B. And it's not a bad plan.

Plan B is leverage. If I can't find a manufacturer who'll pay me a royalty on my idea, then I'm going to go to Sears—just like Mrs. McDonough and her trash separator. I'm going to show them my first-class, uptown presentation portfolio and explain how the price structure would work out, how many sales I predict, and so forth. And I'm going to ask them if they'd be interested in carrying it if I could find a manufacturer.

My guess is that they'll say yes, based on the price and the specifications I show them. Then, with that expression of interest in hand, I'm going to go back to knocking on the doors of a lot of manufacturers. (If Sears isn't interested, by the way, I'll take it to Montgomery Ward and to any other big marketer who seems a likely prospect for that sort of item. The same theory applies.) In other words, I'm going to use leverage—to get a manufacturing deal. My objective, of course, is to sell the idea for a royalty and bring the manufacturer and the marketer together, introduce them and tiptoe out of the picture.

In fact, if my idea really lights 'em up at Sears, they might be able to help me find that manufacturer and do everything but hold my hand while I negotiate the deal.

There are a million variations on how you can use the leverage gained from interesting a big marketer in your idea. With somebody like a Bob Clower to help you in areas where your own expertise may be sketchy, you'll find the going a lot easier. And with an expression of interest from one of the biggies in your hip pocket, you'll find a lot of doors opening

A MIRACLE. JUST A LITTLE ONE

for you in your quest for a manufacturer. Just how you use the leverage depends to a large extent on what your idea is.

Obviously, Bob and the other buyers in the business aren't around for the sole purpose of helping every inventor who comes down the pike. But they are all interested in developing new ideas that fit their markets. If you can turn them on with your product, you've got more than a big sale.

You've got an important ally on your side.

X
LET'S MAKE A DEAL

How much to ask for, how much to expect when you sell your idea.

A while ago I told you that the only way you really want to go with your invention is to sell the idea to a manufacturer for a royalty deal. Now it's time to talk about making that deal. It's one place where many inventors who have been shrewd, calculating and industrious all along, suddenly become bumbling amateurs. And the single factor that trips up most of them at this point is plain old greed.

Believe me, I know whereof I speak because I have done it myself. It cost me, as nearly as I can estimate, $200,000.

December of 1967. We'd had the idea for Stickies in March. We'd been fooling around with it through the summer and we had been selling seriously for three months. In October we sold $8,000 worth of Stickies at wholesale. By December total sales had reached $30,000 at wholesale and the sales curve was taking off like an Atlas-Agena. But it was killing us. We were having an awful time finding enough money to keep up with the growing orders as they came in. (It was cash in front with our suppliers, but our customers took at least 30 to 60 days to pay. The time lag was painful.) We were tired. We were working long days and nights in that little 8′×8′ borrowed office at Goodwill Industries. It was beginning to look as though we might just plain poop out before we got rich in The Marketing Game.

Just then the Lone Ranger arrived. Jack Kuhlberg, then

the president of Chicago Printed String Company and his faithful companion, Dick, the vice-president/sales, wanted to talk about our interesting little product. They'd seen it in a store while they were out here on other business, did a little inquiring and were fascinated by what they heard about Rickie Tickie Stickies.

So the four of us sat down in our sweaty little haven of madness in the midst of tranquillity and we reasoned together. Actually, they and Margaret were together. I was sitting out in the hallway because in an 8′ × 8′ office there's only room for a person at a desk and two other people. Anybody else has to talk through the doorway.

Now this was big-league stuff. Chicago Printed String Company was in the business of making and selling decorative wrapping papers and packaging materials to the gift and stationery trade. On any given day, a hundred salesmen for CPS were out on the road, taking care of business. The Chicago Printed String people were heavy hitters. We were pipsqueaks.

I must say the Masked Crusader of Gift and Stationery was gracious. Looking around our sumptuous headquarters, Jack refrained from laughing and got right down to the business at hand. His company was looking around for new profit areas. They heard that our little product was selling like floral hot cakes. Were we interested in selling the company?

Were we interested? I've always worked on the premise that just about anything is for sale if the price is right, so we had a starting point right there. We talked for a while and parted company with the general feeling that we might be able to do business. Things were looking up for the plastic flower magnates.

The CPS people went back home. I came in from the hallway. We sent samples and price lists to Chicago and began breathlessly waiting to hear from them. In the meantime, things were getting even more hectic than before. January sales topped $30,000—as much as we had sold in the preceding three months combined.

Both Margaret and I were about ready to drop from the combination of long hours, heavy labor and mental strain. The month that went by with no word from Chicago was long enough to fight the Hundred Years' War.

Finally, the summons came. We were to fly to Chicago to

nail down the deal. We were on the threshold of seeing our goofy little flower blossom into a multimillion-dollar business, and we were like two kids on Christmas Eve, waiting for Santa Claus. I don't know how real business magnates handle that sort of thing. We just giggled a lot.

We left Los Angeles International Airport at high noon. It was a beautiful, balmy 86 degrees. Three hours later we stepped off the airplane at O'Hare International Airport where it was two degrees below zero and blowing half a gale. We almost didn't make it to the cab. Next morning wasn't much warmer, but somehow we made it to the corporate offices of CPS. From a grubby little cubbyhole in San Pedro to the hushed sanctums of big business in Chicago. From balmy sunshine to an arctic blizzard. Talk about culture shock!

Fortunately Jack Kuhlberg was a very pleasant man, so our conversation was a lot easier than my sweaty palms would have had me believe. After our first meeting, everything was going well, but Jack was a little dubious about our sales projections and our cost ratios. Would we mind getting him some invoices to show him exactly how we arrived at all that?

No problem. I called our printer in Los Angeles and had him send us the last four invoices, airmail special delivery. A day or so later, the invoices arrived and we went back to the negotiating table.

Already we had arrived at one apparent impasse, though, despite the smoothness of the rest of our discussions. I had been firmly insisting all along on a royalty of 10 per cent of factory gross sales. I figured in my innocence that it was only fair. Jack, who knew better than *that*, wasn't about to agree. In addition, I wanted $30,000 for my assets in the company and I wanted a $20,000 fee to take some of the sting out of the last few wearying months of our lives. The last two items were no major stumbling block, although in retrospect I'm amazed that no one ever seriously questioned our right to have $20,000 in "mad money" just for having the idea.

The royalty question, however, was a problem. CPS would talk vaguely about perhaps going as high as 5 per cent, but 10 per cent was out of the question. So we'd move on to other areas of discussion and carefully skirt the royalty question. Finally, there was nothing left to discuss. We'd covered all the other parts of the agreement and now it was time to do battle over that last problem. Back and forth we went, like a couple of swordsmen in one of those late-late show swashbucklers. I'd chase Jack up the financial stairs, he'd swing out on a fiscal chandelier. I'd thrust, he'd parry. Time passed. Finally, I gave in. We agreed to what I now regard as a fantastically good deal, although I was pretty grumpy about it at the time.

But it was too late.

The time I had spent chasing CPS around the financial castle was the most expensive I've ever spent in my life. The day before we were to sign the final papers, CPS was bought by Paper Kraft, another big company in the same line of business. All bets were off. Instead of being a part of that sale, we were left out in the cold. Breaking off the negotiations, Jack said, "I'm sorry, but I no longer have authorization. I suggest you take your idea and run with it."

It was like being kicked in the stomach. If the deal had gone through, I conservatively estimate that we would have collected over a half million dollars in royalties over the next four years for doing nothing more than we had done. That's in addition to our $50,000 lump payment up front. And the deal *would* have gone through if I hadn't been so damn greedy over that royalty question. If I had started out talking a nice, rational 5 per cent, we could have settled the whole contract in one day. The papers would have been signed before the acquisition left us high and dry.

Oh, we made a decent amount of money by the time it was all said and done. About six years later I did sell the company to someone else. And in the meantime we sold a lot of Stickies, but it was all done on our own, struggling every inch of the way. Without CPS's big, powerful sales organization to give instant saturation of the market, we constantly were playing catch-up with the knock-offs. While we eventually sold some three-plus million dollars' worth of Stickies at wholesale, the knock-offs sold another seventeen-plus million dollars' worth. Most of those lost sales would have been ours instead of someone else's if we had been a CPS product instead of a Don and Margaret Kracke product.

All of this brings me to one point which, believe me, I have never forgotten. Don't let greed get in your way when you're negotiating the sale of your product (or your company, as in our case) to some manufacturer. Most inventors, unfortunately, have a grossly inflated notion of the value of their idea and their rightful share of the product's sales price.

In going into their negotiations with that attitude, a lot of inventors queer their chances of getting something going. They make excessive demands, relative to the value of the idea, and wind up with 100 per cent of nothing.

Don't forget that it's the manufacturer who's going to be taking all the risk with your idea. Bob Clower, my friend at Sears, put it this way: "Take, for example, the decision to spend $60,000 on a mold. The product could fail for any of a hundred reasons. It's the manufacturer who usually must make the hard-dollar investment. *Investment* is the key to a new product, not the idea. It's also a matter of priorities. With the inventor, his idea is *always* the number-one priority and obviously (to him) very valuable. To the manufacturer who is about to gamble maybe $100,000, that idea could fall well down on his list of ways to lose money."

If the profit on your product is big enough to allow it, a legitimate company will be happy to pay you a reasonable amount of royalty. But if your demands cut into his reasonable and proper profit on manufacturing and distributing the product and risking his capital, he'll balk. And he'll be right. Your excessive demands can only show up in one of two ways: increased price of the product, which could price it right out of the market, or in a lower profit for the manufacturer, which could make your invention very unattractive to him. You have to be realistic.

If you've done your homework, you ought to know how much profit spread is available to play with in your negotiations. You can be sure that the company you're negotiating with will know where the pennies are buried. Personally, I'd guess that there is rarely more than a percentage point worth of real negotiating room to play with. An offer of 4 per cent, countered by a demand of 5 per cent is about as freewheeling as these things get. Over the years I've come to the conclusion that the average royalty for a reasonably well-protected, well-developed product-in-being is about 5 per cent of factory gross sales.

While we're on the subject, let's clarify that term "factory gross." Although there may be a slight variation of interpretation from company to company, the following is generally what you should have in your mind when negotiating a deal that will be fair to you and to a manufacturer.

You arrive at factory gross by starting with the price the factory sells an item for. Let's say, for this example, it's

$1.00. From that selling price, the cost of the sale is subtracted. As you've learned, that commission can range anywhere from 5 per cent in the toy industry to 20 per cent in the gift and stationery field. We'll use 10 per cent for this example. Ten per cent of $1.00 is $.10 (as I said early on in this book, you don't have to be a genius to succeed). So you're now at $.90. From that you subtract discounts for other elements of the sale such as cash discounts (usually around 2 per cent) and freight allowances (usually around 3 per cent) or a total of 5 per cent. *Voilà!* You get $.85 as the "factory gross." That's the base number for figuring your per item royalty. Using a 5 per cent royalty, do a little multiplication, and if you come up with $.0425, we agree that that is your royalty per item sold. If the factory sells only one, you won't be retiring any sooner than you had planned. On the other hand, what if they were to sell a million . . .

In the process of writing this book, I talked to a lot of people in the business and without exception they all gave me 5 per cent of factory gross sales as their estimate of the average royalty deal. I didn't even have to prompt them. In a high-risk industry or where the product is not as well protected from knock-offs, a royalty as low as 2 per cent might be eminently fair.

Some years after the Chicago Printed String debacle, by the way, I found myself on the other side of the negotiating table. This time I played Jack Kuhlberg and the other guy did Don Kracke. It was like *déjà vu* in reverse. I'd been there before, but somehow it was all so different now.

The "other" guy was a friend of mine who brought me an idea he had spun off of Rickie Tickie Stickies. But he'd carried it into a whole new direction and had what seemed to both of us to be a highly salable product. He had taken some of my flower designs, and some other designs of his own, and translated them into heat-bonding patches. Bill called them "Snappy Patches." You could just take one of them, lay it on a pair of Levis or a jacket or something, make a couple of fast passes with an iron and you'd have a funky design permanently affixed to it. And if you patched a rip, all the better! This, mind you, was more than a year before the whole patches craze swept the country. Bill was on top of a great idea well ahead of the pack. But we couldn't make a deal.

Bill wanted me to make and distribute the patches and pay him a royalty. Fine. I had the venture capital available, and I thought the idea was worth it. Trouble was, Bill wanted 30 per cent of gross as his royalty. I laid out all the figures—cost of manufacture, all the other costs we went over a few chapters ago, and showed him in black and white that if I paid him 30 per cent, he was going to be making something like three times what I was making. And I'd be taking all the risk. All he had to do was sit back and collect his royalties. Bill didn't see it that way at all. I offered him 5 per cent, which was a pretty generous offer, under the circumstances. No sale. He was determined to take it someplace else and get his 30 per cent. Or, failing in that, he'd do it himself. I shook my head sadly and wished him well.

A couple of years went by and once again Bill was in my office. He'd learned his lesson. He'd tried and failed to get his Snappy Patches off the ground on his own. Now he was ready to discuss that 5 per cent royalty deal. But it was too late. The fad for patches had come and gone and the few patches still around were being discounted just to get them off the shelves. Bill, who had been sitting on top of a dynamite idea a year before the craze hit, never made a dime from it. He—like yours truly before him—had fallen victim to greed.

If the money had been there, believe me I would have been happy to give him his share. Later on, another fellow came to see me with a great idea called "Parent Protest Posters." They were take-offs on some of the protest rhetoric of our era, neatly reversed so it was the older generation doing the protesting. For instance, an old lady in duster cap and apron looking exactly like Flagg's Uncle Sam in drag was saying, "Mom wants you to clean up your room." They were to the point and well done. Jerry wanted me to manufacture and distribute them, printing the posters from his designs. They're still selling, although the bloom is pretty much off the rose by now. Now, this was an entirely different-colored horse from Snappy Patches. The cost of goods was low, so there was plenty of elbow room for a fat royalty. We agreed on 10 per cent, mostly because it would have been embarrassing to offer him anything less. The posters sold very nicely and we both made money. I was happy, under those circumstances, to make a bigger than normal royalty deal.

In the process of researching this book, I did a little experiment of my own, just to see if what I'm talking about is really true. Way back when I got stung on the Little Lumpsie doll and finally sold it off to Fisher-Price, I was glad to get a 2 per cent royalty. At the time, the negotiation on that price took about 30 seconds. Bob Hicks asked me what I had in mind. I said I was thinking about 120 per cent of gross, what was he thinking of? He grinned and replied, "One per cent." I asked if he'd settle for 2 per cent, and the deal was done. Now, some years later, I was picking Bob's brain for this book and I reminded him of the doll. "Do you suppose you would have gone for 5 per cent, at that time?" I asked.

"Nope," he said firmly. "There were too many unknowns about your product, even though you had some good sales results to show us."

"How about 4 per cent?" I asked.

"Nope."

"Three?"

There was a pause. He smiled.

"Yes."

So there it was. We had about a percentage point to play with in our original negotiations. I took a lower figure than, as it turned out, I might have been able to get. But at the same time, I got an advance of $5,000 as part of the deal, and that's fairly uncommon.

Speaking of up-front money, there's another area where many inventors have unrealistic ideas. I know I did. The area is that of options. Boise-Cascade took an option on my Neat Garage idea, as I mentioned earlier. The deal was that for two months I wouldn't sell it to anyone else while they did their homework on the idea. I was delighted. Visions of five-figure options checks danced in my head. I asked how much they were going to pay for the option and they looked blank. "Five thousand, maybe?" I asked, beginning to suspect that this wasn't a five-figure deal after all. Again, no reaction. "Well, how about five hundred?" Pause. "Hey, look, I paid $240 to fly up here, could I maybe get that back?" No deal. They explained that it is not their policy to pay for options. Later, if they took on the idea, they might consider an advance against royalties, but that's about as fast and loose as they ever play with the company checkbook.

In a way, maybe I'm being a little unfair to myself and my fellow inventors. Often as not, it isn't entirely a question of greed, but of simply not understanding how the business of marketing a product works. I've just finished playing matchmaker between an inventor and a rep in a deal where a few weeks earlier there was real animosity in the air. All because of failure in communications between two honest, well-intentioned people over a rather interesting new product.

The inventor is an attractive housewife who lives in Palos Verdes, California, the peninsula where I have my home and my offices. Sondra Cutcliffe is into arts and crafts and she has a highly imaginative mind. She's turned those assets into a fascinating hobby for some years, now. She likes to design Christmas decorations, often making them out of common household objects. This year she designed a clever little doll decoration made from a clothespin, some baker's clay (a dough which turns rock hard when it dries) and a little paint and glitter. The result, in her hands, is a delightfully old-fashioned-looking Christmas tree ornament.

In the past, Sondra had made a few dozen of the Christmas decorations each year and sold them to a few gift stores, making a modest profit and playing at business. This year, she decided to up the ante a little. She'd been successful enough on her own, just taking the ornaments to local stores. What would happen, she wondered, if she took the idea to a manufacturers' rep? Palos Verdes doesn't exactly rank as a poverty pocket, so there would be enough housewives around with time on their hands to form a cottage industry at Sondra's house if the demand got high enough. For the fun of it, of course.

Doing a little checking around, Sondra finally decided on a bright, aggressive young manufacturer's rep named Roger Gruen. Roger sells Christmas stuff—tree lights, ornaments, tinsel and Christmas novelties—so his line was an ideal place for Sondra's product. She showed Roger her clothespin ornaments and he liked them. She told him she could probably make as many as 8,000 of them if she got the neighbors together to form a kitchen-table assembly line. That hardly qualified her ornaments as one of Roger's hot items, of course, but he liked the piece enough to add it to his line for the upcoming trade show in Los Angeles. That's where things got exciting.

All the retailers in the area who sell Christmas items came to the show to see what was new in the line for this year and to place their orders for the holiday season. One of the things that really turned them on was—you guessed it, Sondra's ornaments. The day before the show officially opened, while ev-

LET'S MAKE A DEAL

erybody was milling around trying to set up booths and exhibits, a few buyers managed to get in. Those few buyers placed orders for nearly eight hundred of Sondra's ornaments. And that's before the show even opened! Three days into the show, Roger had orders for 13,000 ornaments and Roger knew he was onto something.

In the midst of the hullabaloo of a major trade show, he did some fast calculating. His orders already had outstripped Sondra's ability to manufacture the ornaments. He quickly made a decision to manufacture and distribute the ornaments himself and work out a royalty deal with Sondra. He figured he could find places to have the ornaments manufactured in the quantities he needed to fill his orders. With her design talent, plus his investment, his contacts and his sources, they could have a really hot product on their hands.

In the meantime, Sondra dropped in at the show, saw 13,000 orders and very nearly fainted. "But, I can't *make* that many!" she wailed.

"Don't worry about it. I'll have them made," Roger told her, flushed with success. In the madhouse of the show, surrounded by surging crowds of buyers, he tried to explain to her about royalties. But all Sondra got out of it was that she was going to be making a whole lot less per ornament than she had agreed to originally. And how on earth was she going to make 13,000 ornaments anyway? She was highly upset and Roger, sensing he was about to get into a real jam, took the ornaments out of his display to forestall disaster. He didn't show them anymore for the rest of the trade show. This was no time for him to conduct a primer course in marketing.

Sondra was convinced that she was being ripped off by Roger, so she called a lawyer and had him call Roger to demand that he cease selling the ornaments and turn all the orders over to Sondra. Meanwhile she asked around the neighborhood and found out that there was this Kracke fellow a few blocks away who was supposed to know something about inventions. She called me and asked to come talk with me, which she did. And I found myself in the middle of no-man's land with a shooting war about to break out between Sondra and Roger.

As far as Sondra was concerned, Roger was stealing her idea and going into business on his own, paying her a mere pittance on each ornament, instead of the whole enchilada minus a sales commission. He had even covered over her name on the display at the show and replaced it with his own name. What's more he had taken orders for an enormous number of ornaments, knowing full well that she couldn't produce that many.

For his part, Roger felt he was being unjustly attacked by some artsy-craftsy suburban housewife who couldn't or wouldn't understand that she had a potential success on her hands and needed his help desperately. He had the means at hand to make them both a lot of money. But as manufacturer and distributor of the ornaments, he was entitled to make a fair profit, too. He couldn't very well take all the risks and do all the work for a 20 per cent sales commission. If only she could understand that a) she *didn't* have to make the ornaments herself, b) he was willing to risk his own money on her idea, and c) he was being totally fair and aboveboard in the whole thing.

I have to admit, having heard only Sondra's side of the story, I was incensed and ready to do battle with that scoundrel Roger. Here, I thought, was a classical confrontation of Good and Evil in the invention business. I would ride in on my white charger, scrag the infidels, rescue the fair maiden and maybe even get a searing exposé for the book.

Then I talked to Roger.

It became apparent very shortly that what we had here was not a dynamite exposé, but rather a regular old garden-variety case of crossed communications. I suggested that the two of them get together and talk it over, offering my services as moderator. (By this time I was fascinated by the whole affair and could no more drop it than you could turn off a good mystery on TV before you find out whodunnit.) Roger wasn't all that excited, frankly. Sure it was a good idea, but life is short. Who needs the hassle? Sondra wasn't eager to sit down with Roger, either. With a little persuasion I finally convinced all hands that this marriage might be worth saving.

I tried to explain to Sondra that a royalty deal was the best possible way for her to make money with her ornaments. I tried to soothe Roger a little bit. By the time the meeting was over, an agreement was reached that should have been ironed out in the first place without all the dramatics. It was a good deal all around.

Sondra would do what she does best: have ideas. She would get name credit. Roger would do what he does best: sell products. They would find someplace that could make a quantity of Sondra's ornaments in time for Christmas sales. They'd study the public reaction to the ornaments to find out if the excitement at the trade show would carry over to the cash register in the retail stores. They'd weed out slow-moving ornaments in the line. And they'd study reorders to get an idea of what sales potential really exists.

Next year, if they decide to continue, Roger will arrange to have the ornaments made in Guatemala or Mexico or maybe the Orient, depending on where they can get the best deal and the most satisfactory workmanship. This year, because of their time problem, the fact that they won't be making a terribly large quantity and because they'll be paying U.S. prices for the manufacturing, there's going to be hardly any profit in the ornaments at all. Sondra probably won't make any royalties and Roger isn't going to get rich either. In fact, he'll probably lose a few bucks. The whole thing is really a market test to get a better idea of where they're going with the ornaments. It's actually to their advantage that the scale is somewhat small. As Roger said, "If the product dies, I'd rather it dies when I'm into it fifteen thousand dollars than when I'm into it fifty thousand dollars." In the meantime, Sondra will be developing new ideas for next year's line. My own feeling is that they have a very good chance of making a success of it. After all, 13,000 orders in three days is not the sort of response you see all the time.

Having now read about some of the fallacies of negotiating a deal with a manufacturer, I imagine you're wondering what the eternal truths are. The first item on the agenda is to take a look at what the manufacturer wants from you in the negotiations.

Fundamentally, any manufacturer you might deal with is looking for the same four things.

FIRST, HE WANTS A GOOD IDEA. That goes without saying, but that's the first thing you have to convince him of. The best way to do that is to provide him with the second thing he wants.

THE SECOND THING HE WANTS IS A GOOD TRACK RECORD. He wants to see that your product is selling, even if it's just in a limited market and only on a test basis. He isn't so interested in the simple fact that some stores have bought the product. That really tells him nothing, other than that you managed to make some sales to buyers for the stores. What he's really looking for is a good record of reorders. Earlier in the book I mentioned that an average product will turn about four times a year at retail. If you can match that, or better it, in a reasonably projectable market sample, you've got a strong selling point.

Okay, suppose you haven't been selling at retail. You haven't got a real-life track record to show him. Then you'll have to make a convincing case with sales projections that make sense, and/or with research results that are believable. One way or another, you've got to convince him that your product will sell. Your own enthusiasm is hardly ever enough to convince the manufacturer of that fact.

THIRD, THE MANUFACTURER WOULD LIKE PROTECTION. Either a patent application or a copyright or one of the other things we talked about earlier in the chapter called "Patent It, Fast!" If the manufacturer thinks he'll be knocked off in the market when he comes out with your idea, he's going to be a lot less enthusiastic about making a deal with you. It's up to you to convince him otherwise.

FINALLY, YOUR COST FIGURES. He needs to know exactly what he'll have to spend per unit to make your product before he can figure out how much maneuvering room he has to play with in the profit margin. Naturally, he'll do his own cost figures, too. But he'd like to see yours.

What about *you*, the inventor? You've got some things you want from the manufacturer, too. THE FIRST, AND MOST IMPORTANT, IS A FAIR ROYALTY. (Or, if you're selling the company, a fair price.) By now you have a pretty good notion of what a fair royalty ought to be on your product. And if you're selling him a company, you have a right to a fair cashout for your assets—including inventory, equipment, accounts receivable and maybe even that nebulous but valuable commodity called "good will."

WHAT ABOUT AN ADVANCE? You've been beating your brains out developing your product, presumably, and it would be nice to have a chunk of money to play with. It will be an advance against royalties, in all likelihood, but it's not unfair to ask for a piece of that in advance. Needless to say, you may not be able to get it. It depends in part on industry practice, in part on policy at the manufacturer's company. It may even depend on his cash situation. However, as a good friend of mine once said, "You really don't have a deal until some money changes hands." He's right! That brings us to another thing you want from him.

HAS HE THE CAPITAL TO EXPLOIT THE MARKET? That is, after all, your best defense against being knocked off. That also implies that the manufacturer has a sales and distribution organization capable of hitting the market hard and fast.

One last thing to think about—primarily if you're selling a company, but even if you're just selling your idea:

IS THERE A MANAGEMENT CONTRACT? If the manufacturer likes your idea, he ought to be interested in any other ideas you come up with. If you're signed on as a consultant to him, giving him right of first refusal, or maybe even exclusive rights to your ideas, you both do well.

Margaret just poked her nose in. Now that she's retired, she seems to do that a lot. Unfortunately, she had a good thought I had forgotten.

More often than not, you'll do better in your negotiations if you decide to hire an agent. Be prepared to pay at least 10 per cent to him, even though he only speaks 150 words on your behalf. I know for a fact most of us cannot be firm enough to bargain on our own behalves. Modesty. Ignorance. Fear. Better you should have a surrogate. Especially if that person likes you and your ideas. By the time you get to the negotiation stage you'll need someone else. Your opinion of your idea and its value will have already gone down the sewer. You'll be bored, embarrassed and really not at all ready to be scorned again.

At this point agents earn their money.

And there's only one thing for you to avoid like the plague.

Greed. It'll kill you, if you don't watch out.

XI
THE WONDERFUL WORLD OF MERCHANDISING

Using advertising, packaging and publicity to sell your product.

To most people, the wonderful world of merchandising is a strip of Madison Avenue about twenty blocks long in midtown Manhattan; a land of Oz inhabited by people wearing blow-dry haircuts and drinking gray flannel martinis saying things like, "run it up the flagpole and see if it gets off in Peoria."

Well, maybe last week you didn't even like merchandisers, but this week you *are* one. Get into your gray flannel suit and put a martini out to dry. You are about to enter the mad, mad world of Madison Avenue.

How come? Because you have a product to sell, that's how come. Getting your product into the stores of America is only half the battle. Now you're going to have to move it *out* of those stores and into people's homes. That takes merchandising.

Merchandising means different things to different people. Advertising, as most of us understand it, is part of the merchandising picture. But for a new inventor trying to get his new product going, advertising is the least of his worries.

So many new inventors I've talked to have grandiose plans for advertising their products. They talk blithely about "taking an ad in a magazine" or even "doing a television com-

THE WONDERFUL WORLD OF MERCHANDISING 155

mercial." Most of them are shocked when they find out the costs involved in doing some of those things. Just for your information, a full page color ad in *Newsweek* will cost you around $35,335 just for the space alone. That's not counting the $5,000 or $6,000 it will cost you for production—getting the pictures, writing the copy, making the separations, setting the type, doing the mechanical layout, getting the plates.

Okay, so maybe you'll make do with something a little less flashy. How about a quarter page black-and-white ad in *Popular Mechanics*? That's around $2,537.50 for the space based on a one-time insertion.

Well, let's just figure on a plain old two-column by six-inch ad in the news section of your metropolitan daily newspaper. We'll take the Los Angeles *Times* as an example. That'll cost you $688.80 for the space. It's $823.20 on Sunday.

And that's just for one shot at it. Any advertising campaign worth its salt comes back several times in a number of different media. For General Motors or the telephone company, that's just part of the cost of business. For an inventor like you or me, that's madness. Big-time advertising is *not* the topic of this chapter.

Anyway, you don't need that kind of advertising. Not yet, at least. Unless you're another Seymour Popiel, the Vegomatic king. Seymour builds something like 50 per cent of the price of his products in as a marketing and advertising allowance. That's because he relies almost exclusively on television promotion of his products to get them moving. For him it works. For you, probably not. Also, at the outset, you'd be much better advised to spend whatever advertising budget you have in trade advertising rather than consumer advertising. Consumer advertising is aimed at the guy you hope will wander into the retail store and be captivated by your product. Trade advertising is aimed at the retailer who you hope will be moved to carry your product in his store. First you get it into the store, *then* you work on consumer sales.

For whatever it's worth, once you reach the big time you'll discover that most companies allow about 3 per cent of their total sales for advertising. To introduce a new product is worth an absolute minimum of 10 per cent of sales. In the case of a General Motors, that gives a pretty substantial budget for advertising media and production and creative and service. A few years ago when Blue Chip stamps came to Southern California, they spent $900,000 in 90 days, just to make 60 per cent of the people in their new area aware of the name "Blue Chip Stamps." In the face of numbers like that, you're likely to disappear into the woodwork without a trace if your total projected sales for the year are a hundred grand or so.

At the beginning of a product's life in the marketplace, there are better ways to get results than to spend your time working on retail consumer advertising. We're going to address ourselves to some of the more practical aspects of merchandising. The subject matter of this chapter, then, includes:

- How to design a package so it sells the product.
- How to make your product sell itself to the public.
- How to get someone else to pay for your advertising.
- How to use "collateral." And what is it, anyway?
- How to knock yourself off for fun and profit.
- How to generate publicity for your product.
- How to put Hollywood to work for you.

Let's start with the most basic advertising medium you have in your arsenal: your package. If you think of the package as just something to hold the product, you're missing out on what may be your only real chance to give the public some sell copy. Remember, you're going very light—if at all—in consumer advertising. At best you've got a little trade advertising, some word of mouth, a few other odds and ends. Most of the public will learn about your product for the first time when they see it in the store. At that point, the most important function of your package is not to hold the product, but to serve as a billboard for advertising your product.

That being the case, your package had better be capable of fulfilling that function. There had better be enough room there to do a little selling. For example, if you are using a "blister pack"—a clear plastic bubble or "blister" on a card holding the product—make sure the card is big enough to hold some words and pictures in addition to the product. If your product is in a box, so much the better. A box is a five-sided billboard, with each side selling your product. Make the most of it. The side you don't use to sell with is the one it sits upon!

Think about how your product will be displayed in the store. If you're using a blister pack, it will be hanging on a

THE WONDERFUL WORLD OF MERCHANDISING 157

rack of J-hooks, probably, so the front of the pack is the only working part. You'll have to use it for all it's worth. If the product is in a box, it may be stacked on a shelf so that only the end is visible. Or maybe the side. It won't matter that the top of the box is a masterpiece of advertising design if nobody ever sees it until he's bought it. Even some of the most seasoned advertising professionals in package design have been known to forget this important little fact. Use all the sides of the box so that each one can stand on its own as a billboard for your product.

The thing to remember is that your package has an awful lot of work to do in a terribly short time. If you're very lucky, the customer may stop to look at your package for as much as ten seconds. That's all you can reasonably hope for. Ten seconds is all the time you've got to convince him that he needs and wants what you have to sell him. In that short moment you've got to tell him what your product is, what it's called, what it does and why that's a good thing.

With a big ten seconds to play with, you're obviously going to have to keep it simple, keep it uncluttered and keep it direct. Show him a picture of the product in use or in some setting that gives him some information about how it works and how it's used. Keep the words down to a minimum, but make sure they're not so terse that they don't make sense. He's not going to stand around reading *War and Peace* on your label but he *does* want to learn something about your product. Otherwise he wouldn't have stopped to read what you have to say. Tell the man quickly and concisely.

That brings up a sore point. You'll remember way back in the Introduction, I told you how I chose the cutesy-poo name Rickie Tickie Stickies and then set it in a totally illegible type face of my own design. That was wrong, wrong, wrong, *wrong!* By doing what I did, I flew in the face of conventional wisdom. I *should* have been wrong. It was just a fluke that I turned out to be right. The rule is that you're much better off with a simple name on your package, especially if that simple name gives the buyer some inkling of what your product is and what it does. And when you put that simple name on the package, for God's sake, make it readable. That's what conventional wisdom says. And usually it's right.

I guess what that means is that what I've told you so far is correct, but maybe not necessarily right for your case. All I can give you is the best thinking I've been able to come up with. If luck or a fluke of circumstances turns all that wisdom inside out—who am I to complain? I benefited from that kind of fluke, too.

Any advertising piece—including a package—has to tread a fine line between being lovely and being informative. As the client, in the case of your product, you'll have to see to that balance when you're dealing with the advertising experts you hire to take care of your design needs. Your package ought to be attractive, certainly. But it doesn't have to be a museum piece, if that gets in the way of its function. On the other hand, it ought to work hard at selling, but it should not look like an ad for a fire sale. It's a delicate balance. All I can tell you is that in a standoff between the two claims, "informative" gets the nod over "pretty" every time. Usually, though, it's possible to be both.

One of the best, most effective ways to increase the sales of a product is to provide the store with a display unit that shows the product to advantage while it does some selling of its own. It's a way to let your product help sell itself. This may be a floor display unit or it may be a display designed to stand on a counter. It might be a multisided rack or any of a number of different kinds of display units. Early on in our Stickies adventure, we discovered that by using a floor display unit we had designed, we could count on selling 40 or 50 per cent more Stickies. (That was a special case and you can't necessarily project those figures to any display unit. But you *can* be sure that displays do improve sales to some degree or other.)

Paperback book publishers have been making use of this bit of knowledge in recent years. Many of them now offer "dump bins" (a form of display unit) to bookstores as a means of displaying their current crop of new titles. These displays take the books out of the anonymous ranks of book spines on the store shelves and put them out in the aisles or on counter tops where they can be seen and where the cover design can help sell books. It's one of the few instances of real merchandising moxie in the publishing business, which seems to be living in the stone age of merchandising in most other respects.

Usually a display unit is shipped to a retailer as a reward for making some larger-than-ordinary order of a product. And it is usually designed in such a way that the order is shipped already packed in the display. That saves shipping cost which, in the case of a standing floor display, can be considerable. There are people who make a nice living designing and selling these displays, and you'll do well to get in touch with some of them. If your order is going to be reasonably large, they may design your display unit as part of the box order. Otherwise you may have to pay a designer's fee. Either way, this is not a job for an amateur.

Almost without exception, these display units have what's called a "header card" or an additional piece which mounts on top of the display and serves as a billboard for the product. The construction of the display can range all the way from plain cardboard to heavy corrugated cardboard to (somewhat rarely) wood and glass and aluminum. It depends on how long you expect it to last and how much you've got to spend. If it's a permanent unit, you may spend quite a bit of money on it—some of which you may recover from the retailer, since it helps him sell, too. If it's strictly for a short-time promotion, it won't have to be built like the Grand Coulee Dam and won't cost as much.

The guidelines for designing a display unit are about the same as the guidelines for designing a package. Make it attractive, make it informative and make it efficient in getting the message across. Find the single most important thing you can think of to say about your product and say it in a way that gives it impact. There's still only about ten seconds to get your message across. The difference is that with a display setting your product apart from the rest of the stuff in the store, you are more likely to be noticed.

I must tell you, by the way, that there are an awful lot of places where you can't use a display, because of store policy. Most of the better department stores won't allow floor displays or counter displays of any kind other than the ones they themselves have put in the stores. (By better department stores, I don't just mean Neiman-Marcus, by the way. I'm talking about stores like Carson-Pirie-Scott or Marshall Field in Chicago, Hudson's in Detroit. Macy's and Gimbels in New York and The Broadway and May Co. in Los Angeles.)

Their theory is that they have spent a lot of money and effort to create a "selling atmosphere" and a "personality" in their stores. Anything that isn't a part of that carefully calculated decor doesn't belong there, even if it increases sales for a specific item. For that very reason, by the way, some department stores and chains around the country have begun branching out into discount operations, usually under a different name. This permits them to participate in the rack-and-display, self-service atmosphere of high-volume sales without sullying their downtown image.

What it all means to you is that you ought to examine very carefully the kinds of stores you plan to be selling in before you invest in display units. If hardly any of them use displays, you'd be wasting money. Also, even if there's no set store policy against displays, you may find that many stores don't use them anyway. Even the biggies get caught in that trap, from time to time. Bristol-Meyers, for heavens sakes, did it once. They spent a lot of money, an absolutely *inordinate* number of dollars, on several thousand standing display units. They were beauties, too. And they sold the product effectively, besides just looking handsome. Bristol-Meyers gleefully shipped 'em out to their retailers and considered it money well spent—until somebody did a survey of the stores. About one out of ten displays was getting used. The rest of the investment was gathering dust in storerooms or had been given the old heave-ho practically on arrival. There was severe chagrin at Bristol-Meyers.

Your best insurance is to call some buyers at the stores you plan to be selling in, or at least the type of store you plan to be selling in. Ask them for the real lowdown on whether or not display units get used. They'll probably be happy to tell you, since it saves them trouble, too.

Let's move on to a somewhat more traditional form of advertising—with a twist. It's called "co-op" advertising and it looks, feels and smells just like regular media advertising for your product. Newspaper ads, maybe radio. Possibly TV, even. The twist is that someone else pays for most of it. You ought to be aware of it because it's a beautiful way to get a lot of mileage out of a practically nonexistent advertising budget. There are a couple of ways you can work it.

We'll take the simplest way first. If a customer is ordering a lot of your product—bigger numbers and more regularly than the average run of your customers—you cut him in on your co-op advertising allowance. What that means is this: Every time he orders from you, he gets to deduct a set percentage of his purchase from your invoice. He uses that deducted money to help pay for advertising in which he men-

THE WONDERFUL WORLD OF MERCHANDISING 161

tions your product. Commonly, the advertising allowance is 10 per cent of his invoice total on any given order. So if he orders $1,000 worth of product from you, he actually pays you $900 and spends $100 on advertising for your product.

What's the catch? None, really. Except that the retailer who's buying from you won't be very interested in advertising your product if it isn't likely to bring people into his store. Therefore, you have to have established some momentum for your product before co-op advertising makes any sense to the retailer. By the same token, you should be getting tearsheets or other proof of the advertising he is running, just to be sure it really *does* mention your product. (In the case of radio or television, he should send you a script and a schedule of where and how often the commercials are appearing.)

Obviously, you have to set some sort of standards for what constitutes a mention of your product. Two words do not a mention make. But if you're reasonable about your demands, the retailer usually will give you a fair shake in his advertising in return for your co-op allowance. There's really no way to set up hard, fast rules on a co-op advertising program. It's all pretty much a matter of judgment and trust between you and the customer. Sometimes that can be a screeching pain. Mostly, though, it's a pretty easy system to deal with and it does both of you some good—it helps out his advertising costs appreciably while it gives you a lot more exposure than you could get on your own.

The next level of co-op advertising is a bit more complicated. But not much. It's the same deal as before, but in this case you also supply the retailer with some of the advertising material he'll use. You make up some newspaper ads, maybe some radio commercials. Perhaps you'll even do some television, if you're feeling particularly affluent and if it makes sense in the light of your customer's advertising plans and your product.

In each of the ads, you feature your product heavily, but you leave room for the local merchant to put his name, his store location and so forth. And you build the ad in such a way that it's your customer who's talking to the public, not you. It's his ad, not yours, even though it's all about your product.

In the case of newspaper ads, you furnish the material to your customer in two different forms. You provide him with fiberboard molds of the words and pictures in your ad, just the way they will appear. At the newspaper, this mold is used to make a casting and the casting will be used as part of the plate which prints the paper. This type of fiberboard mold is called a "mat."

You also provide the same ads already printed on a slick-surfaced paper. This allows him to use the ads in "offset" publications. The ads will be put onto the publication's printing plates by a photographic process. These preprinted ads are described as "camera-ready" and they are called "slicks."

In the case of radio commercials, you can do any of several things. You can provide fully produced radio commercials—announcer, sound effects, music and all—on tape. These commercials will have a "hole" left in them for the station announcer to fill in the local retailer's message. Or, you can provide prerecorded "tags" of five or ten seconds. The retailer drops these tags in at the end of the commercials he is putting on the air. You might just send scripts for five- or ten-second tags to be read "live" by the local station announcer at the end of the retailer's commercials.

The main thing to remember is to give the retailer as much leeway as you can in how he uses your material. In print advertising, give him a selection of different sizes, based on standard column widths. You might give him a one-column by three-inch ad, a two-column by six-inch and a three-column by ten-inch ad, for example. And give him little "plug-in" modules to use as part of a multi-product ad, too. In the case of broadcast material, give him different lengths and diffierent formats so that he can fit you into what he's planning to use. This whole area is one where an amateur could really get himself into trouble and waste a lot of money. Hire, or better yet, involve an expert and let him do his thing. Just be sure the message is clear and has impact. Leave the technicalities to experienced people.

By the way, there may be special cases where you throw the guidelines overboard and give a much bigger co-op allowance on a one-shot deal than you normally would. I ran into a good example of that with the Stickies. A big store in Colorado—at the height of the Rickie Tickie Stickies madness—ran a full-color, full-page ad in a Sunday supplement magazine and the ad featured our Stickies. They were building a promotion around my flowers. The page cost them $1,500 and I agreed to split the cost right down the middle, even though they had only ordered $2,500 worth of my product. I figured it was well worth the exposure to spend that kind of money in this case. And I was right. The store sold out almost instantly and the reorders kept rolling in, thanks to the momentum given us by that store promotion and the ad that kicked it off.

"Collateral" is a word you're going to run into sooner or later when you start merchandising your product. Collateral is advertising and merchandising material that doesn't go into regular advertising media like newspapers, radio and so forth. It includes things like catalogue sheets, store display materials (including those display units we talked about earlier), it even includes things like business forms.

Putting together a good, solid collateral program is pretty basic to your whole merchandising effort, even though much will be seen only by the trade—the salesmen, the retailers and the other people whom you have to reach in order to get your product into stores. That's only half the battle, as I said before, but it's the *first* half of the battle.

Let's take a look at some of the more important parts of your collateral material. First and foremost is your catalogue sheet. This is a single-page, sometimes full-color sheet of paper that goes into a three-ring binder used by your rep when he's taking orders for the products he sells. It explains what your product is and shows whatever different models you have to offer. Doing the catalogue sheet is kind of a litmus paper test of an idea. I've found that if I can't explain a product on one sheet of 8½"×11" paper, it's probably not a good idea. Naturally, you'll want to show your product in its best light, with handsome photos and/or illustrations and with words that not only explain it but help sell it.

Do *not* print your prices on the catalogue sheet. Prices go on a separate mimeographed sheet. That's because they may change during the year. The way things are going these days, the prices will undoubtedly change. Upward. For a number of reasons, you want to be able to change the price list quickly and easily without having to re-do the whole, expensive catalogue sheet. You ought to figure on going through 5,000 or more catalogue sheets a year. I don't know where they go, but they somehow get used up in large quantities over the course of a year, so you might as well go ahead and order a bunch of them at once to take the printing discount that goes with larger orders. All of your reps will want several of them, of course. Some of your retailers will want to keep them on hand. You may mail them out to retailers yourself to stir up some interest in your product. And you may give them out at trade shows, too. You'll need all of them you print, believe me.

When you're printing up your business forms—invoices, order sheets, stationery and business cards, for instance—you might as well put it all to work for you. Plan to design it all so that your product is featured on it in some tasteful form. Maybe you've got an advertising line or a slogan of some sort that has been effective or that you like a lot. Put it wherever it seems to be appropriate. No, you don't want to turn your correspondence into an advertising extravaganza, and you certainly don't want a tacky letterhead, but it can't hurt to plug the product somehow.

There is also a gray area of collateral about which you'll have to make your own decision, based on your product and your market. You can do things like window banners that plug your product, if you think the stores where you'll be selling might use them. They can be just about any size, including jumbo 3- or 4-foot babies. If you do window banners, make sure they can be read from a car passing in the street. The pedestrian is becoming an endangered species in America, so most of your passersby do it in a car. And for heaven's sake, check with your retailers before you plunge ahead and run off a batch of banners. They may have size restrictions you don't know about, and they may have other quirks that could make your banner worthless to them.

Also in this gray-area is something called a "shelf talker." That's a sort of tag or display piece that attaches to the shelf where your product is displayed. Generally they're small—no more than three to six inches wide and maybe one to two inches high, depending on how and where they'll be used. The shelf talker catches the attention of someone walking down the aisle in a store and might make him stop long enough to give you that ten-second shot at him with your package. They do work. You just have to be sure that the stores where you sell can and will use them.

There are any number of different kinds of items like these shelf talkers that you can use. They all fall under the general heading of "point-of-purchase" material. (The name is self-explanatory. And it's a fact that merchandising done right at

THE WONDERFUL WORLD OF MERCHANDISING 165

the spot where the person makes the choice of buying or not buying seems to work very effectively.) Gary Dahl, the father of the Pet Rock, had a stroke of genius and turned a piece of point-of-purchase material into a lot of sales for his baby. The Pet Rock hit its stride in the pre-Christmas period so that lots of dealers stocked up extra heavily for the holiday. Naturally, there were some left over at the end of the Christmas season. Gary was very interested in keeping the ball—or the rock, in this case—rolling, so he designed hang tags to go on the clever Pet Rock carrying case that serves as the package for his product. The hang tags neatly positioned the Pet Rock as the perfect Valentine's Day gift for loved ones with a sense of humor and a need for an easy-care pet, like Gary's purebred igneous rock. Suddenly all the dealers had a whole new selling season for the Pet Rock.

Naturally, Gary can do the very same thing for every holiday from St. Swithin's Day to Tisha B'Av. Nothing about the product or the package changes. All it takes is the addition of an inexpensive piece of point-of-purchase advertising to the original product and the Pet Rock is in position for any special event on the calendar.

At various points in this book, we've been referring disparagingly to knock-off artists. Now we're about to do a full about-face and discuss how *you* can become a knock-off artist. The target: your own product. If it sounds wacko, stick around. There's some very serious method to this particular stroke of madness.

Remember back when we were discussing how to price your product? We talked briefly about how a price that was too high—or too low—could be a problem to you. Well, there's no changing that, but you *can* change something else in that equation. You can change your price. You can knock yourself off by marketing a cheaper version of your own product so that you can fit neatly into other markets.

The first rule of this game is that you have to enter the market at the high end. Make your de luxe model with the fancy packaging and get that rolling. Once that's underway, you build a somewhat cheaper version of the product, if possible. If you can't do that, at least you can do a cheaper package and take a slightly smaller profit per unit to get yourself into a lower class but higher volume market. You can make as many steps down as you can find elbow room for in your price. The only rule is that you have to start at the top and work down. It's very difficult, if not impossible, to start with a cheap version and then market more expensive versions in the classier stores.

While you're doing this, you have to market your product under different brand names, of course. The May Co. wouldn't be very happy to find that the same brand name and the same product was selling at Thrifty-Mart for considerably less, in a more plebeian package. But if you call the May Co. version "Acme" and the Thrifty-Mart version "Amalgamated," you aren't likely to stir up animosity at either store. Retailers expect manufacturers to get knocked off from time to time, so they won't be surprised to see that competition has developed at a lower price level. Since Thrifty-Mart doesn't compete with May Co., no serious harm is done. They both simply address their own individual markets with their version of the product, and everybody's happy. There's nothing illegal about it. I feel it's just plain smart. Your goal is to make a success for yourself, so why not cover all the bases.

The advantages of knocking yourself off are pretty clear. The most basic is that if you don't, someone else probably will! Selling your product at a classy store pretty much cuts you off from a whole market at another price level. By knocking yourself off, you have access to the lower price level, too. Your sales penetration increases and your profits go up. What's more, the lower price level tends to be a much higher volume market. So if there's enough of a profit spread to work with, you can give sales an enormous boost this way. You can hit intermediate steps in the price scale, too. Just be aware that by going from a swanky department store to a discount chain you are getting into a whole different distribution structure, which may have an effect on your pricing. Read over the chapter on "Which Way to Go" before you get too far into knocking yourself off or you may find that you have knocked yourself *out*.

One of the most important areas of merchandising is one that all too many new inventors ignore entirely. Publicity is usually better than the best advertising. For one thing, it's practically free. For another thing, it usually gets the kind of audience you couldn't buy for any price. And finally, it is more effective because people are more likely to read and be-

THE WONDERFUL WORLD OF MERCHANDISING 167

lieve something in regular news media than they are in an ad. Take it from me, publicity is worth its weight in solid-gold ads.

The very first step to take in generating publicity is to spend a few hundred bucks for a first-class, professional photographer. You will probably be needing photos of your product for your package, for your catalogue sheets and for other purposes anyway, so you'll need to spend the money no matter what happens. With a set of good photographs in hand, you have the first and most important element of a publicity campaign. Here's how to use it:

The object of your exercise is to get a story about your product published, so the next thing to do is figure out where you'd like it published. An obvious place to think of is the trade press. There are all kinds of magazines published, each catering to some very specialized audience. Everything from the *National Nurse Anesthetist Journal* (try saying that three times, fast) to *National Knitted Outerwear Times*. There must be at least one trade publication designed to serve the kind of retailers who will be selling your product. Find out the name of the publications that reach your trade audience. How? As we keep telling you all the time, ask. Call a store you think will carry your product. Ask for the buyer of your kind of item (as Mrs. McDonough did with her trash separator). Ask that buyer what trade publications he reads. It's that simple. Then go after them.

Don't stop there, of course. Another natural for you is a newspaper wire service, like United Press International or Associated Press. These services are always on the lookout for a good feature story—something with a newsy slant but basically just an entertaining or informative article. Think also of other publications you'd like to be in with your product. In our case, with the Rickie Tickie Stickies, a natural place to try was the Los Angeles *Times* Sunday supplement, called *Home* magazine. Our flowers were sort of free-spirited and funky, which matched the way *Home* magazine views the Southern California scene. It made sense. In the case of your invention, you can pick out equally appropriate publications.

The next step is to figure out a story angle. Why would the publication run a piece about your product? What's in it to interest their readers? Those are the very same questions the editor has to ask himself, so put yourself in his place. Figure out what kind of story he'd really like to have and his readers would really be interested in, then see what you can do to fit your product neatly into that kind of story.

If it looks as if your product were dragged into the story, kicking and screaming, just to get some publicity, you won't get into print. Stay away from far-out angles. Look for a good, solid, realistic, interesting slant and build the story so that your product is a logical part of it.

Once you've figured out a good angle for the story, do a very brief outline of the way you see the story. Type that up neatly and send it, along with a good selection of photographs that match the story, to the editor of the publication you have in mind. Include your address and phone number so that the editor can get in touch with you for more information, photos or whatever else he'd like to have for the story. And don't expect to see any of the pictures again, whether the story is used or not. Editors are swamped every day with press releases. They can't afford to spend the time to return them. It's just part of your cost of doing business, like so many other things we've discussed in this book.

If the publication uses color photos, send them nothing smaller than 4" × 5" transparencies and never send color prints. Small transparencies and prints on paper give the publication problems in production, so they give the editor an excellent reason to forget about your story. If you send black-and-white photos, send top-quality 8" × 10" glossy prints. The kind you get at the drugstore or the overnight photo places tend to be fuzzy and not terribly well developed. Spend a little extra to have your photographer make studio-quality glossy prints.

I said earlier that you'd be needing photos for a lot of purposes, so you should get good ones that can be used for publicity. But if you are aiming at a big, important general-circulation magazine like a Sunday supplement, you'll probably want to set up a special shooting session, either in a studio or on location somewhere, to make special pictures that match the story slant. That sounds like a big deal, but it's not as expensive as you might think. A few hundred dollars, maybe a thousand, judiciously used should get it done for you. Especially if you can get models who are not professional (but who look professional). When we were shooting some of the Rickie Tickie Stickies stuff for our package design, we used neighbors and friends and their kids. We got signed releases from all of them, in return for a dollar, and

THE WONDERFUL WORLD OF MERCHANDISING 169

we had a supply of soft drinks and snacks on hand at the session. Later we sent all of them nice sweaters as a follow-up gift. They had a good time and enjoyed seeing themselves on the package in stores, and it all cost a great deal less than using professional models. (The signed releases are very important, by the way, even if you use professional models. The releases can keep you out of trouble later on. In our case, they also helped us beat that Canadian knock-off outfit I mentioned earlier.)

But except for the amateur models, we were professional in every respect at our photo sessions. Well, maybe with one exception. If you were to look very closely at a photo on the front of our display box you'd find a small dark spot on the rug in a photo of a bathroom where the flowers are liberally used. That happened well after midnight on the last night of shooting. We were using our own home as the location for the shooting and Margaret had just run the rug through the washing machine and dryer so it would be nice and sparkly-bright for our photo. It took a couple of hours to dry that rug and we all sat around impatiently, watching the minutes tick by, waiting for that stupid rug to dry. Finally everything was ready. We laid out the rug, set the lights and began preparing the camera angle to make the shot. Just about that time, our cat wandered into the bathroom and—dazzled by all the big-time photography—had an accident in the middle of the rug. No way were we going to go through another whole wash-and-dry-and-dry-again cycle of the washer for that rug. We cleaned up the mess as best we could and took our pictures. And that cat has haunted us ever since.

The benefits of a little effort in the area of publicity can be astounding. We got our story placed in *Home* magazine partly because we had done a pretty fair job of getting a good story together. But it was also partly because of a fluke. What I didn't know at the time was that the editor was in desperate straits. A story he had been counting on for the next issue of the magazine had fizzled out on him and he was looking frantically for another good story to replace it. It had to be good, of course, but it had to turn up pretty soon or he would have a lot of leftover space in the magazine.

Our little story came to him like a gift from the gods and he snapped it up. We got a two-page, full-color spread featuring our little flower as part of the new design scene in good ol' easy-living Southern California. It was incredible publicity for us, of course, and it was a good, colorful, appealing story for the magazine, too.

Then the ripples began to spread.

Editors and associate editors of newspapers and magazines read all the other magazines and newspapers they can get their hands on. It's part of their job, scouting story ideas, keeping up with what the competition is doing. Somebody at the Chicago *Tribune* saw the story in *Home* magazine and thought it was a gas. So, several months later, the Chicago *Tribune* Sunday supplement had a very similar story on our flowers. They called us, we sent them the pictures they wanted and we had our first spin-off story.

The next thing that happened was that one of the buyers at Marshall Field, the big Chicago department store, saw the story and liked the flowers. He placed a big order with us and we gained a solid foothold in the Chicago market.

Meanwhile, we had managed to stir up interest at UPI, and the next thing we knew we had a nice feature story, with picture, on the UPI national newswire. By the time we quit counting, we had seen that story run in more than two hundred newspapers all over the country. What happened next, I'm still not sure I believe.

Whether it was the UPI story, the Chicago *Tribune* Sunday supplement feature or the *Home* magazine piece, I don't know, but somebody at CBS in New York got interested in Rickie Tickie Stickies. One thing led to another and the next thing we knew we had a network news crew dragging cables and lights into our living room to film a segment for the Walter Cronkite news. We got something like seven and half minutes of national network coverage out of it—something no amount of money could ever buy. You couldn't even match that kind of exposure with an hour of network commercial time.

Years later we had the same kind of experience, parlaying a feature piece into a whole series of media events. This time the product was those Parent Protest Posters I mentioned in an earlier chapter. Nearly thirty months after we hit the market with the product, an editor at *Newsday* on Long Island in New York saw us in a store and got in touch. To the editor, it was a brand new product which she had just discovered. Did we have any pictures and information she could use to do a story? You betcha, ma'am! So we got a nice, long story in *Newsday*—a very highly regarded newspaper—about

THE WONDERFUL WORLD OF MERCHANDISING 171

our posters. It was great exposure in a very important market area. Better still, the *Wall Street Journal* was working on an article for its widely read front-page daily feature. The subject? New products on the market. The *Journal* picked up details of the story from the *Newsday* article and we found ourselves on the front page of the *Wall Street Journal* all over the country.

Then the producers of the "Today Show" called us. They had seen that piece in the *Journal* and were fascinated. Would we mind if they did a number on us. No! And there we were again, on national network television.

As you can see, if you do a good job of generating publicity, you can get benefits you never dreamed of. Maybe you won't wind up rubbing elbows with Walter Cronkite and Barbara Walters, but you could sure get a lot of coverage by important news media.

One of the smart things we did was to hire a news clipping service as soon as it became apparent that we were going to be showing up in a lot of different publications. For a relatively small fee, the service clipped out every story that mentioned us and they sent all the clippings to us. Later we were able to use those clippings to demonstrate the kind of interest we had stirred up across the nation. It was a valuable sales tool that helped us cash in on all that publicity.

I've just finished doing a little name-dropping. You can, too, with a little bit of effort. If your product seems to be working out well, you may find that you can get an endorsement from a big-name celebrity to use in your merchandising efforts. I mean a *big* name. You may not have the cash to afford the celebrity's usual endorsement fee, but by doing some calling around to agents, you may be able to work a deal anyway. You could pay the star by cutting him in for a percentage of your profits on the product. A lot of big names might find that a very attractive deal for tax reasons. If they can find a way to spread their earnings out over a few years and avoid taking a big lump sum for their services, they're usually interested. After all, fame is all they have to sell, and fame is a perishable commodity. Stars and celebrities tend to make the bulk of their money in a span of a few years, which means that the Internal Revenue Service gets a very healthy portion of it. By deferring or spreading out that income, they can save some of it from the eager clutches of Uncle Sam. If you offer them a way to do that, you might be able to attract one of the bright stars of sports, television or Hollywood to endorse your product.

Is it worth giving away a piece of the action for a celebrity endorsement? Probably it is. Certainly some of the big companies in the world have paid huge sums to have people like Arthur Godfrey and Joe Namath and O. J. Simpson endorse their products. If it makes sense for them, it might just make sense for you, too. You'd be surprised how much a little celebrity glamour can do for sales of a product.

There's another way you can put Hollywood to work for you. The people who make movies and television shows constantly are faced with the problem of "dressing the set." They have to put props into every scene to help the illusion of realism along. (Hardly any "room" you see on film or TV is really a room. Almost all of them are sets, built on a sound stage and filled with props.) Naturally, they can't keep using the same tired old props, so they're constantly on the lookout for something new to use in the scenes. Your product might be just the thing. If people buy it and use it, then it is presumably a real part of everyday life. Anything that helps the film people portray everyday life is all to the good.

You might consider sending a sample of your product—or at least a photo and some descriptive material about it—to the three television networks and to several of the major film studios.

Ideally, you would send your material to the art director in charge of each individual series currently in production and each feature film currently in production. That may not be possible for you, since it involves keeping up with the trade papers to see who's producing what and where. So, less ideally, you would send your material to the vice-president in charge of production at the three networks and the studios.

How do you find all the addresses? Simple. You order a book called "West Coast Theatrical Directory." It's published by H. M. Gousha Co., P. O. Box 6227, San Jose, California 95150. It tells you more than anybody would reasonably want to know about the film business. You'll not only have the addresses of the studios—including the independents, as well as biggies like Fox and Universal and Warner Brothers and the like—but you'll even know where you can rent a crab dolly or a 10-K light, complete with stand and sandbags, if you ever need it.

Every art director in film keeps something called a "production book," which is a loose-leaf binder full of sheets listing sources of things he needs in making a film. Find a way to fit your information for him on a standard three-ring sheet (your catalogue sheet is a good thing to include) and send it to him in that form. Enclose a note saying that this is for his production book and that you'd be happy to co-operate with him if he ever needs some of your product for a production.

You may strike out at every one, but then again you might find yourself on television or in the movies. I sent samples of Rickie Tickie Stickies all over Hollywood and they turned up on a number of TV shows that I'm aware of and probably some I missed. They weren't necessarily prominently displayed, but they were sure there on the flickering silver screen. Every little bit helps.

Anyway, it's worth a try. Besides, how can you be a Madison Avenue merchandising biggie if you don't have a few movie studios and television networks in your address book?

XII
WHO'S GOT THE MONEY?

Marketing your idea means spending money. Here's how to finance at least part of your venture.

There are times when it seems you have to be rich to begin with if you're going to make a success of your invention. There were times at the early stages of our adventure when I was convinced the whole thing was going to die from acute fiscal anemia.

All the money you have to spend! In the last chapter, we talked about getting people to design packages and display units, hiring copywriters and art directors to do your advertising and collateral material, not to mention photographer costs and models. Then there's the cost of all those 4"×5" color transparencies and 8"×10" black-and-white studio prints you'll be sending around in the hope of generating publicity. If you wind up manufacturing the product yourself, even as a market test, you'll face the cost of tooling, of manufacturing, of packaging and distribution. Even getting a patent costs money.

Where does it all come from?

Well, there's good news and there's bad news. The good news is that I'm going to tell you how to get a lot of work done without paying any cash. The bad news is that you'll still have to spend some big money. Worse, there's a financial problem I haven't completely explained, yet.

The new financial problem is something I call "pocketbook lag." The pros call it cash flow. To illustrate, remember how

I told you I sank $1,000 into that first batch of Stickies? (That's not counting the photography costs for our publicity pictures and package design, nor does it include the cost of the special dies we had to provide the printer so he could make the Stickies for us.) To get that money, we had dipped into the vacation slush fund which we figured we could afford to risk on this new idea.

Shortly we sold out all that first batch of Stickies and had a new stream of orders coming in. It was time to go back and print up another batch. This time it was going to be a bigger order, too, so we could at least break even on the printing costs.

That's when we discovered our principle of pocketbook lag. The money hadn't come in yet from those first sales. You see, in business a really good account is one that pays in 30 days. It's not uncommon to wait 60 or 90 days or even longer to be paid for your product. In fact, the area of business in which we were operating—gift and stationery and department stores—is notoriously slow-pay. At the same time, suppliers expect to be paid cash up front, especially when they're dealing with a brand new business like ours. That's pocketbook lag.

We needed $2,500 more now. Hitting the vacation fund was one thing, but now we were going to have to go into hard savings, and that was painful. Still the idea was giving indications that it was going to pay out well, so we bit the bullet and spent the savings.

Just about that time, though, we hired a rep and our publicity efforts began to pay off. On the basis of his contacts in the trade and the fact that we had a story about to break in *Home* magazine, our rep got orders from five hundred more stores around Southern California. The ink wasn't even dry on our second batch of Stickies and already we needed a much bigger batch. This time it would be $5,000 worth, to meet the demands of our expanding market. Money from the first order was trickling in, but we were already way behind the eight ball on our second order. And now there was this new demand. The vacation fund was empty. There wasn't enough money left in hard savings to pay for this third order of Stickies, and we were frittering away the checking account on things like food, clothing and shelter. This was a crisis.

The only place left to look was the kids' education fund. We had an ironclad rule that the education fund was sacred, not to be touched for any reason, ever, under any circumstances.

That afternoon I paid the printer for the new batch of Stickies out of the education fund.

And suddenly that found money wasn't enough, either. Right on the heels of that order, we needed more Stickies—$10,000 worth this time. Sales were climbing sharply. All of this incredible growth had taken place in the space of about two and a half months, so there was never time for the incoming money to catch up with the outgoing money. I was becoming a Stickies addict, and my habit was getting awfully expensive to support.

Anyway, there we were, facing the same dilemma you'll be facing. Expenses and the pocketbook lag were eating us alive, and the fact that we had a winner on our hands only made the problem worse. We had to find a source of capital or we were going to drown in bittersweet juices of success.

The choices that face an inventor at a time like that are these: He can borrow from a bank. He can take on partners. He can go public and sell stock. He can start holding up liquor stores in his spare time.

We'll dispose of the last two alternatives fairly quickly. Moral considerations aside, you're not going to have enough time on your hands to be running around sticking up liquor stores. And as for selling stock and going public, it's remotely possible, but unlikely. By the time you go through all the red tape it takes to go public and by the time you've met all the requirements for a corporation that sells stock, it'll be way, way too late to do you any good. In any event, as a brand new company with a brand new product, you can't make it to the big board. Or the little board, for that matter.

The next possibility is a bank loan. That's what I decided to try next when things got tough. I needed someone to loan me capital to keep my booming new business growing. Isn't that what bankers would have you believe they do all day? So I began groping around in my mind for a bank that seemed likely to listen to me. The best one I could come up with was a local bank that had once made me a loan—cosigned by a friend—for some other venture. I had paid the loan back promptly, so my credit record was good with them. My name wouldn't be on their no-no list, anyway.

Better still, this bank had a reputation as a real go-go operation. They were supposed to be real swingers. Also, the branches of this bank were all autonomous. You could go down there and get an answer and get your money right away without waiting around for a stuffy bunch of cigar smokers at the central headquarters to make up their minds. I called the manager of the local branch—the guy I had dealt with on that previous loan—and told him I had a new product which was testing very well. Could I come talk to him about financing? I was running out of my own resources.

"Sure," he said. "Come on down."

There was hope. I really don't remember now why it was that I drove Margaret's car down to the bank. But it was in the flower-covered station wagon that I made my grand entrance to the bank parking lot. I tooled in, found a parking place in the shadow of that vast expanse of chrome-and-glass architecture and stashed the Rickie Tickie Stickie-mobile.

The meeting was very pleasant. The manager expressed interest in the numbers I had worked up for my presentation. Then he wanted me to tell him a little more about exactly what this product was.

Just at this moment his receptionist—bless her heart—strolled past the big window overlooking the parking lot. She took one look at the station wagon with all those flowers on it and came running the whole length of the bank, yelling to the manager. (I guess she was an old-time employee of the bank and didn't worry about formalities or the fact that this was the manager.) She came running up, screaming, "You've got to see this, quick!" She literally took him by the hand and dragged him over to the window and said, "Isn't that great! That's the greatest thing I've ever seen!"

He was sold. We got the loan, I'm convinced, strictly on the basis of the receptionist's excitement over Margaret's car with the flowers on it. Unfortunately, we had to put up the house, the mountain lot and just about everything we owned as collateral for that $10,000 loan. But I was sure that in just a short time the money would catch up with the expenses and I'd be in a position to pay off the loan and fund the whole venture on my own. As it turned out, it was quite a while before that happened.

That brings us to a point about trying to borrow money from a bank to fund your idea. Banks are not very interested in ideas. They like collateral, thank you. The banker's human instincts told him that the flowers were really neat. His business instincts told him that my figures indicated a potential success. But his banker's instincts told him that the loan had to be backed by collateral, not by numbers.

I've since been convinced that banks are not a very logical place to find funding for an idea. But I first learned it to my own satisfaction some months later when I went looking for another loan.

I was still suffering from pocketbook lag. But by now I had a good, solid sales curve to show. And I had a much more elaborate presentation. I had asked my accountant for professional advice and we put together a cash-flow projection for 1968 that should have warmed the heart of any knowledgeable investor or, as they prefer to be called, "financial partner." We had a full-bore presentation, complete with charts and graphs, full of impressive details. Then we spent days meeting with groups of bankers—swinging, go-anywhere, do-anything bankers; dour, pin-striped bankers; young bankers; old bankers—bankers who never could see the slightest connection between our little flower and their money.

One day was especially memorable. I had wangled an appointment with a bank known in the trade as bright, innovative, daring and ready to take a flyer. Our kind of people. They would understand.

My part of the presentation was easy. I simply stood up and told the money men all about Rickie Tickie Stickies. It's like being asked to show pictures of your children. Anytime. Anyplace.

I showed samples. A sales brochure. Sales figures to date. Cost of goods ratios. Plans for national distribution and future new products. Advertising and promotion plans. All the stuff dreams are made of.

Thirty minutes of polite, if silent, attention was extended to my little dog-and-pony show. Then came time for Ken, my accountant, to do his thing. I've always been amused by the fact that great ideas are presented vertically, like a page from this book. Financial support for those ideas, however, always appears horizontally. The cash-flow charts ran off the right-hand side of the conference table.

Ken made all kinds of sense, it seemed to me. All we were asking for was a little credit line up to a million. "Up to one million what?" was the first question after a very long silence. I don't think I've ever heard a silence quite that long.

"Dollars," Ken replied. Then all the heads around the table

WHO'S GOT THE MONEY?

swiveled back to me. "What, again exactly, Mr. Krack, was that idea of yours?"

"A gaily colored plastic flower that sticks on things, sir," I shot back. And I added that the name was Kracke, as in *Business Week*.

More silence. To this day, I'm convinced that if our product had been a small black box that could be sold to the then-flourishing aerospace industry we would have had our credit line in five minutes flat. "Financial partners" don't understand black boxes any better than you or I. But, aerospace was a good thing.

If a black box flopped, you could at least feign confusion. But a gaily colored plastic flower? How do you make excuses to your lending committee when the plastic flower you backed with a million dollars turns out to be a loser?

We tried other banks. Same pitch. Same results. No bank was at all interested in lending that kind of money without collateral. I, of course, had no collateral left to put up. All I had was a wildly successful, profitable product and the bank wasn't interested in that. It had all happened in the space of a few months and banks like to watch a product perform for a good long time before they are willing to consider making a loan on it.

In the meantime, while they're watching your product perform, of course, and you're stuck in pocketbook lag, you may even be knocked off by some competitor and you are generally under-financed, overextended and ready to turn turtle. By the time the bank has watched you long enough to be convinced that you're a success, they probably will have another problem. "You've peaked," they'll say. "Your idea was a nice novelty item, but we think that the demand is ready to slack off. We can't loan you any money on a product that will be slowly going downhill from now on."

And that will be that.

I suppose it's not really their fault. Bankers are trained to be cautious about lending money, to make sure that there's collateral backing any big loans. Their whole operation simply isn't geared to deal with a quick success. Mediocrity they can fund. A product that plods along for years with no great spurts of growth can probably find bank backing. But that kind of product usually doesn't need bank funding. They don't get caught in pocketbook lag. A product that takes off like a skyrocket needs money to fuel that growth. But that's precisely the kind of product that banks are unwilling to look at.

Let's leave banks, for the moment, and look at the other alternative I mentioned: partners. That's where I went, finally. The trouble with getting partners is that they want a share of the action in return for their investment in your product. That's not an illogical demand, but it does take some of the sweetness out of your success. Every profit dollar that rolls in has to be split up and doled out among *all* the partners. You're just one of them. You may be the major partner, but you still don't get all the profit from that marvelous idea of yours. It's a little galling. Especially when you're the one who had the idea, you're the one who's doing all the work and you're the one who's taking the biggest risk.

Still, finding partners is a viable solution. I found two partners, when the pinch really hit. And instead of getting $120,000, which would have been enough to let me finally catch up, comfortably, with the pocketbook lag, I had to settle for much less. It was big money, of course, but it wasn't big enough to make things comfortable. Knock-offs were beginning to show up and skim the biggest part of the market I was trying to reach. I needed a lot more money and a lot more distribution to catch up with them. We had been through our negotiations with Chicago Printed String, by now, so that avenue of escape was closed. It was up to us to run with the Rickie Tickie Stickies the best way we knew how. The investment by my two new partners made it possible to do that—but barely.

And in getting those two partners, I had to give away a hunk of my company. *My* company, shared with strangers! (Well, they weren't strangers. As a matter of fact, they were friends and the deal they asked for was not unreasonable, under the circumstances. I just hated to give away part of my dream.)

If you have to take on partners to keep your idea going, try to avoid giving away any more of the action than you absolutely have to. And if possible, keep open the option of buying them out at some later point in the life of your product. If your idea is going well, you may make enough money from your share of the profits to be able to buy out your partner at the current value of his share of the company.

The earlier you can buy out your partner, the better, of course. Then, as the business continues to grow, you will recoup the cost of that buy-out. For example, at the point when you buy out your partner, his share of the company may be worth $50,000. He's doing well because he's been sharing in profits all along and maybe invested only $10,000 originally. Now, as your business continues to grow, the share you bought back for $50,000 might become worth $75,000 or more. So you wind up doing well. So does he.

Obviously it's also always better to have "silent" partners—that is partners who invest money but don't participate in the management of the company. If you're doing a good job of developing your idea, you don't need any more cooks in the broth. They're unlikely to be as well versed in your business as you are, anyway, so you're better off—and they're better off—with you running things. If they weren't satisfied with the way you were handling the business, they wouldn't have invested in the first place.

There also is another kind of partner. This partner doesn't invest money, nor is he a "silent" partner. What this partner invests is his time and his expertise.

For instance, you'll need professional advertising and merchandising help to design your package, write copy for your collateral material, do your layouts for the collateral, design your letterheads and all those other technical jobs I mentioned in the chapter on merchandising.

That can be expensive. A professional copywriter or art director can command anything from twenty-five to fifty dollars an hour for his services if he or she is good. And the kind of work they do is slow. It takes a lot of time to write even a catalogue sheet or a window banner. It's not just a matter of sitting down at a typewriter and pounding out a sentence or two. Likewise, in designing packages and layouts, the work goes slowly and carefully if it is done well. To do all the little jobs I mentioned in the merchandising chapter could easily cost you several thousand dollars' worth of creative time by these professionals.

You may be able to convince them to do the work on their own, with no money coming in, if you offer them a share of your business. Needless to say, that share ought to be proportional to the amount of work they do for you. But if your product does well, they could be much better off with a share of it than with a regular fee. A job that might have brought one of them a thousand in cash might eventually bring in five or ten thousand. Gary Dahl is a writer by trade. So when he needed to have someone design the package for the Pet Rock, he offered an art director a percentage of the business as a fee for doing the work. The art director agreed and spent several days working out the design, which was excellent. By the time Gary's business grew enough to permit him to buy out that art director's share in the company, the art director got $50,000 in cash for it. That's not bad wages for a design job. Especially when you've been making $15,000 a year!

Advertising agencies often frown on letting their people do free-lance work like this, but almost every creative person I've ever met has moonlighted at one time or another. So, by getting to know someone at an advertising agency, you can get a line on who might be willing to work for you in developing your new product. Art schools, too, are a good source of technical help in this area. Either the instructors themselves or some of the advanced students in commercial art and design courses might be able to handle the job for you.

All of this is relatively insignificant, though, compared to another way you can work this same angle. Think, for a moment, about who is the most involved and most aware of your product other than yourself. Your suppliers, who else? The person who's printing your packages, the fellow who is manufacturing your product, all the people with whom you deal and to whom you have to pay money to get your product moving in the marketplace are potential sources of operating capital.

Give your printer a piece of the company in return for his services. It's probably a better deal for him than a straight cash operation in a couple of respects. First, as I said before, the value of his share in the company could become far greater than what he would have made in cash strictly as a supplier. Second, I don't know a printer anywhere who doesn't have down time on his presses. So by slipping your work into those periods of idle time in his shop, he won't even be losing regular business. He can provide you with what you need at very little cost to himself. That's an attractive deal if he has some faith in your product. And if you've been dealing with him, paying your little bills promptly and being straight with him, he's probably willing to listen to you. He's seen what has been happening, and he's probably picked up on some of your enthusiasm.

Let's face it, it's a lot easier to make one of your suppliers understand the problems you're trying to beat than it is to get a banker or an investor to understand them. Your supplier has been living with those problems every day, the same as you have. He knows the score.

Since the manufacturing of your product and the printing of your packages and so forth represents such a large portion of your expense, you can turn a share of your business into the equivalent of an enormous amount of financial backing.

Of all the different ways you can choose to put some money behind your product, this one is far and away the best of them all. It not only gives you a lot more maneuvering room in your finances, but it gives you partners who are highly motivated to help you succeed. After all, the more money you make, the more money they make. Your success is their success.

XIII
SERENDIPITY-DOO-DAH

After all the hard work is done, there's one more factor to consider: luck.

I've been doing a lot of talking about hard work and perseverance and doing your homework and keeping your nose to the grindstone and all that. It must sound like a lecture on the work ethic by now. You'll be happy to know that there's a more romantic factor involved in making a success of an invention. In all the talk about hard work, I've neglected to mention this one factor which is the most important influence on many a success story. It turns up too many times to be ignored.

The factor is luck.

Serendipity.

Chance, happenstance, coincidence, call it whatever you want. It's always waiting in the wings to make its fateful appearance on stage and change everything around. There are stories I know of that would never make it as pieces of fiction because nobody would believe them. For instance:

Some time ago I was draped over the helm of a sailboat out in the Pacific one dark and stormy night. There wasn't much chance of us winning the race anymore. In fact, we were already beginning to meet some of the boats coming back from whatever island our navigator was supposed to find.

There wasn't much left to do but think beautiful thoughts and pray for daybreak. Suddenly, I had a brilliant idea. It

SERENDIPITY-DOO-DAH

was a jacket for sailors like me—the ones who can't recall whether port is green lights or red lights, and which one is right or left? (There's a mnemonic device you can use to remember, but I forgot it.)

My sailing jacket was in two colors: the entire left side was red (I looked it up) and had the word "Port" lettered boldly on the sleeve. The entire right side was green and had the word "Starboard" lettered on the sleeve. As a real memory prompter and as a gag, it was a natural. I couldn't miss. The jacket priced out nicely, so I had some samples made and set out to make my fortune in the garment game.

After all the biggest manufacturers on my list had turned it down, I began to have nagging doubts about the success of the Port-Starboard jacket. But, eternally the optimist, I stuck a photo of the jacket into my attaché case and carried it around for months just on the off chance that some stranger on a bus might turn out to be the idea man for a leisure-wear manufacturer. In fact, I carried it around so long I almost forgot I had it.

Then one day I found myself in a meeting with a lot of Sears, Roebuck executives. We had been working on a totally unrelated project and suddenly there was a lull in the meeting. Somebody started a conversation about sailing, to pass the time. I figured that my story of the Port-Starboard jacket was probably worth a giggle, so I told it and started to describe the jacket. Then I remembered that ratty, dog-eared old photo in my attaché case, so I pulled it out and showed the people.

One woman, a market researcher, was delighted with the idea and offered to take it upstairs later on and show it to the sporting wear buyers at Sears.

You probably think you know how the story ends, but you're not quite right. Sears turned the idea down, although they said they liked it a lot. And they made a suggestion to the housewares buyer, a suggestion that she had already decided to make on her own. Both of them told me to take the jacket to a Chicago firm called Land's End—a marketer of nautical gear and attire.

Now, two people coming to the same conclusion could be a coincidence. But months earlier one of my colleagues had made the same suggestion. At the time, I simply filed the idea away in my mind for someday when things slowed down a little. Now I'd heard the very same suggestion from three separate sources. Serendipity was afoot, and I've had enough experience with luck to pay attention.

On my next trip into Chicago I paid a call to Land's End. The people there turned out to be very pleasant and very interested in my jacket. The upshot is that I've made a sale—all because of some lousy navigation and two chance conversations that happened some months and more than 2,000 miles apart.

Then there's the "Corned Beef Hash Affair."

I was in Chicago to make a presentation of my modular storage system—Neat Garage—to a manufacturer. This was going to be my big chance to finally get the idea turned into a product, and I was doing my best to talk them into giving me a nice royalty deal. I got out my portfolio with all the market estimates, sales projections, glowing descriptions and full-color 8"×10" glossy photographs of my garage before and after Neat Garage. I talked. I waved my arms. I cajoled and explained and sold. Nothing happened. The company wasn't interested.

So I packed up my traveling minstrel show, whistled up my dogs and ponies and headed back to the hotel where I was staying. By now it was well after lunch time, and I was hungry, so I dumped the presentation portfolio in my room and went back downstairs to the dining room to see if I could still get something to eat.

By this time of the day the great, cavernous dining room—it must be built to accommodate at least two hundred people—was echoing and almost empty. There were only two other people sitting down to a late lunch by the time I got there, and the hostess seated me next to one of them. I took a look at the menu and wasn't really inspired by anything I saw there. The guy next to me was working on something that looked promising, so I turned to him and asked, "What are you having?"

He looked up. "Corned beef hash," he said.

"Any good?"

"Try the omelette," he said, smiling.

I chuckled at that and pretty soon we had a conversation going. Good grief! His parents live in Palos Verdes, just about a mile from my house. We went through the whole "small world, ain't it," routine, and he asked me what I was

SERENDIPITY-DOO-DAH

doing in Chicago. I explained that I was trying to sell this marvelous idea for a modular storage system.

"Hey," he said. "That's kind of interesting. It sounds like something my company might be interested in. Tell me about it."

It turned out that he is a marketing executive for a major national building products company. Within minutes, we were back upstairs and I had dragged my whole dog-and-pony show to his room where we were poring over my portfolio of market data and pictures. He loved it. It was just the kind of thing he was looking for, so he set up an appointment for me to make my presentation to his new products committee.

A few weeks later I made a presentation to the committee. When we were done going over the details of the idea, the committee was as interested as my friend, the hash expert had been. As we go to press, they're still interested and are working out all the details to see if they can manufacture Neat Garage.

If it hadn't been for a bad batch of corned beef hash at the hotel that day, I might never have gotten into that conversation. I would never have had my shot at that new products committee. For all I know, the corned beef hash might turn out to be a million-dollar stroke of good luck disguised as bad cooking. Come to think of it, I wonder what business the other guy in the dining room was in? Supposing I'd sat next to him? I guess I'll never know.

The Serendipity Goddess put a lot of time and effort into Rickie Tickie Stickies. The idea itself was born because of a stroke of coincidence. When we were driving down that L.A. freeway and came upon those decorated cars, we might not have paid too much attention if they had appeared one at a time. But fate sent all three of them past us in a row! That was too much to ignore.

The mental wheels started rolling and the idea was born. I might never have become the Head Stickie if it hadn't been for those three specific cars showing up simultaneously at that particular spot on the freeway that day. Do you have any idea what the odds are against any three specific cars showing up together at a given spot on the freeway? I'll bet you'd be more likely to be dealt a natural royal flush in five-card poker.

The story of Polyoptics is partly a story of luck and partly a story of sticktoitiveness. Polyoptics is a company that makes those plastic strands that conduct light the way a pipe conducts water. You can shine a light on one end of the strand, then weave the strand through all kinds of complicated curves, tie knots in it and string it around corners. When you get to the other end of the strand, you've got a light shining brightly wherever you choose to point it. It's nifty and a highly creative bit of technological work.

The company had been making the strands for a number of industrial and commercial applications, but there wasn't a whole lot of demand for it. Nobody was really geared to make use of the idea, and Polyoptic's sales were pretty slow. So, to keep from going stir crazy around the office and to try to find a new outlet for the product, the company's designers worked up a table lamp for the home. It used bunches of the Polyoptic fibers to conduct light out of a hidden central source. It looked like some sort of turned-on sea anemone or a wild bunch of electronic hair on a lamp base, so it had quite a bit of novelty appeal. Some different versions of the new lamp were made and the company took them to the next trade show in San Francisco, where they hoped to break into the consumer market with this new application of their industrial product.

It began to look like a total flop when, after three days at the show, not a single sale had been made. People were staying away in droves. Finally, one store placed an order, just in time to keep Polyoptic from packing up and going home. Then another order came in. Pretty soon the trickle had grown to a respectable flow of orders, getting the product off the ground. That broke the ice.

As the lamps hit the stores and people began buying them, orders grew larger and more frequent until Polyoptic had sold literally millions of dollars' worth of lamps and was pulling in a solid profit. They even made money on the knock-offs, since they manufactured the crucial fibers. Better still, the sales of the lamps at retail began to put the strange new fibers out before the public eye. Industrial engineers and designers became aware of them in large numbers, and before long a lot of new industrial applications were being developed. So, as a rub-off from the retail sales of the lamps, the company's industrial sales began to move out smartly, too. None of it, of course, would have happened if Polyoptic had packed up and left the disappointing San Francisco trade show before the first order came in to break the ice. Needless to add, that bit of serendipity wouldn't have happened if Polyoptic hadn't stuck to its guns after three days at the show. Sometimes Lady Luck needs a little help, too.

I don't want to end this chapter leaving you feeling that somehow the Serendipty Goddess will bail you out with your idea. She won't get you out of the job of doing all that homework. You'll still have to do all the work, take all the right steps and probably spend an uncomfortable amount of money if you are really serious about making your invention a success. But every now and then, Lady Luck *does* turn up where you least expect her and she does the damndest things.

XIV
YOU HAVE REACHED ROCK BOTTOM

How the hot rock turned into a cool million in one year. The story of the Pet Rock.

Gary Dahl, the guy who gave birth to the Pet Rock, has a unique sense of humor. When you call his company, Rock Bottom Productions, the person who answers the phone says, "Good morning, you have reached Rock Bottom."

I suppose that's no longer funny to the people who have to answer the phone that way. After the fourthousandsixhundredeighteenth time, any one-liner wears a little thin. But it gives you an idea of the kind of thinking that went into the Pet Rock. Gary is a person who makes you laugh by turning something inside out and giving it back to you in a way you never thought of before. The Pet Rock is proof.

A lot of people think the Pet Rock is the greatest gag of all time—a rip-off that makes people cheer for its success. I mean, it's just a plain old rock packed in excelsior in a miniature pet-carrying case, accompanied by a training manual that's a perfect parody of every one you've ever seen. And it costs four bucks!

That's part of the turning-inside-out of it all. All of those people cheering the great rip-off are right, of course. But they're also wrong. It's not a rip-off at all. Nor is it a rock. Gary knows that the rock, the carrying case, the excelsior are all fragments of madness brought together by the training

YOU HAVE REACHED ROCK BOTTOM

manual. That's what makes the joke work. The Pet Rock is really a book, sold with some props. And that book has brought Gary well over a million dollars, paid by people who thought they were buying something else.

That's what makes it so funny, when somebody says on the phone, "You have reached Rock Bottom." Rock Bottom, hell! You've reached exactly what this whole book is all about. You have reached a man who had an idea, took risks, worked hard and made it a success. You also have reached the richest man in town.

Maybe being the richest man in all of Los Gatos isn't terribly impressive, but it sure beats working for wages, living in an 800-square-foot rented house and paying big bills. That's where Gary was before the rock. In less than one year, Gary Dahl went from being a bill-burdened working stiff to being a millionaire and then some. Today, Gary has a Mercedes and a grand new house where the swimming pool is bigger than the place he lived in when it all began.

The Pet Rock was born on April Fool's Day, 1975, in a bar in Los Gatos, California. The bar isn't anything to get excited about, but it's a congenial sort of joint and on that night there was a raucous crowd sitting around a couple of tables toward the back of the room. The crowd had drifted in after work—some of them from a small advertising agency in town. Gary, a young fellow with a bushy beard, was one of those admen. He was pouring a glass of beer and laughing at the conversation, which had gotten onto the topic of pets. People were telling all sorts of outrageous stories about their dogs and cats.

Gary slid into one of the chairs and somebody asked, "Hey, have you got a pet?"

"Oh, hell yeah," he replied with a grin. "I got a pet rock, man. Real easy to take care of and cheap, too. Never have to feed him or anything. Plus he's smart. Knows all kinds of tricks. He can lie down and play dead, he can roll over, and he can do all that stuff."

That cracked them up. Pretty soon everybody was picking up on the thread of the idea and throwing out wilder and weirder things that pet rocks are good for. Everybody was laughing and scratching over it. But Gary wasn't laughing quite so hard anymore. In fact, he was beginning to do some heavy thinking. He went home that night musing about the possibility of actually doing something with that crazy idea of a pet rock.

He spent much of the next two weeks at the typewriter, hammering out his parody of the pet-training manual. In between writing sessions, he began making decisions—all of which turned out to be right. Gary had no more experience at inventing things than you do. What's more, he didn't even have a book to guide him. He was just instinctively figuring out all the steps he'd have to go through if he wanted to make a success of his oddball idea.

The very first decision he made was probably the smartest of them all. He decided that every rock had to put at least one dollar in his jeans. In other words, he built his cost figures backward, starting with the profit and letting everything else fall into place accordingly. It worked because the Pet Rock would be able to command a price far beyond its actual, physical worth. (Remember when we talked about "value pricing" in the chapter on "Doing Your Homework"?)

It's instructive to take a look at an analysis of his cost-of-goods figures. These are my own estimates, based on some of the things Gary told me and some things I've calculated myself. I think they're pretty accurate.

I know from Gary that the rock costs a penny. When he started out, he went to a builder's supply place in San Jose and discovered that there are all kinds of different grades of gravel available. So he spent some time pawing through bins of rocks, trying to decide on what would be the best pet.

"I didn't want just any old rock. It had to be something special," he explains. He finally decided on the most expensive rock in the house—a size-graded, uniform variety called "Rosarita Beach Stone." It cost a whole penny apiece. (He's a practical man, by the way. He chose that rock in part because it was size-graded, so he wouldn't wind up with a pile of slag after he was done. He could use nearly every rock in the order.)

During the course of the publicity avalanche that followed the rock's success, Gary put out a lot of tongue-in-cheek information, including a story that his people went personally to Rosarita Beach in Baja, Mexico, to test each rock for obedience before selecting it. He also advised reporters to buy property in Bakersfield, California, because by the time he was done, that was going to be valuable beachfront property.

YOU HAVE REACHED ROCK BOTTOM

(Bakersfield is way out in the hot, dusty inland part of California.) But the reality of the matter is that the rock came from far-off exotic San Jose, a truck load at a time being brought up from the Baja.

Okay, so the rock is a penny. Gary also told me that the booklet costs six and a half cents, now that it is being printed in large quantities. (The last order was a million books.) The excelsior packing probably costs two cents. The box costs four cents. That's a total hard cost-of-goods of $.135.

Add to that an estimated 10 per cent interest on the money borrowed from a friend to finance the operation, or another 1.3 cents per unit. It probably costs Gary $.30 for sales commission (15 per cent of the $2.00 wholesale price) and there's probably another $.40 in there for G.&A. costs—overhead, publicity, travel, all the other expenses of being in business. Finally, he's paying something like $.04 each to have the rock packed in the box with the book and the excelsior.

That's a total of $.888. Gary's factory selling price is $2.00 each, which means he's getting over a dollar per rock in profit—the target number he started out with. More important than the fact that he built that profit margin into the price is the fact that he's *getting* it. His retail price is right for the market, allowing him that kind of profit per unit.

In the spring of 1975, Gary had a price structure and a draft of the training manual parody. Now he had to figure out exactly how to go about packing and selling the Pet Rock. He needed a design for the box, for one thing—something that would say "pet" at first glance, something that would fit his cost ratios, something that would help sell the product. He also needed a layout for the booklet, plus illustrations. But he had no cash to pay out for that kind of work, so he did what I talked about in the chapter on "Who's Got the Money." He offered a piece of the action to an art director friend, Pat Welch, if Pat would do the design and artwork for him. He offered him a percentage of the deal for it. (As I noted earlier, by the time Gary bought out Pat's share, it was worth $50,000—enough for Pat to pay off his bills, quit his job and retire for a couple of years, Gary says.)

Although there were a couple of redesigns along the way, the box and the booklet are still basically the way Pat first laid them out. After a few weeks, they had some prototypes of the product and Gary began working on how to distribute the rocks. He heard that there was a trade show in San Francisco coming up in August, so Gary took his prototypes to a manufacturers' rep there and asked if he would carry the Pet Rock and put it in the show. The rep laughed, but finally said, "What the hell, it won't take up much room. Sure, I'll give it a try."

By the time of the trade show, Gary had spent a total of maybe $500 on the idea—making prototypes, going to San Francisco and so forth. He hadn't started manufacturing yet, although he had set the type for the boxes and the booklet. He had his prototype samples to sell with. He was going to hold off until he saw the response from the trade show before he plunged ahead. That's called market research. Any orders taken at the show were to be for October delivery, giving him a couple of months to crank up production. He was being cautious.

At the San Francisco show, it was his rep's number-one best seller. Some 3,000 orders were taken, and Gary began to suspect that he might have a viable product on his hands. But he was still playing close to the chest. He decided to put the Pet Rock into the New York trade show later that same month, before making any irrevocable decisions. Again, it was a success. Although the prototypes arrived three days late and so had only two days of exposure at the New York trade show, another 1,500 orders were taken. It was decision time.

Gary was still unsure, though. It was one of several times in the life of the Pet Rock that Gary came very close to backing out of the whole thing. He could think of a million reasons why the rock wouldn't sell, he said. The thing that tipped him over the edge and sent him hurtling on to fame and fortune was one order. In the midst of his deliberation, an order came in from Neiman-Marcus, in Texas, for 500 Pet Rocks. That did it. Gary ordered some books and boxes and rocks and excelsior. He was in the manufacturing business.

"We went on the hook for ten thousand units," Gary said. He went to see his ex-employer at an advertising agency he had left two years earlier, and asked for two things—a loan, and the use of some office space. He got both. By the end of October, all 10,000 rocks had sold and orders were beginning to flood his operation.

At this point, he was still trying to run a "mom and pop" business. His wife, Marguerite, was at home typing up orders all day, working as a cocktail waitress at night. Gary was spending his lunch hours licking mailing labels, sticking them on shipping cartons and waiting around for the U.P.S. truck. That didn't last long, under the pressure of the growing business. By the end of October, orders were coming in at the rate of 10,000 a day, and Gary had to quit his job. That wasn't easy because everyone at the news agency tried hard to talk him out of it. "Why give up a solid job for some crazy flash-in-the-pan idea?" they kept asking him.

"Finally, one day I just showed up at the office with a big cardboard box and started packing up my stuff," Gary said. "They came up and asked, 'Why do we get the impression that you're leaving?'"

Gary used what he called the "World War I" theory of business. "As the pressure increased, we just threw more bodies in front of the machine guns," he explained. "We just kept hiring more and more part-time people as we needed them. At one point we had twelve girls working full time all day, every day, just typing invoices."

Packaging was getting completely beyond the capability of Gary, his wife and their friends, so he came to the same decision Margaret and I came to with the Stickies. He went to a sheltered workshop—in his case it was Hope Workshop, an organization for the mentally handicapped. It worked out just as well for him as our arrangement with Goodwill Industries worked out for us. By the end of the Christmas season, the workers were packing thousands of rocks a day to keep up with the demand.

In the meantime, he had outstripped the capabilities of his local printer so he was ordering boxes and books from Los Angeles. A box manufacturer there also altered the box design slightly. The new one looks identical to the original box, but instead of having to be folded together, this one simply snaps open to accept the rock, the book and the packing on the assembly line, making possible those thousands of units a day.

With the business growing completely out of control, there were strange occurrences nearly every day. Once some store back East ordered 72 Pet Rocks, then placed a panic-stricken call to Gary when the order arrived. Instead of 72 rocks, they got 72 *cases* or 1,728 rocks, and they had no idea what to do. "I guess one of the girls here misread the order, or maybe the handwriting was really bad or something," Gary said. "I told 'em to keep the rocks. They'd sell 'em all."

And they did.

Another time, shortly after Christmas, the May Co. Department Stores returned 3,000 rocks, afraid they had grossly overbought. Less than a week later, May Co. ordered 5,000 more.

Amid all the mishaps and confusion, there was also a stroke of unbelievably good luck. Warehousing of the Pet Rocks in their existing facilities was impossible, in the quantities that were being handled during the Christmas season. So throughout the whole month of December, thousands and thousands of boxed Pet Rocks stood in stacks out in the open, with no shelter from the weather. And for the first time in anyone's memory, not one drop of rain fell in Los Gatos during the whole month of December—usually the rainy season in that part of California!

The pace of sales was so hectic that it wasn't until the spring of 1976 that Gary was able to sit down and figure out just exactly how many Pet Rocks he *did* sell. It was well over a million. Now one of his biggest problems is how to deal with all the money. Somehow he has to make some investments and put some of it under shelter from the Internal Revenue Service.

"I've hired a business manager, a show-business guy who works with people who make a lot of money in a short time. In the meantime, I've got money stuck in savings and loans all over this whole county. All over the Bay Area, in fact," he said.

Gary isn't very complimentary about the average accountant and business manager. He had hired one man at the beginning of the Pet Rock's success, just to watch over his earnings and do what he could to protect them. One day the man walked into Gary's office and cheerfully announced, "Well, I guess you'll have to write a check to Uncle Sam for half a million dollars, Gary, but look at it this way, you'll have half a million dollars left for yourself." Gary's reply was succinct:

"You're fired."

Why should he simply acquiesce to the government taking away half of everything he's been able to make? After all, it's the most silent partner you'll ever have. Especially if your idea and *your* money go down the tube. The number-one project of the new business manager is to make sure that no more money than is necessary goes into taxes. Gary's not trying to avoid his responsibilities, but on the other hand he's not volunteering to do more than his share, either.

Now that sanity has begun to creep back in, Gary has had time to look back on it all and put it into some kind of perspective.

"You know, when I started out I figured I had a good novelty-gift idea. As it turned out, I had an international phenomenon. My own best guess was that I'd be damn happy to sell 100,000 units. And I would have been happy, too. That would have been enough money to pay off all my bills and set me up for a good long time."

Part of the reason for his success was that the whole Pet Rock phenomenon was such a happy story. It was, in fact, a Horatio Alger story of a poor boy making good. The press helped it along enormously by jumping on the story and getting a sort of bandwagon effect going with the goal, as Gary says, of "making Dahl a millionaire by Christmas."

On Christmas Eve, news photographers took pictures of Gary holding up the millionth Pet Rock. It had worked. The poor boy had made good. He was a millionaire by Christmas.

Actually, that was a little bit of media hype, Gary now admits. He really has no idea what day the millionth Pet Rock was sold. But that's part of the success story. He never spent a nickel in advertising. All the notoriety that came his way came from publicity, not advertising. And there was plenty of publicity.

It started when Gary sent out a press release to the news magazines in the fall of 1975, when he was underway and sales were beginning to pick up. *Newsweek* latched onto the release and gave Gary and his Pet Rock almost half a page in November, including a picture. From that point on, there was no stopping the tide of news and feature stories about the crazy new gift item.

By Christmas there had been interviews on more than three hundred radio stations, there had been stories in 1,400 of the approximately 1,800 daily newspapers in America, he had appeared on all of the major television networks at least once and even the BBC had done a series of interviews. (That's because Gary had licensed an entrepreneur in England to sell the Pet Rock there. The original shipment included 4,000 complete units, rocks and all. Those were sold out immediately at the Birmingham trade show. Now Gary simply sends boxes, folded flat, and books. The rocks and the excelsior are from the realm.)

As you might expect, there have been a bunch of knock-offs trying to cash in on Gary's success. Some of them are marketing their own pet rocks, including one which bills itself as "The Original Pet Rock." Some are trying to market spin-offs, like Pet Rock Stud Service, Pet Rock Obedience Lessons. There's even a Pet Rock Burial-at-Sea Service! Together, all of them are scrambling for about 5 per cent of the market, according to Gary's estimate.

There are several reasons the knock-offs have been so unsuccessful. For one thing, Gary has been careful from the very start to make a connection between himself, Gary Dahl, and the Pet Rock. He is the original, his is the real thing. And it has worked.

Another reason for his success in beating the knock-offs actually began as a stroke of bad luck. The Pet Rock got off to a very late start for the 1975 Christmas season. He was delivering in October. A lot of the business has already been done by that late date. It worked out to his advantage, though, because the rock took off so quickly and over such a short period of time that the knock-offs really couldn't get cranked up in time to make the Christmas season once they saw Gary's rock was becoming a smash hit.

Most important of all, though, is that Gary got there firstest with the mostest. He built up a nationwide network of reps very early, so that he was able to flood the market quickly and reap all the sales before the knock-offs could match his distribution. It was a beautiful example of what we talked about in "The Plaintive Plaintiff" chapter:

An idea is *some*thing.

Distribution is *every*thing.

Gary went through the proper motions in getting legal protection, but he's very unimpressed with its value. "I've got a design patent, the box and the book are copyrighted, and the trademark is registered. I'm covered here and in Canada and in England. But I'm sure getting tired of paying a lot of legal fees that don't do me any good in defending myself." An example of the kind of results he's had in depending on his legal protection happened in the state of Washington. Someone

YOU HAVE REACHED ROCK BOTTOM

there had made a photocopy of Gary's Pet Rock box—right down to the copyright symbol. This person was marketing the counterfeit box and pet rocks and even going so far as to claim to merchants that he was working for Gary. Gary and his lawyer went up and talked to the local district attorney, who discouraged them from prosecuting, despite the fact that it was not only copyright infringement, but probably fraud as well.

A few days after Gary returned to Los Gatos, his clipping service sent him a story from the papers in Seattle. The district attorney had called a press conference to make a statement about some weirdo from California coming up and trying to make trouble for a local citizen with some lawsuit. The D.A. said that Gary must have "rocks in his head." Yuk yuk. Gary was unamused.

How has all the fame and money affected Gary's life? Not an awful lot, really. The house and the car, of course, are new. But he doesn't dress any differently or act any differently than before, when he was just another copywriter. It has changed some of his relationships, though.

"My wife came home one night, crying," he said. "She'd been at a public function, and there was a very close friend of hers, a girl she'd worked with long before any of this happened. And the girl had snubbed her completely. That was really hard to take. I suppose maybe the girl was insecure and didn't know what to say to her, but it hurt a lot."

On the other hand, there are a lot of friends who haven't changed a bit. "Most of 'em are the same as ever. In fact, they're happy we've got that new house with a pool, because they can come up and swim there," he said, grinning.

I thought I'd leave you with Gary's story, after spending the thirteen previous chapters talking about all the hard work you were going to have to do. Maybe you won't make a million dollars with your first idea. Or your second. Or maybe you won't make a million dollars ever. But you'll never know until you try. The very worst fate I could imagine—the awfulest thing that can happen to you—is to fail because you didn't take a chance at it.

It *can* be done. You *can* have a million-dollar idea. All it takes is some time, some work and some luck. Do it! Get out there and be another Gary Dahl. Have your run at marketing your idea. And whenever things begin to look impossible, when it seems there's just no way you can make your idea work out, think about this:

When I was walking out of Gary Dahl's office the last time, he was leaning back in his chair, looking like a kid with a new toy and telling me,

"I've got four more ideas. Wait'll you see 'em!"

APPENDIX I THE INVENTOR'S CHECKLIST

Here is a chronological listing of the steps you should follow when an idea pops into your head. At several points in the checklist, you will be confronted with GO/NO GO decisions. These are the points at which this checklist could save big money. Your money. Relevant chapters are noted at most steps.

Is there a guarantee that if you follow this outline faithfully to its logical conclusion, you will make money with your idea?

No!

However, if you follow this outline, are you guaranteed that your idea will have been given the best possible chance of success?

Yes!

☐ 1. Have the idea (Ch. I).

☐ 2. Start a diary listing every action you take along the way, and have it notarized periodically.

☐ 3. Evaluate your idea for need, desirability and profitability (Ch. II).

☐ 4. Do some testing of the idea, either on your own or by hiring professionals to back up your own evaluation (Chs. II, V, VI).

GO/NO GO

If, at this point, your idea can't cut it, it's a good time to stop and get another idea. If you're still convinced you've got another Pet Rock, keep going regardless.

☐ 5. Work out the physical design by making a model, prototype or sample run (Ch. VI).

☐ 6. Determine your "cost of goods" including materials, labor, packaging, plus such one-time costs as package design, production art, special dies or molds, etc. (Ch. VI).

☐ 7. Select the primary method of distribution for your product (Chs. VI, VII).

☐ 8. Set up your own "knock off plan" for selling the same product under different names through different distribution systems (Chs. VI, VII, XI).

☐ 9. Plug the costs of each system of distribution you'll be using, into your cost calculations (Ch. VI).

☐ 10. Arrive at your wholesale and retail price (Chs. VI, VII).

GO/NO GO

If everyone along the line of distribution can't make the kind of money he normally expects, this is the next place to consider stopping. Or at least weeding out the distribution channels that don't seem to make sense for your product.

☐ 11. Apply for a patent, copyright or (if applicable) trademark registration (Chs. III, IV).

GO/NO GO

If it turns out to be a protectable idea, move on. If not, but you think you can get massive distribution quickly, move on. If it is not protectable and you don't think you can saturate the market before the idea thieves notice you ... do some soul searching before deciding to continue.

THE INVENTOR'S CHECKLIST

☐ 12. Watch out for the rip-offs. They get their mailing lists from the patent applications, among other places, and they'll be getting in touch with you (Ch. V).

☐ 13. Prepare your presentation. You'll certainly need it for selling your idea to a manufacturer. You may also want it to use in the search for financial backing (Chs. VIII, XII).

☐ 14. Choose the manufacturers to whom you will try to sell your idea (Chs. II, VII, X).

☐ 15. Find out who is in charge of "new product ideas" at those companies and call or write them. Don't be discouraged if that person tries to talk you out of even trying (Ch. II).

☐ 16. If all else fails, say that your idea is already in the mail.

☐ 17. Then run like hell to the post office.

☐ 18. Request a copy of the target company's "idea submission form" and sign it. It marks you as a professional (Ch. VIII).

☐ 19. Note in your "idea diary" the names of all the people you contact and the companies they work for (See Step 2 in this checklist).

☐ 20. Plan what demands you will make, what deals you will accept in your negotiations with a manufacturer (Ch. X).

☐ 21. Negotiate. If they agree to buy your idea, ask *them* to prepare the contract and let *your* attorney review it. That saves you some money, and if they're interested in your idea, they won't mind (Ch. X).

GO/NO GO
If nobody is interested in your idea after your whole sales pitch is given, it's time to consider abandoning the idea

and getting a new one. On the other hand, if you're still convinced you have a viable concept, take the next big plunge.

☐ 22. Set the wheels in motion for a limited, local test-marketing sales effort (Ch. VII).

☐ 23. Try to use "leverage" by getting a major distributor on your side (Ch. IX).

GO/NO GO
At this point, money definitely rears its ugly head. If you can't finance the local test marketing, and if you can't get financial backing or leverage on your side, bail out. If you can lubricate the financial wheels somehow, keep moving!

☐ 24. Produce a prototype run of your product—enough for a reasonable number of reorders (Chs. VII, XII).

☐ 25. Produce your merchandising tools (Ch. XI).

☐ 26. Start selling, either on your own or with reps (Ch. VII).

☐ 27. Record your sales results and the amount of play your publicity gets. Consider using a clipping service to keep track of the "ink" you get (Chs. II, VII, XI).

☐ 28. Wait six months. (It takes that long to get a good idea of sales performance, unless your idea takes off like a rocket.)

GO/NO GO
If the public reaction to your publicity and your product is a giant yawn, perhaps this is a good time to think of a new idea. If, however, your product is performing respectably, move on.

☐ 29. Try to sell your idea to a manufacturer again, using your test-market performance as a major selling point in your up-dated presentation. Go back to some of the people

THE INVENTOR'S CHECKLIST

who turned you down before, as well as some new people.

☐ 30. Revise your notion of the deal you'd accept. With hard sales performance, you can afford to ask for more (Ch. X).

☐ 31. If some manufacturer buys your idea, have *your* attorney prepare the contract and let *their* attorney review it. You'll be putting their feet to the fire this time, so your man ought to write out the terms. Just don't be too greedy (Ch. X).

GO/NO GO

If you still can't find a buyer for your idea, you have a really tough decision to make: Should you take the plunge and roll out nationally on your own? Or is this the time to pack up your grits and gravy and shuffle back to the drawing board?

☐ 32. If you're still game, analyze the costs of a full-scale national rollout, including the costs of staffing up, of a national sales program and of market support (Chs. VI, VII).

GO/NO GO

If you can't afford it, the game is over. Deal out a new hand and go back to Square One. If you can afford it, or you can get leverage or financial backing to make it possible, get back into the fray!

☐ 33. Rewrite your marketing plan, including one- two- and three-year sales projections. Work out cash-flow charts. Reanalyze your distribution channels (Chs. VII, VIII).

☐ 34. Roll out.

The ultimate GO/NO GO is now riding on public reaction to your product. If it's "GO" and you succeed—smile a lot. You've earned it. And get to work on your next idea.

If it's "NO GO" and your idea fails—cry a little. You've earned it. And get to work on your next idea.

Good luck! From those of us who have succeeded. From those of us who have failed. From all of the above.

APPENDIX II SOURCES

Nearly every business or trade in the world has its own special publication. These trade journals can be a great source of information on what's going on in the field your invention fits into, sources of materials and manufacturing equipment, lots of other things you'll need. Herewith, then, is a listing of some of the more prominent source publications. It is not exhaustive, but it's a beginning.

Advertising & Marketing

MAC, Western Advertising News (wkly.)
6565 Sunset Boulevard
Los Angeles, Calif. 90028

Catalog Showroom Business (mo.)
1515 Broadway
New York, N.Y. 10036
(catalogue showroom industry)

Incentive Marketing (Incorporating Premium Travel)
633 Third Avenue
New York, N.Y. 10017
(premium incentive merchandising)

Innovation World (quar.)
230 Park Avenue
New York, N.Y. 10017
(no ads ... marketing of new products)

Premium Incentive Business (mo.)
1515 Broadway
New York, N.Y. 10036
(advertising premiums)

Canadian Advertising Rates & Data (mo.)
481 University Avenue
Toronto, Can.
(Rate & Data information)

Automotive Trade

Auto Merchandising News (mo.)
1188 Main Street, Suite 500
Bridgeport, Conn. 06604
(automotive)

NTDRA Dealer News (wkly.)
1343 L Street, NW
Washington, D.C. 20005
(tire dealers)

Automotive Aftermarket News (mo.)
300 West Lake Street
Chicago, Ill. 60606
(news for auto jobbers & salesmen)

Jobber Topics (mo.)
7300 N. Cicero Avenue
Lincolnwood, Ill. 60646
(auto jobber & warehouse distributors)

Jobber & Warehouse Executive (mo.)
53 West Jackson
Chicago, Ill. 60604
(auto warehousing & jobbing)

Automotive News
965 East Jefferson Avenue
Detroit, Mich. 48207
(auto industry)

SOURCES

Ward's Auto World (mo.)
28 West Adams
Detroit, Mich. 48226
(auto industry)

Autoproducts Magazine (mo.)
21590 Greenfield Road
Oak Park, Mich. 48237
(motor vehicle original equipment marketing)

Motor (mo.)
250 West 55th Street
New York, N.Y. 10019
(auto trade)

Automotive Chain Store (mo.)
11 South Forge Street
Akron, Ohio 44304
(auto supplies)

Modern Tire Dealer (mo.)
P. O. Box 5417
Akron, Ohio 44313
(tire & car service)

Speed & Custom Dealer (mo.)
11 South Forge Street
Akron, Ohio 44304
(automotive)

Tire Review (mo.)
11 South Forge Street
Akron, Ohio 44304
(tire dealer news)

Warehouse Distributor News (mo.)
11 South Forge Street
Akron, Ohio 44304

Automotive Industries/International (mo.)
Chilton Way
Radnor, Pa. 19089
(Automotive Original Equipment Market)
Also same w/o "International" same data (s-mo.)

Automotive Marketing (5 times a year)
Chilton Way
Radnor, Pa. 19089
(automotive mass retailing)

Motor Age (mo.)
Chilton Way
Radnor, Pa. 19089
(automotive maintenance & service)

Chain & Variety Stores

Chain Store Age (mo.)
2 Park Avenue
New York, N.Y. 10016
(chain stores in all fields)

The Discount Merchandiser (mo.)
641 Lexington Avenue
New York, N.Y. 10022

Discount Store News (bi-wkly.)
2 Park Avenue
New York, N.Y. 10016

Non-Foods Merchandising (mo.)
124 East 40th Street
New York, N.Y. 10016
(supermarket general merchandising)

Retail Directions (9 times a yr.)
48 East 43rd Street
New York, N.Y. 10017
(department store management)

Sew Business (mo.)
127 Avenue of Americas, Suite 3560
New York, N.Y. 10020
(sewing, notions, variety stores)

Automotive Chain Store (mo.)
11 South Forge Street
Akron, Ohio 44304
(auto supplies)

Clothing

Men's News (wkly.)
1016 South Broadway Place
Los Angeles, Calif. 90015
(garment industry)

Men's Week (s-mo.)
1016 South Broadway Place
Los Angeles, Calif. 90015
(men's retailing apparel)

Needle's Eye (bi-mo.)
404 North Franklin Street
Chicago, Ill. 60610
(sewing industry)

Daily News Record (dly.)
7 E. 12th Street
New York, N.Y. 10003
(men's & boys' clothing and textiles)

Men's Wear Magazine (s-mo)
7 E. 12th Street
New York, N.Y. 10003
(men's & boys' clothing and furnishings)

California Apparel News (wkly.)
1016 Broadway Place
Los Angeles, Calif. 90015
(women's apparel industry)

Homesewing Trade News (mo.)
129 Broadway
Lynbrook, N.Y. 11563
(home-sewing industry)

Women's Wear Daily (dly.)
7 E. 12th Street
New York, N.Y. 10003
(women's & children's apparel, home sewing, textiles)

Conventions and Fairs

Association & Society Manager (bi-mo.)
825 S. Barrington Avenue
Los Angeles, Calif. 90049
(association management)

Meetings and Conventions (mo.)
1 Park Avenue
New York, N.Y. 10016
(business meetings & conferences)

Meetings and Expositions (mo.)
10 E. 39th Street
New York, N.Y. 10016
(conventions)

Successful Meetings
1422 Chestnut Street
Philadelphia, Pa. 19102
(conventions, meetings & exhibits)

Cordage and Twine

Paper & Twine Journal (mo.)
1860 Broadway
New York, N.Y. 10023
(industrial paper representatives)

Dry Goods

Stores (mo.)
100 West 31st Street
New York, N.Y. 10001
(retailing management)

Electrical

The Electrical Distributor (mo.)
111 Prospect Street
Stanford, Conn. 06901

Battery Man (mo.)
100 Larchwood Drive
Largo, Fla. 33540
(battery electrical parts trade)

Electrical Wholesaling (mo.)
1221 Avenue of the Americas
New York, N.Y. 10020

Merchandising Weekly (wkly.)
1 Astor Plaza
New York, N.Y. 10036
(appliances, housewares)

EE-Electrical Equipment (mo.)
172 South Broadway
White Plains, N.Y. 10605
(electrical manufacturing & Industrial electrical marketing)

Audio
134 North 13th Street
Philadelphia, Pa. 19107
(sound & communication)

General Merchandise

Camping Products Merchandising (bi-mo.)
1718 Sherman Avenue
Evanston, Ill. 60201

Modern Retailer (mo.)
50 Hunt Street
Watertown, Mass. 02172
(discount & self-service stores)

National Mall Monitor (bi-mo.)
Pennsauken, N.J. 08110
(shopping-center industry)

Shopping Center World (mo.)
461 8th Avenue
New York, N.Y. 10001
(shopping-center industry)

214 HOW TO TURN YOUR IDEA INTO A MILLION DOLLARS

Stores (mo.)
100 West 31st Street
New York, N.Y. 10001
(retailing management)

Gifts, Toys, Novelties

Gift and Tableware Reporter (s-mo.)
165 West 46th Street
New York, N.Y. 10036
(gifts, art goods, china & glass)

Gifts and Decorative Accessories (mo.)
51 Madison Avenue
New York, N.Y. 10010

Greetings Magazine (mo.)
95 Madison Avenue
New York, N.Y. 10016
(card, stationery, novel gift suppliers & retailers)

Toy and Hobby World (mo.)
124 East 40th Street
New York, N.Y. 10016

Hardware

Pool News (s-mo.)
3923 West 6th Street
Los Angeles, Calif. 90020
(swimming pool trade)

Swimming Pool Weekly/S.P. Age (wkly.)
P. O. 11299
Ft. Lauderdale, Fla. 33306

Southern Hardware (mo.)
1760 Peachtree Road
Atlanta, Ga. 30309
(hardware)

Sports Merchandiser (mo.)
1760 Peachtree Road
Atlanta, Ga. 30309

SOURCES

Hardlines Wholesaling (6 times a yr.)
7300 North Cicero Avenue
Lincolnwood, Ill. 60646
(wholesale hardware)

Hardware Merchandiser (mo.)
7300 North Cicero Avenue
Lincolnwood, Ill. 60646
(home-improvement merchandise centers)

Locksmith Ledger (mo.)
2720 Des Plaines Avenue
Des Plaines, Ill. 60018
(physical security)

Hardware Retailing (mo.)
964 North Pennsylvania Street
Indianapolis, Ind. 46204
(hardware, building material)

New England Home Supply (mo.)
P. O. Box 146
Hingham, Mass. 02043
(hardware, home supplies)

Northern Hardware Trade (mo.)
5901 Brooklyn Boulevard, Suite 203
Minneapolis, Minn. 55429
(hardware & sporting goods)

Tack 'n Toys (mo.)
P. O. Box 67
2501 Waygata Boulevard
Minneapolis, Minn. 55440
(marketers of products for horse & rider)

Snow Goer Trade (5 times a yr.)
1999 Shepard Road
St. Paul, Minn. 55116
(snowmobile trade)

Hardware Age (mo.)
Chilton Way
Radnor, Pa. 19089
(hardware trade)

Hardware Merchandising (mo.)
481 University Avenue
Toronto, Ontario, Can.
(hardware trade)

Le Quincaillier (mo.)
481 University Avenue
Toronto, Ontario, Can.
(hardware trade—*en Française*)

Home Furnishings

Budget Decorating & Remodeling (bi-mo.)
699 Madison Avenue
New York, N.Y. 10021
(home furnishings)

Home Furnishings Daily (dly.)
7 East 12th Street
New York, N.Y. 10003
(home furnishings)

Housewares (mo.)
757 3rd Avenue
New York, N.Y. 10017
(housewares, home furnishings & electrical)

Home Goods Retailing (mo.)
481 University Avenue
Toronto, Ontario, Can.
(house furnishings)

Indexes to Periodicals, Books, Pamphlets

Business Service Checklist (wkly.)
U.S. Dept. of Commerce
Office of Publications
Washington, D.C.
(list of news releases, reports, periodicals of Dept. of Commerce)

Applied Science & Technology Index (mo.)
950 University Avenue,
Bronx, N.Y. 10452

Business Periodical Index (mo.)
950 University Avenue
Bronx, N.Y. 10452

Vertical File Index (mo.)
950 University Avenue
Bronx, N.Y. 10452
(pamphlet index)

Lighting & Lighting Fixtures

Home Lighting & Accessories (mo.)
1115 Clifton Avenue
Clifton, N.J. 07013

Lighting Design & Application (mo.)
345 E. 47th Street
New York, N.Y. 10017

Lighting Systems (bi-mo.)
P. O. Box 188
S. Milwaukee, Wis. 53172

Machinery

Plastics Machinery & Equipment (mo.)
1129 E. 17th Avenue
Denver, Colo. 80218

Modern Applications News for Design and Manufacturing
  (bi-mo.)
1282 Old Skokie Road
Highland Park, Ill. 60035

Mail Order Trade

Progressive Mail Trade (mo.)
Box 1302
Springfield, Ill. 62705

Small Business Digest (quar.)
P. O. Box 839
Long Beach, N.Y. 11561

Notions

Souvenirs and Novelties (6 times a yr.)
Bldg. 30, 20-21 Wagaraw Road
Fair Lawn, N.J. 07410

Packaging

Western Material Handling/Packaging/Shipping (bi-mo.)
606 N. Larchmont Boulevard
Los Angeles, Calif. 90004

Good Packaging (mo.)
1313 E. Julian Street
San Jose, Calif. 95116

Package Printing & Diecutting (mo.)
41 E. 42nd Street
New York, N.Y. 10017

Packaging Digest (mo.)
1120 Chester Avenue
Cleveland, Ohio 44114

Pets

Pet Age (mo.)
2561 N. Clark Street
Chicago, Ill. 60614

Pets/Supplies/Marketing (mo.)
1 E. 1st Street
Duluth, Minn. 55802

Plastic and Composition Materials

Plastics Engineering (mo.)
656 W. Putnam Avenue
Greenwich, Conn. 06830

Boxboard Containers (mo.)
300 W. Adams Street
Chicago, Ill. 60606
(packaging industry)

Package Engineering (mo.)
5 S. Wabash Avenue
Chicago, Ill. 60603
(package design and production)

Paper, Film and Foil Converter (mo.)
200 S. Prospect Avenue
Park Ridge, Ill. 60068
(package industry)

Package Development (bi-mo.)
P. O. Box 225
Briarcliff-Manor, N.Y. 10510
(package design & production)

Modern Packaging (mo.)
1221 Avenue of the Americas
New York, N.Y. 10020
(package industry)

Plastics Design & Processing (mo.)
700 Peterson Road
Libertyville, Ill. 60048
(Plastics processes)

Plastic Materials & Machinery (bi-mo.)
221 Columbus Avenue
Boston, Mass. 02116
(Plastics machinery)

Plastic World (mo.)
221 Columbus Avenue
Boston, Mass. 02116

Modern Plastics (mo.)
1221 Avenue of the Americas
New York, N.Y. 10020

Plastics Technology (13 times a yr.)
633 Third Avenue
New York, N.Y. 10017
(Plastics industry)

APPENDIX III A TYPICAL MARKETING PLAN

The following is an outline of the marketing plan used by Sears, Roebuck and Co., for any new product in its line. It asks the questions any manufacturer or marketer will want to know about *your* product when they're considering selling it. You ought to know the answers to all of these questions, if you plan to make a sale.

I. How does the idea fit into the existing product category? (In other words, why is there an opening for such a product in the line, how will consumers perceive it, how does it find its place in the existing line?)

II. Where does the new product fit into the existing channels of distribution?
   A. CATALOGUE/RETAIL The ones you and I know about already.
   B. COMMERCIAL Most of us aren't aware of it, but Sears sells to commercial users of products, too.
   C. INDUSTRIAL Many Sears products are bought and used by industry. One example is Sears' "Craftsman" line of hand tools—wrenches, hammers, chisels and the like.
   D. SERVICE CENTERS For every group of retail outlets, Sears has a service center to maintain and repair what it sells. These centers are also retail outlets for products, including replacement parts.
   E. EXPORT Yes, Sears sells overseas, too.

III. Sales and Profit Objectives.
   A. How many units does Sears plan to sell? For how much?

A TYPICAL MARKETING PLAN

IV. Marketing Strategy.
   A. POSITIONING Top of the line? Cheapest? Most versatile?
   B. PRICING STRUCTURE Are there de luxe and standard models? At what prices do these sell?
   C. GEOGRAPHY If it makes a difference where the product is sold, where *will* it be sold? A new kind of snow shovel might be a gas in Minneapolis and a bomb in Phoenix, for instance.
   D. COMPETITIVE REBOUND Will the competition react strongly? How soon will they come out with a similar product? How similar? Will it be lower or higher priced, and how can Sears counter their move? In short, how long can Sears expect to have an exclusive on the new product, and what should Sears expect to have to do when the competition moves in?

V. Tactics.
   A. ADVERTISING AND PROMOTION EXPENDITURES How much?
   B. NAILING DOWN OF ALL DETAILS When will the product be introduced? Will it roll out on a geographic basis or on a calendar basis or what? Where should the product be warehoused and in what quantities? A million different questions.
   C. PREPARATION OF ALL CAPITAL EXPENDITURES How much will it cost to get this idea rolling, and when will Sears have to start spending how much?
   D. MEASURE FEEDBACK What's the expected reaction?
      1. From customers.
      2. From sales people.
      3. From service people.
      4. From the credit department.
   E. FOLLOW-UP POSITIONING
      1. Can the new product lead to a couple of new products? E.g., can the new paint scraper in the hardware department find a place in the sporting goods department as a boat-maintenance tool? Will the new chafing dish lead to sales of chafing dish fuel? Will the new back-yard barbecue lead

to an interest in a new line of outdoor entertaining equipment?

VI. Measurement (all products are measured on market penetration).
    A. On its own, as a single item in a total universe of retail items.
    B. As part of a line—sporting goods, for instance.
    C. Catalogue sales response can be used to predict retail sales.
       1. The catalogue is usually the first place you see a new item at Sears.
       2. Catalogues are also considered—by Sears—as part of the advertising media mix, along with radio, newspaper, television and the like. The catalogue not only sells a product, but it actually advertises it, too. Sears has found that people who have a Sears catalogue spend 2½ times as much in their local Sears retail store as they spend in the catalogue. (For whatever it's worth, Sears credit card customers also spend 50 per cent more in cash than they charge, so Sears can use bill stuffers stuffers as an advertising medium and as a means of testing response to a new line.)

INDEX

INDEX

Accountants, use of, 124, 196
"Actual reduction," 34
Advertising, 154–65; catalogue sales and, 108; collateral material, 163–65; consumer, 155, 156; co-op, 161–63; copywriters, 181–82; costs, 155, 160–61, 181–183; creative directors and, 13; ideas from, 13; "Inventors Wanted," 58; mail-order distribution and, 101–103, 104; merchandising and, 154–65; packaging and, 156–57, 158–70ff., 182; premium items, 112–13; publicity and, 166–73
Agents, royalty negotiations and, 152–53
"Agreement to Review Idea" form, 127
Air freight, use of 78, 79–80
Alcoa, 125, 126–27
Amortization (amortizing of costs), 74, 75, 77, 103–104, 135
Art work: directors, 13, 182–83; percentage of business in exchange for, 181–87; renderings, 21
Attorneys, patent, 37–39, 41, 42, 43, 56; fees, 41, 53

Banks (bank loans), financing and, 120, 124–25, 176, 178, 179, 180; collateral and, 177–80; presentations and, 120, 123–25

Barbie Doll, 23, 29
Blister pack, 156, 157
Boise Cascade, 137–38, 147–48
Bonds, restraining orders and, 53
Boxes, advertising displays and, 6–7, 156–57, 159
Box-top premiums, 110–11, 113, 116, 117–18
Brand names, 5–6; advertising and, 157–58; knock-offs and, 166; selecting, 5–6; trademark registration, 35–36, 43
Business forms, 164
Business managers, 196–97
Buyers, store, 7, 13

Capital investment (*see also* Financial backing; Investors): amortization and, 74–75 (*see also* Amortization); royalty deals and, 152–53
Cash discounts, 145
Cash flow, 174, 178, 179; charts and presentations, 124
Catalogue sales, 104–11; markup, 109–11; testing, 108–109
Catalogue sheets, 163–64; 181–82
Celebrities, endorsements by, 171–72
Checklist, inventor's, 201–206
Chicago Printed String Company, 141
Claims, patent applications and, 40–44, 42–43; broad

versus narrow, 40
Clipping services, 171
Clower, Bob, 13–15, 28, 59, 131–32, 134–35, 138–39, 144
Collateral, bank loans and, 177–80
Collateral material, advertising and merchandising and, 163–65
Commissions, salesmen and 71, 77
"Comps" (comprehensive drawings), 21
Conception, legal protection and proof of, 33–34, 39
Concurrent development phenomenon, ideas and, 127
Consumer advertising, 155, 156. *See also* Advertising
Contracts: royalty deals and, 152–53; suppliers and bids and, 83, 84–85
Co-op advertising, 160–63
Copyrights, 35, 44–46, 51, 52, 55–56, 51; new law (1978), 45–46; renewals, 45; symbols, 55–56
Copywriters, 181–82
Cost of goods (C.O.G.), 76–77, 80, 81, 190–93; presentations and, 123
Costs, 6–7; advertising, 155, 160–61, 162–63, 181–83; amortizing (*see* Amortization); catalogue sales and, 107–108; C.O.G., 76–77 (*see also* Cost of goods); copyright, 44–45; distribution, 78–85, 87–88; financing, 174–83; fixed, 76, 79–80; G.&A., 77, 81; initial idea and, 6–7; labor, 74, 75–76; mail-order sales and, 102–103; market research and, 73–74, 67; packaging, 71, 74–77; patenting, 33, 37, 40–42, 53; production (manufacturing and materials), 71, 73–74, 75–77, 79–85, 106–107; and profit, 80–81, 85ff.; sales, 76–77; shipping (*see* Shipping); sliding, 76–77; supplies, 71, 73, 82–83, 84–85; trademark registration, 43–44

Coupons, premium item sales and, 115–16
Creative thinking, 10–18
Cronkite, Walter, 2, 170
Cutcliffe, Sondra, 148–51

Dahl, Gary, 97, 128, 165, 182; and success of Pet Rock, 190–200
Design: advertising and, 74–77, 156–57, 181–82; packaging, 75–77; patents, 36–37, 39, 41–42, 54–56
Desirability, evaluating product ideas for, 20–31; and price acceptability, 30
Diaries, use of for ideas, 201, 203
Die-Hard battery, 29
Discount chains, 166
Discounts: cash, 145; catalogue sales and, 109–11; foreign sales and brokers', 109–11 freight, 145; quantity, 109–11
Displays, advertising, 156–57, 158–60, 163–65; boxes, 6–7, 156–57, 159
Distribution (distribution methods and systems), 31–32, 81–85, 87–88, 89–119; basic distributor/wholesaler system (chart), 99–100; catalogue sales, 104–11; choosing, 81–85, 89–119; factory-direct-to-retailer, 98, 100–101; geographic and vertical lines of, 94; leverage and, 130–39; mail-order, 101–104; markup and, 98–101, 109, 114–15; premium item sales and,

INDEX

111–17; private-label sales and, 117–19; profit and, 31–32, 130–39
Drawings: patent applications and, 38–39, 40, 41; trademark, 43–44
Dumping, discounting and, 110

Ecology, trash sorter and, 131–36
Endorsements, product, 171–72
Exclusive rights: catalogue sales and, 105–106; legal protection and, 37
Experts (professionals), use of, 4, 74 (*see also* specific kinds); and presentations, 124–25

Factory-direct-to-retailer distribution system, 98, 100–101
Factory gross sales, royalty deals and, 144–45
Family Farm, 26–27, 29
Financial backing (financing), 102, 174–83 (*see also* Capital investment); bank loans and (*see* Banks); cash flow and (*see* Cash flow); costs, 174–83; manufacturers and, 95–96; partners and, 180–83; presentations and, 120–29
Fisher-Price Toys, 21–22, 23, 25, 26–27, 59, 83, 96, 97–98, 147
Fliers, catalogue sales testing and, 108–109
Foreign sales, 94–95; brokers' discounts and, 110–11
Freight allowances, 78–79, 145. See also Shipping
"Fulfillment house," premium item sales and, 115–17

Games, 98 (*see also* Toys); market research rip-offs and, 61–65
Garbage compactors, 26–27

Garbage sorters, 131–36
General and administrative costs, 77–81
Gift and stationery industry, 97, 101
Goakes, Ruby, 75–76
Good will, selling price of company and value of, 118, 152
Goodwill Industries, 76, 110, 195
Greenland Studios, 105
Gruen, Roger, 148–52

Hallmark Cards, 15, 16; Creative Services, 59
Halper, Lewis, 106–107
Handicapped or mentally retarded, the, packaging work and use of, 172–73
Hanover House, 105
Header card, display unit, 159
Hicks, Bob, 25, 28–29, 59, 96, 97–98, 147
Hope Workshop, 195
Horchow Collection, 89
Horizontal and vertical idea development, 17

Iaia, Joseph A., 48–51, 53, 57
Ideas (inventions, products), 10–18; checklist for inventors, 201–206; choosing marketing and distribution systems and, 95–119; creative thinking and, 10–18; diary, use of, 201, 203; evaluating and testing for need, desirability, and profitability, 19–31, 71–88; evolutionary not revolutionary, 29; and financing, 174–83 (*see also* Financial backing); horizontal and vertical development, 17; and legal protection (*see* Legal protection); luck and, 188–89; and negotiating deals, 140–53; and presentations, 120–29; price and

INDEX

success or failure of, 29; profit and leverage and 130–39; research and rip-offs and, 58–70; royalty deals and, 140–53; source publications listed, 207–19; typical marketing plan outline, 220–22
"Idea Submission Form," 125–29
Indexes to periodicals, books, pamphlets (listed), 216–17
Industrial designers, 74
Industrial engineers, 74
Injunctions (restraining orders), legal protection and, 52–53
International Handbook of Jockstraps, The, 87
Interviews, market research and, 21, 22–26, 67–70; "in-depth," 23–26
"Inventions Wanted" ads, 58
Inventor's checklist, 201–206
Investors (investment), 174–83 (*see also* Capital investment); and financing, 178, 179, 180–83; as key to new products, 144; presentations and, 120ff.

Jack-in-the-Box premiums, 112–13
J. C. Penney, 56, 89, 105, 136
Johns, Bill, 6

Knocked-down ("K.D.") items, shipping costs and, 107
Knock-offs: legal protection and, 52–57, 151–52; and pricing, 164–65
Kool cigarettes, and premium items, 113
Kuhlberg, Jack, 141–42

Labor costs, 74, 75–76
Legal protection, 32–47, 48–57; copyrights, 35, 44–46, 51, 52, 55–56, 57; kinds, 35–36; patents, 32–47, 152; suits and (*see* Suits, federal); trademark registration, 35, 43–45, 57
Leverage, 130–39
Little Lumpsie doll, 83, 96, 146–47
Loans. *See* Banks (bank loans)
Los Angeles *Times*, 155; *Home* magazine, 167, 169–70, 175
Luck (serendipity) factor, 184–89

McDonald's stores, and premiums, 114
McDonough, Suellen, 132–36, 138
Magazines: advertising and, 101, 154, 155, 162; publicity and, 167–72
Mail-order sales, 101–104; advertising and, 101–102; shipping and, 103
Management contract, 153
Managers, business, 196–97
Manufacturers: basic distributor/wholesaler system chart, 99–100; catalogue sales and, 104–11; choosing, 96ff.; mail-order sales and, 104; markup structure and, 98–101; presentations and, 120 (*see also* Presentations); production costs and, 71, 73–74, 76, 80–85; profit and leverage and, 130–39; representatives, 92, 93–94, 99, 100, 118; royalty deals and negotiations and, 90–92, 95–96, 140–53
Marketing, 89–119 (*see also* Merchandising); advertising and (*see* Advertising); basic distributor/wholesaler system, 99–100; catalogue sales and, 104–11; choosing method of, 89–119; and distribution systems and markup structure, 98–101;

INDEX

factory-direct-to-retailer, 98, 100–101; financing, 174–83 (*see also* Financial backing); mail-order sales and, 101–104; manufacturers and, 140–53 (*see also* Manufacturers); premium items and, 111–16; private-label sales and, 117–18; profit and leverage and, 130–39 (*see also* Profit); research and (*see* Market research); typical plan outline, 220–22

Market research (test marketing), 60–70, 86–88; catalogue sales and, 108–109; evaluating product desirability and profitability and, 21–31; interviews, 21, 22–26, 67–70; premium items and, 114–15; and price acceptability, 30–31; reports and rip-offs and, 58–70

Markup (markup structure), 81, 82, 83; catalogue sales and, 108–10; distribution systems and, 98–101, 109–10, 114–15; premium item sales and, 114–15, 116

Marshall Field, 159, 170

Materials (*see also* Supplies): cost of, 71, 73, 83, 84–85

Mattel Toy Makers, 14, 16–17, 97, 98, 121; and evaluating product desirability, 22–23

May Co. Department Stores, 166, 196

Media (*see also* specific kinds): advertising and, 102, 154–55, 160–63; buyers, 102; mail-order sales and, 102; publicity and, 167–72, 197–98

Merchandising, 154–73 (*see also* Marketing); advertising and, 154–65; collateral material and, 163–65; knock-offs and, 165–67; publicity and, 166–73

Models, 22, 72, 74, 122. *See also* Prototypes; Samples

Montgomery Ward & Co., 89, 104, 105, 109, 118, 136, 138

Movies (films), publicity and, 172

Names. *See* Brand names

National Premium Sales Executives Organization, 114

National sales and distribution, 92, 95, 99–100 (*see also* Distribution; Marketing); catalogue sales, 101–104; mail-order sales, 101–104; manufacturers and, 96ff.; premium item sales, 111–19; private-label sales, 117–18

Neat Garage, 136–39, 147–48, 186–87

Negotiations (negotiating), 42–43; for patents, 42–43; and royalty deals, 140–53

Neiman-Marcus, 194

News clipping services, 170–71

Newspapers: and advertising, 155, 160, 161, 162; and mail-order sales, 102; and publicity, 168–72, 197–98

Newsweek, 102, 155, 197

Options, 147–48

Overhead costs, 77, 81

Packaging, 75–77; advertising and display design, 156–57, 158–60ff.; costs, 71, 75–79; trade journals, listed, 218

Paperback book displays, 158–59

Paper dolls, 29

Parent Protest Posters, 146–47, 171

Parker, George, 15–16, 59

Partners, financing and, 178, 179, 180–83; buying-out, 181; "silent," 181; and supplies, 181–83

INDEX

Patent and Trademark Office, 38
Patents, 17, 32–47, 48–49; applications, 38–39, 40–41, 46–47; attorneys (*see* Attorneys, patent); costs, 33, 37, 41–42, 53; defending (infringement suits), 52–57; design, 36, 41, 54–56; federal statute on, 37–38, 51; "interference proceeding," 42; kinds, 36; "office action" letter, 42; plant, 36; point-of-purchase, 165; renewing, 41; royalty rights and, 37, 50–51; search, 39–40, 41; utility, 36, 41
Patton, Warren, 37, 38, 46
Pecan sheller, 27–28
Penney. See J. C. Penney
Percentage of business, in exchange for supplies, 182–83
Perkins, Max, 11
Perseverance, creative ideas and, 15
Pet Rock, 97, 128–29, 175, 182, 190–200; Gary Dahl and success of, 190–200; publicity and, 197–98
Photography (photographs), advertising and publicity and, 167, 168–70, 174; and presentations, 122–23
Plant patents, 36
Pocketbook lag, financing and, 174–75, 176, 178, 179
Pocket Fisherman, 25
Point-of-purchase advertising, 164–65
Polyoptics, 188–89
Popiel, Seymour, 25–26, 155
Popular Mechanics, 155
Premium item sales, 89, 111–17; box-top, 111, 113–14; "fulfillment house," 115–17; markup structure, 114–15, 116; self-liquidating, 112
Presentations, 120–29; cost-of-goods calculations and, 124; financial backing and, 177, 178–79, 181–83; photography and, 122–23; physical format, 121, preparing, 120–29; professional, 125; sales performance and, 123–24; submission forms and, 125–29; "velvet" approach, 121–23
Press releases, 168–69, 197
Price (pricing), 30–31; acceptability, 30–31, 85–87; knock-offs and changes in, 165–67; markup and (*see* Markup); profit and (*see* Profit); retail and wholesale calculations and, 71, 73, 80–81ff. (*see also* Retail price)
Printing (printers), 75, 182–83
Private-label sales, 117–19
Problems (problem-solving), ideas and, 12–13
Production: costs, 71, 73–74, 76, 80–85; sample run, 72–74, 93
Production book, film, publicity and, 173
Profit (profitability), 80–81, 85ff., 130–39; costs and, 80–81, 85ff.; evaluating ideas for, 20, 31; knock-offs and, 165–66; leverage and manufacturers, and 130–39; markup and (*see* Markup); partners and, 180–81; Pet Rock, 193, 196–97; royalties and, 90–92, 144
Promotions, premium, 111–16
Protection, legal. See Legal protection
Prototypes, 6, 22, 72, 122. See *also* Models; Samples
Publications, source, listed, 207–19
Publicity, 166–73. See *also* Advertising
Published material, copyrights

INDEX

and, 35, 44–46, 51, 52, 55–56, 57
P.X. (B.X.), selling to, 94

Questionnaires, market research and, 24–25, 67–70; "in-depth," 24–25

Radio: advertising and, 160, 161, 162–63; publicity and, 197
"Recycl-it Basket," 132–36
Redbook, 102
"Reduction to practice," legal protection and, 34–35
Registered mail, legal protection and, 33, 34–35
Registration, trademark, 35–36, 43–44, 52, 57; T.M., 44
Releases, photography models and, 169
Reorders, 86–87
Reports, market research rip-offs and, 60–70
Retailer: and advertising, 160–63, 164–75; distribution systems and markup structure (charts), 98–100
Retail outlets, 91, 92–94ff.
Retail price, 73, 80–81, 82, 85–86, 87; calculating, 71, 73, 80–81ff.; catalogue sales and, 109–10; mail-order sales and, 102–104; market research and, 87; markup structure and (*see* Markup)
Rickie Tickie Stickies, 29, 97, 101; and advertising and publicity, 157, 158, 162, 168, 169–73; background and start of, 2–9; and financing, 175–83; and foreign sales, 94–95; initial costs and, 6; legal protection and, 54–56; name, 5–6, 157; packaging, 75–76; pricing, 84, 85–86; and royalty deals, 140–44; sales, 85–87; selling the company, 118

Risk, invention ideas and, 15
Rotocasting process, 133, 134
Royalties, 89, 90–92, 95–96, 140–53; average and fair, 144–45, 152–53; greed and negotiations, 144–45, 146, 147, 153; and legal protection, 37, 50–51, 57; and negotiations with manufacturers, 140–53

Sales: charts, 124; commissions, 145; costs and, 76–77 (*see also* Costs); performance and presentations, 123–24; representatives, 90, 92–93, 99, 100, 175; testing and, 86–88
Samples (sample production run), 72–74, 91, 134 (*see also* Models; Prototypes); costs, 73–74
SAS, foreign sales and, 95
Saturation, idea protection and, 56
Schools, selling to, 94
Sealing systems, patents and, 49–50
Search, patent, 38–40, 41; "preliminary novelty," 41; "state of the art," 41
Sears, Roebuck and Co., 13, 29, 56, 59, 89, 105–106, 112, 117, 130, 131–32, 133–35, 137–39, 146, 185; marketing plan outline, 220–22; and research, 26, 27–28
Self-liquidating premiums, 112
Shelf talkers, 164–65
Shipping: catalogue sales and, 108; costs, 71, 76, 77–80, 81, 103, 107–108; freight allowances, 79, 145; mail-order sales and, 102–103
Simpson, O. J., 172
Slides, presentations and, 123
Smith, Billy, 127–29
Snappy Patches, 145–46

INDEX

Source publications, listed, 207–19
Specialty catalogue sales, 89, 104–11; markup structure, 110–11
Spiegel, 89, 104
Spin-off ideas, 128–29, 145–46
Submission forms, idea, 125–29
Suits, federal, legal protection and, 52–57; posting bonds, 53; preliminary injuctions and, 52–53
Sunset House, 89, 105–106, 109, 112
Supplies (suppliers): costs, 71, 73, 83, 84–85; percentage of business for, 182–83; presentations and, 120

Television: advertising and, 13–14, 23, 25–26, 155, 160, 161; ideas from, 13–14; product research and, 23, 26; publicity and, 171, 172–73, 198
Testing. See Market research
Thrifty-Mart, 166
"Today Show," 171
Toys (toy and game industry), 96–98; choosing manufacturers and distribution systems and, 96–98; and evaluating product desirability, 21–23, 27; new products and ideas and, 13, 21–22; research and rip-offs and, 61–65

Trade journals (trade press): and advertising and publicity, 155, 167; listed by industry, 207–219
Trademark registration, 35 43–45, 52, 57; T.M., 43–44
Trash compactors, 26–27, 43
Trash separators, 131–36
"Turns at retail," 86–87

Underhill, Nick, 121
United Press International (UPI), 167, 170
U.P.S., shipping and, 78, 79–80
U. S. Post Office, 78
Utility patents, 36, 41–42

Value (need), evaluating ideas for, 20, 31
"Value pricing," 80
Vegomatic, 26

Wall Street Journal, 171
Welch, Pat, 192
West Coast Theatrical Directory, 172
Wholesale price, costs and, 80, 81–95. *See also* Price (pricing) Wholesaler/distributor system, basic (chart), 99–100
Williams, Richard, 112–13, 114
Window banners display, 164
Wire services, publicity and, 168
Wolfe, Thomas, 11